Penguin

The Larw

Harold Larwood, arguably the fastest bowler in the history of cricket, was born in the Nottinghamshire mining village of Nuncargate in 1904. At thirteen he became a pony pit-boy and a year later he began work down the mine itself. Cricket, however, was Larwood's 'reason for living' and in 1923 he joined the Nottinghamshire groundstaff, playing his first senior game for the club a year later. In 1926 Larwood's dream was realized when his fast bowling won him a place in the England team to play Australia in the final test of the series at the Oval. He and the 48 year-old Wilfred Rhodes bowled England to a famous victory and the Ashes were recaptured. Larwood made a successful trip to Australia in 1928, but the explosive form of Don Bradman resulted in a lean test series in 1930 and the loss of the Ashes. After topping the national bowling averages in 1932, Larwood was chosen to spearhead the England bowling attack on the winter tour to Australia. Always the dedicated professional, he carried out the controversial orders of his amateur captain, Douglas Jardine, with awesome efficiency. Australia were destroyed and the Ashes regained, but 'bodyline' acrimony remained. The M.C.C. asked Larwood to make an apology for his bowling: he refused and never played for England again.

Larwood retired from first-class cricket in 1938, and in 1950, at the invitation of an ex-Australian test cricketer, he emigrated to Sydney where he still lives with his wife, Lois.

Kevin Perkins, Larwood's collaborator, was himself a promising fast bowler, coached by Larwood in Sydney in the 1950s. Larwood described him as the best young prospect he'd ever seen, but an arm injury ended his ambition of opening the bowling for Australia. By a strange twist of fate, Perkins came from Bowral, home town of Bradman – Larwood's greatest antagonist on the field.

Mr Perkins has been a journalist for more than thirty years. He is now news editor of the *Sun-Herald* in Sydney.

The Larwood Story

•

HAROLD LARWOOD
with
KEVIN PERKINS

Penguin Books

Penguin Books Ltd, Harmondsworth, Middlesex, England
Viking Penguin Inc., 40 West 23rd Street, New York, New York 10010, U.S.A.
Penguin Books Australia Ltd, Ringwood, Victoria, Australia
Penguin Books Canada Ltd, 2801 John Street, Markham, Ontario, Canada L3R 1B4
Penguin Books (N.Z.) Ltd, 182–190 Wairau Road, Auckland 10, New Zealand

First published by W. H. Allen and Company 1965
First revised edition published in Australia by Bonpara Pty Ltd, 1982
Published in Penguin Books 1985

Printed and bound in Great Britain by
Cox & Wyman Ltd, Reading
Typeset in Baskerville

Contents

Acknowledgements

From the author and his collaborator to the late Hugh Buggy, Melbourne journalist, who saw every ball bowled on the bodyline tour and made available his well-kept records and newspaper reports and was able to recall various incidents with encyclopaedic certainty.

Thanks, too, and no less warmly, to many former Test cricketers and loyal friends – 'flannelled fools' all – for their generous help at all times.

HAROLD LARWOOD   KEVIN PERKINS

But what good came of it at last?
  Quoth little Peterkin.
Why that I cannot tell, said he
But 'twas a famous victory.

SOUTHEY

CHAPTER ONE

The Hangman's Name is Larwood

A RECORD CROWD of just under 50,000 had swarmed into Adelaide Oval on this day. It was Monday, 16 January 1933. The sun streamed down on the excited spectators, spangling the grass-verged wicket out in the middle with patches of russet brown. A faint breeze stirred from somewhere in the direction of the cathedral and helped to make it a splendid day for cricket.

But this was no ordinary day, nor was it an ordinary cricket match.

This was bodyline.

The cream of English and Australian cricketers were locked in the most bitter combat in cricket history.

The blackest day known to cricket, one critic called it, and his fellow-writers joined the chorus; the most sensational era since cricket began; the greatest upheaval the game has ever known; the most controversial – the most unpleasant; unfair! unsportsmanlike! illegitimate! disgraceful!

To bowl bodyline you had to be fast. Fast enough to make thunderbolts rear from the pitch in the direction of the batsman's ribs, shoulder or head. The faster the better. It left him with an even finer split-second to decide whether to attempt a stroke, dart out of the way or take a rib-roaster.

They said I was the fastest bowler in the world. I hurled the ball at the batsman at close on 100 miles an hour, giving him less than half a second from the precise moment of delivery to make a decision and act.

Larwood the Wrecker, the newspapers called me.

Lightning Larwood. Larwood the Killer. The Silent Killer. Hoodoo Larwood. Murder on Tip-Toe!

My bodyline bowling consisted of a series of short-pitched, catapult deliveries shooting up on the leg stump in line with the batsman's body. Up to six fieldsmen waited in a tight umbrella on the leg side, tensed for an easy catch that might be faint-heartedly popped up. Two fieldsmen stood on the legside boundary hoping for a catch from a hook shot.

All hell broke loose on this day when I hit Bert Oldfield. It was the third Test and Australia were 6 wickets down for a little over 200 runs, chasing England's first innings total of 341. I was not bowling to a bodyline field setting at the time. Australia's star batsmen were back in the pavilion looking on, and members of the 'hutch' were at the wicket or padded up waiting to face the Nottingham Express.

Bert wasn't a recognized batsman in the true sense, but he was a player not without style and could, on occasions, get his 50, or thereabouts. In this innings he had scored almost 40 and was settling down nicely and becoming a thorn in England's side. Now he delighted the crowd with a beautiful leg glance to the fence hit off one of my deliveries.

Running in on tip-toe, I decided to drop one short to unsettle him. Oldfield swung at the ball, attempting a hook. He mistimed the stroke and, as he spun round, the ball struck the right side of his temple with such force that later he was found to have a fractured skull.

Critics and spectators had been prophesying that bodyline would kill somebody sooner or later. It now seemed that the dark moment had arrived.

Bert dropped his bat, clutched his head in both hands, staggered away from the wicket and fell to his knees.

As a low rumble of hooting and rage swelled from the crowd, I ran up to the crumpled figure. 'I'm sorry, Bertie,' I said.

The plucky little wicketkeeper tried to collect himself as the English side, realizing how gravely hurt he was, hurried over to gather round him.

'It's not your fault, Harold,' Oldfield mumbled as soon as he was able to speak.

The scene that followed was one that had never erupted on any other cricket field, and it is difficult to imagine it ever being repeated.

Woodfull, the Australian captain, sitting with members of his team in the enclosure outside the dressing-room, was normally a reserved and circumspect individual, but on this occasion, still nursing bruised ribs from one of my deliveries which had hit him two days earlier, he vaulted the pickets and bustled on to the field in ordinary attire.

'This isn't cricket, this is WAR!' he boomed.

As towels and hot water were rushed from the dressing-room to bathe Oldfield's head wound, the crowd worked itself into a frenzy, and with every passing moment the situation became uglier and more dangerous.

If anybody fires a pistol, they'll lynch us, I thought.

If one man jumps the fence, the whole mob will go for us.

I moved towards the stumps so that I might grab one in readiness if they came at us. Some of the other lads also moved nearer the stumps.

Thousands of almost hysterical onlookers began counting me out as Oldfield staggered groggily from the field, assisted by Woodfull. They also counted out England's skipper, Douglas Jardine.

Suddenly the editor of an evening newspaper dashed along one of the terraces under an open stand where bewildered members of the press box were standing on tip-toe to get a clearer view of the scene.

Waving a white panama hat to attract the attention of Hugh Buggy, the newspaper's cricket reporter, he yelled, 'This is disgraceful. Put the boot into them! Put the boot in!'

Fleet Street men, riled by this display, promptly cabled back to their papers that an Australian editor had instructed his reporter to 'put the boot in' to the visiting players.

The anger of the crowd needed no stoking.

'One, two, three, four, five, six, seven, eight, nine OUT you BASTARD!' they bawled at me from the outer ground.

'Go home you Pommie bastards!' they yelled.

'Bastards! Bastards! Bastards!'

Although hostility had spread to every stand, this particular epithet appeared to be used only by those in the outer ring.

Although the next Australian player, Big Bill O'Reilly, had now come to the wicket to take strike, his jaw set firmly, the counting-out and hooting continued unabated.

Several police officers were rushed in and reinforcements called for by the oval authorities. More were hastily mustered and, together with mounted troopers, were held in reserve at headquarters, awaiting developments.

The Melbourne *Herald* reported at the time: 'No such unrestrained hooting and abuse has ever been heard, even at a tense football match in Melbourne.

'O'Reilly missed three balls from Larwood with wild swings, and each time the crowd vented its vocal fury on Larwood. No bowler in a Test has ever faced such a tornado of angry shouting. The crowd lost all interest in the Australian innings and concentrated at howling at the fast bowler.'

In an unprecedented scene, rubbish galore was pelted on the normally immaculate arena, and the crowd continued its yelling and abuse until the Australian innings ended soon after for a total of 222.

More, however, was to come. As we left the field in silent anger, we were hooted off. Hooted, not jeered. I remember that as we walked through a crowded stand to reach the dressing-room indignant members leapt from their seats yelling insults, some shaking their homburgs and velour hats at us. This outburst was all the more amazing because cricket spectators in Adelaide, the City of Churches, had the reputation of being among the most sedate of Australian sports crowds.

In the dressing-room, Sutcliffe and Wyatt began to strap on their pads in readiness to open England's second innings. It was quieter but not much, and we could still hear them. Greatly to everybody's surprise Jardine, who was expected to go in about number four, had strolled over to a corner and was putting on his pads.

Sutcliffe and Wyatt looked quizzically at each other. Then Sutcliffe went across to his captain.

'What's the order, Skipper?'

Jardine did not answer at once. He cocked an ear towards the scattered shouts filtering through from outside.

Finally, he spoke: 'Listen to the bastards yelling. I think I'll go in myself and give the bastards something to yell at.'

Australian crowds hated Jardine. He, in turn, hated Australian crowds.

Reaching into a small bag in which he carried several colourful Harlequin caps, he chose the most outlandish, a long-peaked creation splashed with most of the colours of the rainbow. Out on the field, but a few minutes ago, he had been wearing the standard England cap.

Jardine knew the Australians resented his millinery, regarding it as sheer snobbery, a symbol of the despised old school tie back in the Old Dart. He wanted to rile the crowd for their coarse insults, and this was one way to do it.

Jardine certainly cut a brave figure on the way to the wicket. The crowd's hoots and abuse soared to a crescendo at the sight of the tall, spare, Cassius-like Englishman who showed so little concern as he faced the bowler that he might have been engaged in a game on the village green. The cap, perched atop his lean sunburned face, accentuated his hawklike features.

Before Jardine played each ball a raucous section of the crowd on the mounds roared: 'You're out, you bastard! You're out, you bastard!' Australian newspapers politely reported this as: 'You're out. You're out.'

South Australian fast bowler Tim Wall, a local schoolmaster, thumped them down with great vigour, the crowd's encouragement injecting a super lease of life into him.

'Hit 'im on the bloody head, Tim!' some of them yelled.

'Knock 'em over.'

'Knock the bastards over.'

'That's got you, you bastard!'

Jardine defied the attack with a dogged display of batting, ignoring the crowd's taunts and going on to score 56 in an innings that was, even for him, a painfully slow knock of four hours and fifteen minutes.

The crowd's anger was the climax of mounting resentment at the shock attack launched by Bill Voce and yours truly and which led to such a battering of the Australian batsmen.

Bill Ponsford, Australia's opener and one of the all-time greats, was still in pain from eleven blue-black bruises on his ribs, shoulder, and back, which he sustained in the first innings on Saturday while making a fighting 85. The heavy padding he wore under his flannels failed to protect him. He was hit more often by my flyers than the tell-tale bruises indicated.

Spectators had carried resentment into the match because of trouble at the nets. It was an Adelaide tradition to allow spectators at the practice nets of the visiting team before a Test, but the Englishmen had been barracked and, when Jardine demanded that they be barred, the authorities pulled down the shutters. As one Australian cricket writer observed, we practised in Scotch mist behind locked gates.

Their resentment grew on the Saturday, second day of the Test, soon after Bill Woodfull and Jack Fingleton opened Australia's first innings. Fingleton was out for a duck, groping at a swinger from Gubby Allen, giving Australia another poor start.

Then, in the last ball of my third over, bowling to an orthodox field, I struck Woodfull a stunning blow over the heart. Not only was the ball travelling at about 100 miles an hour but it broke back from the off in whipping from the pitch.

The Australian captain had stepped across his wicket to

play the ball, only a slightly short one, and found himself standing square in front when he decided to play a defensive stroke. Absorbing the full impact, he dropped his bat, clutched his chest and staggered away from the wicket.

Don Bradman, who came in at the fall of Fingleton's wicket, was standing close enough to hear what followed. Jardine walked across to me and said:

'Well bowled, Harold.'

The spectators hooted, and heatedly counted me out for the injury to Woodfull, who was unable to continue for several minutes.

But what followed provoked an even rowdier outburst.

As I began my next over to the Australian captain, who was still shaken, the field was swung over to the legside placing – a clear indication that he was about to face the full fury of my bodyline onslaught. Only four men were posted on the leg, but it was enough to send spectators into a frenzy.

My second ball to Woodfull was a rearing bumper, which knocked the bat out of his hands.

Bradman, after ducking several bumpers, played a semi-defensive shot at a ball on the leg stump, popping up a soft catch, which Allen embraced at short square leg.

Stan McCabe, hero of the first Test in Sydney, gave Jardine the easiest of catches at short leg, and I had thus taken 2 wickets for 8 runs. Woodfull completed a courageous knock for 22 runs, his stolid effort lasting for an hour and twenty-nine minutes and doing much to save his side from total collapse

Voce, my bodyline partner, went off the field with an ankle injury. Although the crowd didn't know it was for him, a call was made over the amplifiers for a doctor, and immediately the news was passed from one to another that Woodfull was in a bad way. I came in for a fresh burst of jeers and catcalls.

The Australian captain, although not seriously hurt, was at this very moment lying on the massage table in his team's dressing-room receiving treatment for a great livid bruise on his chest.

Plum (later Sir Pelham) Warner, England's joint team manager, entered the Australian room to offer his sympathy. It was then that Woodfull, normally a man of quiet dignity and highly respected in Australia, made the remark that was to go down in cricket history.

'I don't want to see you Mr Warner,' he began. 'There are two teams out there on the oval. One is playing cricket, the other is not. The game is too good to be spoilt. It's time some people got *out* of the game.'

By this forthright avowal Woodfull brought bodyline into the open and summarily dismissed the views held by many people that it was nothing less than a newspaper invention.

The Australian captain's stunning rebuff of Sir Pelham Warner upset all of us, especially when news of it leaked out to be avidly seized upon by every Australian newspaper. The English journals angrily referred to the snub and its implications.

For the record, Woodfull's imputation was never withdrawn.

The Monday crowd which seethed with such hostility after I had knocked out Oldfield (he was taken to hospital by ambulance) had been stirred up to some considerable extent by Woodfull's vehement protest two days before.

But the ball that struck the Australian keeper, ironically not a bodyline ball, was the one that caused all the trouble. From that moment, bodyline, essentially a bowler versus batsman affair, was taken out of the hands of the players. At the end of the day's play I was given police protection. Thousands of angry spectators were waiting near the dressing-room and outside the ground. We were dressed and ready to leave when a police officer entered our dressing-room.

'Which one is Larwood?' he demanded.

Bill Voce pointed. 'That's him.'

'What have *I* done wrong?' I asked.

'Nothing, but there's a big crowd outside gunning for you.'

'Ar, we don't want any police protection, we'll look after him,' Voce said. I was glad of 'Tangy's' friendship at that moment. He was a big fellow, 6 feet 3 tall, and could hold his own anywhere.

'You might be safe, but I think I'd better come with you just in case.'

The crowd looked menacing, and other police officers stood around to keep them back. I walked out by myself, followed by my escort. Bill Voce, and one or two others were just behind, and although we came in for a fair share of abuse, nobody laid a hand on us.

That afternoon, with the crowd's deep-throated roars of anger still ringing in their ears, members of the Australian Board of Control met in what every correspondent of the time surely agrees was an atmosphere of haste and confusion.

They sent off the historic cable to the MCC at Lord's protesting that bodyline bowling was unsportsmanlike, menacing the game, causing injury and intensely bitter feelings among the players and threatening the friendly relations between England and Australia.

The Marylebone Cricket Club, in an indignant rejoinder, suggested the situation was not as serious as had been claimed and offered to cancel the rest of the tour if this was what Australia wanted.

Wiser counsels prevailed, however, and we continued our tour. But it was only the beginning of the real controversy for me. That form of bowling, which Jardine called legitimate leg theory, I called fast leg theory and the Australians bodyline, might never have detonated at all but for certain ineluctable factors involving the unjustness of the scales between the batsman and the bowler, the genius of Don Bradman and the immense strength of Jardine's personality.

I have no hesitation in saying that in 1930 the dice was loaded against the bowler, and cricket as a spectacle was in danger. It was not a sudden development and began some time in the twenties when groundsmen, experimenting with various fertilizers, produced plumb, easy-paced wickets, so that life became simple for batsmen but for nobody else. This uneven contest was, in many ways, more pronounced in Australia than England and, for my own part, I can say that bodyline would probably never have originated if Test matches had been played in England alone. Only the conditions peculiar to Australia led to its introduction.

But despite this state-of-the-wicket imbalance bowlers, even before 1930, struggled on, protesting occasionally with bumpers and praying for a drop of rain and a quick burst of sunshine to tip the odds their way and give them a chance.

Then came Bradman, and his presence made the difference. He was the human catalyst for whom the sharp prong of bodyline was shaped.

And here let me confirm what so many people have always believed and about which I have remained silent for more than thirty years: *bodyline was devised to stifle Bradman's batting genius.*

They said I was a killer with the ball without taking into account that Bradman with the bat was the greatest killer of all. Cricket fans today can have no idea how dynamic this little chap was. Bradman would murder you if you gave him any stuff that was even slightly loose. A fast, good-length ball, enough to keep other Test players quiet, would fly to the boundary like a shot out of a gun when Bradman was at the crease.

He was phenomenal, striking top form immediately after landing in England in 1930 and 1934. On those tours he was scoring near the 300 mark within a week after stepping off the ship.

In 1930 the slender 21-year-old boy from Bowral astonished the cricket world with his brilliant attacking play. His Test aggregate of 974 runs for an average of 139 enabled Bill Woodfull's team to turn the tables on England and regain the Ashes.

Bradman pasted me unmercifully in two of the three Tests I played in during that series.

Bradman's supreme achievements on that tour included 236 (right off the ship), 131 in his first Test in England, first visiting batsman to score 1,000 runs before the end of May, 254 in his first Test at Lord's, 105 before lunch and 309 in a single day (final score 334) at Leeds a fortnight later.

In those days cricket was King and a bond of Empire much stronger than is the present Commonwealth. The game gripped the imagination and set fire to the emotions.

After that overwhelming 1930 tour, England had a rare problem to solve. *Something* had to be done to curb Bradman.

The answer was found in bodyline.

Bodyline *was* a plot, and I was involved in it, having been given the job of spear-heading the attack to put the brake on Bradman.

I had a job to do, and I thought I did it pretty well. I was asked to bowl bodyline, and I carried out instructions.

Bowling to Australia's batsmen was rather like potting pheasants on the wing, but with Bradman it was like trying to trap a wild duck, his movements were so swift.

In the final split-second before my arm whipped over, I used to watch him, trying to anticipate his intentions. If he moved one way or the other, I would vary my direction at the last instant to keep it in line with his body. He made it happen that way. It was either him or me.

I finished that tour with 33 wickets in four and a half Tests – an all-time record for a fast bowler — at an average of 19 runs each against some of the best batsmen in Australia's history. Eighteen of my victims were either clean bowled or out leg-before. I took a wicket every 40 balls.

Bradman was my victim four times in eight Test innings, twice hearing his stumps rattle, and whereas he was my boss in England, I called the tune in Australia.

I bowled myself to a standstill on Australia's concrete-hard grounds so that England might take home the Ashes. We triumphed by four matches to one.

Then the political storm broke. The gentlemen who sent me 'bravo' cables, congratulating me on my bowling feats in Australia, turned against me, as did my own club.

The honest toiler who had bowled his innards out was sacrificed to cement the bonds of Empire. But he kept his pride.

When the balloon went up, I couldn't let any of the boys down. I couldn't let anybody down.

I took it the only way I could – on the chin. No man can beat the establishment. A black cloud has hung over my name ever since.

British diplomats were called in as mediators to soothe ruffled feelings and heal the Empire breach, which was even splitting family loyalties. Bodyline became not quite the thing to talk about in English drawing-rooms, but you could buy a quick fight in any English pub by calling me a bodyline bowler or saying that England's tactics were unfair in beating the Australians.

As Whitehall entered the fray, it is reasonable to assume that my bodyline tactic caused some heartburn even at the level of the throne.

Dominions secretary, Mr J. H. Thomas, who conferred with MCC officials when cricket matches between England and Australia looked like being abandoned, admitted years later that no Empire problem had caused him as much trouble as bodyline.

Not half as much trouble, though, as it caused me.

When I began bowling bodyline, the famous phrase 'it isn't cricket', was still in currency and was self-explanatory.

I changed all that. Within a few weeks, the term 'bodyline' was being used, especially by politicians, as a synonym for skulduggery or anything that implied hitting below the belt.

The argument raged throughout the Empire. Was Larwood's leg-trap bowling unfair and against the spirit of the grand old game? Was the purpose of bodyline to maim the Australians deliberately? Was I bowling *at* the man or were they frightened of me and retreating in terror?

Bodyline even made the headlines in America, probably the only time any sport played in the British Empire ever got such attention.

In Australia I was tagged as 'Jardine's hatchet man'.

I smote the Aussies hip and thigh – only too literally so.

One Australian Test batsman claimed publicly that when he took block a yard outside his leg stump, my bodyline balls still came straight at him. He was right.

An Australian Quarter Sessions judge even gave this considered opinion for the newspaper columns: '"Leg-theory" bowling is covered by the criminal law, under which it is an offence recklessly and wantonly to harm any person, even without malice!'

Wisden, the bible of cricket, wrote of the bodyline affair: 'The whole atmosphere was a disgrace to cricket.'

Most Australians, but not all, condemned me. Many English writers denounced the Australians as a race of squealers and congratulated me for shaking up cricket in Australia. Some English critics wrote what a good sight it was to see Australia's batsmen edging away discreetly when I was letting them slip.

Although Australia was in the midst of a grim economic depression, when most people had to turn a bob over twice before spending it, crowds fought to pack the grounds in every state to watch the tense conflict.

My bowling inspired poems and limericks in newspapers and magazines and on the stage, and scores of these were sent to me from many parts of the Empire. Cartoonists were on clover.

Before bodyline was outlawed, Jardine and I were blamed for almost wrecking the institution of Anglo-Australian Tests, perhaps even cricket itself.

Cricket lovers of a new generation today cannot possibly imagine the bitterness, the hostility generated throughout the tour.

Although I was threatened with murder and told, in other letters, what a pleasure it would be to tar and feather me, strangely, it was in many ways the most enjoyable tour

I ever had. My notoriety on the field encouraged hospitality to the point where Australians off the field almost killed me with *bonhomie*. The convivial glass flowed marvellously.

But because of the bitter argument the inside story of that tour was not allowed to be told, nor have the details of what followed in England ever been revealed. None of the players was permitted to discuss the conflict with pressmen, and Jardine would not even tell members of the Australian press corps the time of day from the moment we landed there.

Among many hundreds of letters I received in England and from Australia, South Africa and New Zealand; I was most intrigued by those from the Australians who, in characteristic manner, told me exactly what they thought of me.

I threw most of them away, especially the abusive ones which my countrymen sent to me. But I still have half a suitcase of letters.

I reproduce some of them to show the feeling of the time:

Australia,
18 May 1933

From a Two-Eyed Australian. To H. Larwood Esq., BLB, Chicken Farm, England.
You poor boob – what a hell of a show you have made of yourself and all others connected with you – In a cabled report of an interview of yours with a member of the *Sunday Express* you let yourself go – (money talks).

The 'supposed leg theory' bowling attack was prearranged (on board prior to arrival) – Cigars, whiskey, etc., I suppose. Very nice – We are getting down to tin tacks.

Leg theory be damned – If you confirm the theory that you were not bowling at the MAN you're a damned liar – Your elongated snob of a captain used you for this set purpose – You're not to blame as it were, you were bowling to instructions, but you're a lousy cow to have done so –

Your dear old mother must be proud of you – you Sweet Thing –

So soon as your team won you were sent back 'ome. Why didn't you go to New Zealand? No, you had done your dirty work. You poor pom – what a hell of a time you will get if you come out here again.

Now a later report states 'cheque returned'. That would hurt? Also, you gave insufficient thought to the interview – just what might have been expected. Not sufficient intelligence is more like it.

Woodfull is a better man than ever you will know how to be – and Bradman broke your heart in England – and he will never be afraid of you, not while you have a hole in your behind · Sorry about the cheque. Cheerio.

Many of the acid ones came from England. Here is one I happen to have kept over the years:

Hearts of Oak, Yorks.
May Day

Dear Larwood,
I enclose a piece of sackcloth as a very befitting accompaniment to the ashes which you helped so ingloriously to filch from Australia.

You know, only too well, what sportsmen think of you in the Antipodes; the enclosed might convey to you the opinion of some of your countrymen. The fact that the enclosed is unclean, needs no apology. It is in keeping with your method of play.

Yours disgustedly,
John Bull

An Australian in England appears to have been the author of this, written on a letterhead of the Clarendon Hotel and dated 7 May 1933:

Mr H. Larwood,
Annesley Woodhouse,
Notts.
Sir,
I have read with a feeling of contempt your utterly disgusting remarks about Australians in today's *Sunday Express*. I suppose

there is no reason to doubt that the printed story is as you gave it.

I understand that before you became a professional cricketer you were a pit-boy. It certainly sounds as if you were.
R. G. C. Hodge, Adelaide, S. Aus.

Among a great number of supporters who wrote was one signing himself 'Scots Joe'. His letter was sent from Footscray, Melbourne, on 17 January 1933. It read:

Mr Larwood.
Dear Sir,
Send them down like hell. Give us something new in cricket.

Don't be bluffed by their howling, that is about all they are fit for. Oh, they are great sports. Yes, just when they are winning. If they come at it too much Jardine is quite justified to take the whole team off the field.

This letter came from Fremantle, dated 1 June 1933. It was signed by J. Payne, of Victoria St. It ran:

Mr 'Arrold Larwood, the Bodyline Poultry Farmer. At last your rambling story is told. No press in the world would have printed such a lot of loose muck except for the unusual circumstances attached to it.

There is no doubt you are a dirty swine. You will never have the chance of showing yourself up again. If you were half a man you would not have used bodyline here. The Australians refused to use it. All the kidstakes talk about leg theory was meant to make the English crowd think about leg theory.

Your reputation was gained by methods which threatened the lives of our men. Great sport for you. You felt quite safe when you knew you didn't have to face it. If you had killed one of our men you would have been King. But your mission was not a complete success.

If you attempted your bodyline in England you would be hunted off the field. But there is no danger of your trying it on . . .

You hadn't enough brains to write any sort of a story if it wasn't slandering Don Bradman from beginning to end . . .

What else can be expected from a village Bonehead like you?
The Hangman's name is Larwood.

The Hangman's name is Larwood! I have never forgotten those words.

In my heart I feel I must take the blame for all the trouble that occurred. I know I shouldn't, but the position is similar to the hangman's. If the judge orders him to hang a man, he has to do so.

But he must take the responsibility for that man's death.

CHAPTER TWO
In the Beginning

TIME HUNG HEAVILY on the hands of a two-year-old boy one
June day in 1907 in the tiny Nottinghamshire mining
village of Nuncargate.

Discovering a pint of paraffin in a bottle in the scullery of
his father's modest cottage, the child promptly swallowed
part of the contents.

A hastily summoned doctor pumped out the oil in time
to save the child's life.

The incident started something, for the boy's father
decided that his son needed some kind of interest to keep
him out of mischief.

From an old fence paling he fashioned a tiny cricket bat
and presented it to his son together with a rubber ball to
push about the garden. It solved the problem, and the boy
began spending hours in the backyard playing with his new
toys.

It wasn't long before young Harold Larwood was
pestering his father for more bats and balls. At this time two
of his brothers, Ernest and Tom, were taking music lessons,
but Fred, the eldest, was interested neither in sport nor
music.

Harold, too, would have none of music. His father,
Robert Larwood, threatened and coaxed, but he couldn't
be persuaded. All he wanted to do was play with bat and
ball.

I can remember only from the time when I was about
five. From that age I hardly spent any leisure moments
without a bat or ball in my hands. Kicking a soccer ball also
became an important part of my life.

I kept my father poor buying me ninepenny cricket balls. They usually lasted about a week because I hit them so hard and so often. I became so attached to the game, as far as I understood it, that unless my father kept me in bed under threat of punishment – he could dish it out – I would even get up before breakfast to play. My brothers didn't care much for cricket. By now I was carving my own bats out of any old piece of wood I could find.

Nuncargate, where I was born, an undersized baby, on 14 November 1904, was typical of many small villages in the Midlands at that time. It existed only because of a coal mine at Annesley, about 3 miles away.

Times were hard, and there was no money about. My father, a miner, was as poor as our neighbours and had four boys to bring up. At an early age, Tom, the brother next to me, became seriously ill and was never able to do any hard work. He eventually got a job with an insurance company in Manchester. Later another brother, Joseph, arrived.

My parents were God-fearing people and staunch members of the local United Methodist Church, working hard in its interest. Father was treasurer of the Chapel and Ernest became its organist. For all of us it was a case of *having* to go to church every week, which I did until the age of sixteen.

Sometimes concerts were held in the village, and my brothers took part. I was made to feel a bit out of things but still had to go along. People in any numbers terrified me, and I have never lost the shyness I always felt as a boy. If my parents mentioned my name at home to visitors, I'd get up and quietly leave the room.

School I hated. I was pretty good at arithmetic but hopeless at most other subjects. My mother worried over my lack of ability and often said I spent too much time on sport. Three of her relatives were in the teaching profession, but it made no difference. I hated school.

Every morning at school we had to line up for inspection. The teacher would come along and inspect our fingernails and shoes. I used to kick a football on the way to school, and my shoes were always dirty. I copped it regularly. And they didn't have any limit to the number of strokes either. They used to give you just as many as they thought you needed.

One big teacher, in particular, used to pick on me, and when I failed to answer the difficult questions he reserved for me, he would haul me out in front and cane me. It used to sting on those cold mornings. Sometimes, when he had given me as many as he could manage, he'd send me to the headmaster for some more. He said it was for misbehaviour – usually playing cricket or football in the streets.

Then, when I got home, I often copped it again from my father, angry because of my lateness. He knew what I had been doing.

'All right,' he would say. 'Take your trousers off.' He used to really hurt my bare backside with his great ham of a hand.

When the teacher picked on me, I would glare at him and say to myself, One of these days I'm going to knock you down.

I threatened him a few days before I was due to leave. As he waved the cane at me to punish me for misbehaving, I boldly told him in front of the class, 'You can cane me this week, but I'm leaving next week. You'll want to be careful then.' He stung that day.

When we met a few years later, we became friends.

My liking for football grew less as I became older, and cricket was the only game I cared for.

After school, the village youngsters usually gathered at the recreation ground, picked sides and had a game. Sometimes there'd be nobody there, and I'd trudge back home. Now and again my father, noticing how despondent I was, would come out and give me a game in the street. It had a dirt surface like all the others in the village. These occasions made up for all the thrashings.

Father was a slow bowler and captained the Nuncargate team from the Annesley colliery where he worked. The village had nothing to offer in the way of entertainment. I used to smash a lot of the windows of our neighbours playing cricket, but they didn't mind. Mining folk understand.

My mates on the recreation ground used to call me Lightning – not because of a natural inclination to hurl a ball as fast as my frail frame would allow, but because I always beat them at running.

A rare treat was to see the silent movies. When my father could afford it, which wasn't often, I would walk 2 miles to the cinema and pay a penny at the 'Saturday afternoon rush'.

Although life was austere and simple, it was happy. It revolved around going to school, playing the most wonderful games, and going to bed every night at 6.30. It was secure, too, because my parents, although very strict, made our humble home a warm and loving shelter.

My father bought our house out of money he saved from working in the mine. It cost something like £200 – an enormous amount of money in those days. When one considers his meagre wages, it is easy to understand the extent of his sacrifices and my mother's skimping.

Father never drank a drop of liquor in his life, I am sure. He didn't swear, and the only luxury he allowed himself was an old pipe he would smoke sitting at the fireside every evening after supper. He used to tell us that we must always do the right thing, the right thing by everybody.

I thought he was tough on me at times, but it wasn't until later in life that I realized how good he had been to all of us. I was to see the time when I hoped I could be as good a father to my children as he had been to me. He was a good man.

A boy living in Nuncargate in those days learned that life was real as he approached his teens. There was little ahead of you except a life of hard work.

No parents in Nuncargate could afford to send their children to school beyond the primary level unless they won a scholarship.

This was out of the question for me and at thirteen, in order to get my mind more on the business of earning a

living, my parents set me to work in the colliery co-
operative stores. I used to weigh up flour for the customers.
I was only 4 feet and sometimes humped sacks bigger than
myself.

One morning, while carrying a case of margarine down
the cellar, I slipped on the stone steps, fell head-first, and lay
unconscious for four hours. They thought then I would
never waste any more time on cricket, or for that matter, on
anything else.

My friends were earning more money in the mine at
Annesley. I wanted to join them, hardly able to wait until I
had turned fourteen, the legal age a boy could work down a
mine. My parents didn't want me to go because I was so
small and frail-looking. But finally they relented.

So I became a pony pit-boy. On the very first day I
mustered a team of pit-boys, played a team of local boys
and bowled them out in three overs.

Each day, a short, skinny youth, I walked 3 miles to the
mine, did a hard day's work and walked home again.

Every morning, after being taken down in a cage to the
bottom of the shaft, I had to make my way in pitch-
blackness to the coal-face, 2 or 3 miles off the main road and
through narrow tunnels.

That's where I worked most of the time. My father and
brothers were nearer the surface, and I never saw them
underground except perhaps at the cage when we were
coming up. My job was to drive a pony which pulled a kind
of miniature train. The 'train' was made up of four or five
heavy tubs in which the coal was carried. The tubs, a little
bigger than an average-sized television set of today, each
held about 2 hundredweight of coal, and, coupled together,
ran on rails.

The only illumination down there was a small oil light
carried by each man. It shed such a poor light you couldn't
see who the man next to you was unless you held it right
against his face.

Often my light snuffed out. It was then literally as black
as coal. In the total darkness I had to feel my way along the
tunnel, either to the coal-face or to one of the turn-arounds

where men were working. As a pit-boy I drove a pony along the tunnels. They were only pony high and so narrow I had to walk behind or in front of the loaded tubs. There wasn't enough headroom to sit on top of the loaded tubs even if you wanted to.

At the seams sweating coalmen toiled, stooped and bent in cramped corners like figures in some eerie dream. On hands and knees they cracked away the brittle coal with pick and shovel.

Noisily the men shovelled the hard-won coal into the tubs. I'd set off on the long trek through the blackness, the pony straining and pulling but invisible. This monotonous journey was broken now and then when the pony's hooves struck a stone, sending sharp echoes up and down.

On reaching a turn-around, a widened section where two sets of tracks ran, the full tubs were taken off and connected to a wire rope and hauled to the bottom of the shaft.

I would then turn my pony round, fasten him to an empty set of tubs, and return to the coal-face for another load.

It went on day in and day out, although it was always night! Often before leaving the turn-around I climbed into one of the empty tubs to get a ride back and tucked my head well down so I didn't bump it on the tunnel roof. Even this little variation had its frustrations. You ran the risk of a wheel jumping off the track, and unable to climb out because there wasn't enough headroom, found yourself trapped and had to shout for help.

You couldn't waste any time because coal would be piling up at the seams. Sometimes a loaded tub wheel would jump off the track. Straining and lifting, grunting and holding, it was often too much for a small boy to lever a heavy tub back on to the track. At times I would have to uncouple one or two tubs to get at the one causing the trouble.

In those moments of desperation, alone in the dark, a boy learns the pitmen's language fluently. Somehow it doesn't seem so bad below. It's an earthy language, close to the honesty of sinew and sweat.

I remember one day my pony got his hoof caught in the rail along a tunnel. A wire rope was cutting into his fetlock. Nothing I could do would release the poor animal. I gave vent to my helplessness with a scorching burst of language, echoing and dying along the tunnel.

Stumbling along the 400 yard cavern in search of help, I was surprised by being grabbed and held by the shirt.

'Calm down and tell me what's happened,' a voice said.

I recognized a prissy cousin of mine, a man who never swore in his life. His job was to look after the small steam motors which drove the drag ropes. For weeks after that I was worried in case he told my parents about the way I had cursed. If he did, they never mentioned it.

Anyway, he helped me release my pony, a white one named Tinker. He was my favourite and a friendly little fellow to whom I used to talk. He used to answer me. I couldn't afford to bring him anything from home, but sometimes I got little tit-bits at the mine for him. The ponies were very well fed.

There was nobody to talk to, and the isolation was overwhelming at times. But it was worse for the ponies, they never got any fresh air. Only once did I see them emerge from the mine and that was when there was a strike and we were out of work for two or three months.

I remember going along to a field where the ponies were galloping about, to see if Tinker was all right. He wouldn't come near me.

I was a pit-boy for three years. On pay days I gave every penny to my mother. My wages were 32 shillings. It was a lot of money.

When I was seventeen, I took a job on the night-shift at another mine nearby, the Langton Colliery. It was winter.

The exertion of working was enough to keep me warm on those chilly nights. Wearing nothing but trousers and thick boots, I had no more than a 3 foot clearance to work in at the coal-face.

Crouching down, the gloom pierced only by the

flickering half-light of an oil lamp, I cleaned away dirt with pick and shovel laying bare the coal seams for daytime workers.

Night after long night I tore skin off my back knocking against the jagged coal edges as I reached and dug and shovelled and half straightened up, my back screaming, my sides aching.

I got used to it. I had to.

Cricket was my outlet. I played often in the late summer evenings although very tired after a day's work. As a slightly built boy of fifteen, I played in the Nuncargate second eleven as a fast bowler, the other players being men in their twenties. In my first season I took 76 wickets at an average of less than 5 runs.

Two years later I was promoted to the village's first team. Bowling in sandshoes because I didn't own a pair of boots, I sent down 20 overs during the match, even though I'd worked down the mine all the previous night.

I remember the game as if it were last week. After a few overs my nose began to bleed. Team-mates, men they were, urged me to leave the field.

I refused and kept on bowling. Down the mine I dreamed of cricket; I bowled imaginary balls in the dark; I sent the stumps spinning and heard them rattling in the tunnels. No mishap was going to stop me bowling in a real game, especially this one.

My nose bled worse than ever, spattering my shirt. I was again advised to go off, but I continued to bowl. Then a ball caught the middle stump. My next delivery scattered the incoming batsman's wicket. Although feeling a bit weak by now, I got ready for one more and hit the off stump. It was my first hat-trick.

Cricket was my reason for living.

CHAPTER THREE

Into the Sunlight

A HUSH OF EXPECTANCY fell on the crowd at Trent Bridge, Nottingham, in a match in the summer of 1922. Surrey were playing the home county and Jack Hobbs, one of my idols whom everybody knew as the Master, was about to take strike.

It was my second visit to Trent Bridge. Realizing nothing could stop my passion for cricket, my father two seasons before had brought me here to see my first big match, Notts against Warwickshire. The view wasn't very good then because we only had sixpenny seats. We were so far away the players looked like models, but it didn't stop me plying my father with questions on the identity of the flannelled heroes and quizzing him about the game.

I was seventeen before I was to go again. The Master was playing, and I begged my father to let me go. He told me if I could get myself to Trent Bridge he would pay my admission to the ground.

We lived 12 miles from Nottingham, but the solution was at once simple. I walked. It was nothing for me to walk a few miles for a game of cricket.

And now Jack Hobbs was facing fast bowler Fred Barratt to take the first ball. I watched enthralled as the ball whipped down. The Master played it to short leg and was out caught! It made no difference – I applauded as hard as I could. And after the match I trudged home, happy to have seen my idol in action for the first time.

On the way back I thought about Barratt. He was a professional, and he'd come from a Midlands mine. From Annesley. I knew a lot about him. For instance, in 1919, against Yorkshire at Sheffield, he'd hit three sixes in successive balls off that greatest of slow bowlers, Wilfred Rhodes. I didn't know what that ball to Hobbs had done but it must have been a beauty.

William ('Dodge') Whysall, Notts and England batsman, had been a miner. He used to work in Newstead Colliery, a couple of miles from Annesley. Then there was another Notts professional, Sam Staples, who in his first season with the county had scored over 300 runs and taken 42 wickets at 21 runs each with excellent medium-paced bowling.

Joe Hardstaff was another famous Nottinghamshire player. He had gone to Australia in 1907–08, and was still playing for the county. He happened to live a few doors away from me and used to work with my father in the Annesley mine. A son, young Joe, was aged eight at this time.

I thought about them all.

One day about a year later I got the shock of my life. Joe Hardstaff came up to me in Nuncargate and said 'Harold, my boy, how'd you like to go to Trent Bridge for a trial?'

I couldn't believe my ears. It didn't seem possible.

'Surely not, Mr Hardstaff?'

Joe, who was later to go on the Lord's ground staff and then become one of England's greatest umpires, told me he had been watching my progress for some time. It surprised me greatly because although he and my father were on friendly terms, I had never imagined that he might be interested in me.

'I think you have possibilities,' he said. 'You might even become a great cricketer one of these days if you really wanted to.'

If I wanted to! It gave me a thrill, but it seemed all too fanciful.

To be frank, I did not believe I would get as far as a trial with Notts. But Joe Hardstaff arranged it otherwise it might never have happened. I had to have proper gear. It cost my father £9 – a small fortune at the time – to fit me out with flannels, sweater and sprigged boots that were not the best fit. I'd have been laughed off the ground without them.

It was 1923, and I was then eighteen. My father accompanied me to Trent Bridge, home of the Nottinghamshire County Cricket Club just outside Nottingham and not far from the River Trent. The famous old ground was founded in 1838 by William Clark, whom records show was the top-hatted lessee of the Old Trent Bridge Inn that once stood nearby.

My appearance at the nets obviously shocked members. I looked skinny and was only 5 feet 4 inches in height. I was pale from underground work in the pits.

As I took off my sweater and measured off twenty paces, some members of the committee laughed openly at the idea that they were seeing an outstanding young fast bowler.

'Good heavens,' I heard one say. 'He'll never run that far let alone bowl when he gets there.'

'He'll never bowl fast, he's too small,' said another.

I think everybody must have been smiling, sympathetically, when I moved in.

Gritting my teeth I began slowly, pace quickening, stride lengthening, then the ball shot towards the batsman. I was nervous and a little frightened, but their joking had spurred me on. I kept letting them go without let-up. I might have looked of little physical account, but I was wiry. And I had a strong back.

I bowled to several batsmen at the nets, but they played me all right. They were county cricketers, and experienced players. One or two made encouraging remarks. I must have made a good impression because a club official took us into his office and asked me if I would sign on for a year with a view to becoming a professional.

He asked me how much I was getting at the mine.

'Thirty-two shillings, sir.'

'Would you be prepared to accept the same here?'

'Yes, sir.' I jumped at it.

When we got outside my father said sharply, 'Why didn't you ask for more?'

'Why didn't you speak up?' I replied.

During the next three seasons I was put through my paces and pretty thoroughly. I couldn't have had two better coaches than Jimmy Iremonger, the old cricketer who was the county's coach, and Fred Barratt. Joe Hardstaff and Sam Staples also helped me.

Fred took me under his wing because he and my father were friends, and I think he also took a fancy to me because I was so small and keen to learn. He taught me how to swing the ball. Three years later when I was to bowl Ponsford with a bender, it was no fluke. Nor was it the result of a natural action. It was because experienced men taught me, and I had practised hard.

Fred never played for England in any Test, but about 1930 he visited Australia and New Zealand in an English team. A big powerful fellow, he was pretty fast. Once be broke two stumps bowling R. H. Williams of Worcestershire. In 1928 he got the cricketer's double – 1,167 runs and 114 wickets, the first Notts man to do so since John Gunn in 1906. He was one of the biggest hitters I've ever seen.

When I went to the nets for the first time, I didn't know how to hold the bat properly. I don't think I'd ever heard of footwork. Jim Iremonger taught me patiently, even though I felt uncomfortable wearing pads.

A class batsman and good off-break bowler, Iremonger surprised the visiting Australians just after the turn of the century with his ability. For Notts in 1904 he scored three centuries in a row against other counties. He figured in century opening partnerships with A. O. Jones on thirty-four occasions and twice with Jones made century partnerships in each innings – 134 and 144 in 1901, and 102 and 303 in 1904.

These then were the men who were my guides and mentors. Iremonger taught me more than anybody else. He it was who gave me a smooth run-up, balance and follow–through most important factors for the bowler who hopes 'to turn 'em pale'.

'Every step of every run to the wicket must be the same,' Iremonger drilled into me. At first my bowling stance was not side-on enough to gain the full body swing needed to impart that devil into the ball. The action not high enough. I kept at it. There was some speed in my delivery, but I had a lot to learn. I was not to perfect my run-up and delivery for about three years.

Iremonger prepared such good lively wickets that many famous batsmen when playing Notts used to have special practice on them. Several visiting county cricketers played for England after they sought and received coaching from Iremonger. One was C.J. Barnett.

At that time a group of us travelled to Trent Bridge each day from the minefields. Kirby–in–Ashfield station was a meeting place for Whysall, Barratt, Staples, 'Old' Joe Hardstaff and me. I had a half hour walk to the station, rode in the train for half an hour, then walked twenty minutes to the ground unless a tram was there, which wasn't often. It was the same thing in reverse at the end of the day after playing cricket.

Among my chores I used to help the Notts dressing-room attendant clean the boots of visiting county players. I can remember Maurice Tate, another of my idols, playing against Notts for Sussex. I sat there enraptured watching Tate and Gilligan bowl.

I cleaned Maurice's boots (you could have eaten off the soles), and when he left at the end of the match he flipped me two shillings as a tip. Little did I dream that within two years I would be sharing England's opening attack with him or that later I would be the cause of this great bowler not getting a game in England's Test touring team.

A year after joining Notts as a probationer, I was given my first county game, against Northants, and I took one wicket. I wasn't ready and was sent back to the nets. But it was a start, and I think the late Johnny Tyldesley helped me get it by dropping a favourable word. Coaching at Old Trafford after his retirement, he was playing in Lancashire's second eleven when I took 8 for 44 for Notts second team.

I gave up working in the mine but continued to give Mother all my money from the Notts club. She said I needed it myself and promptly returned some of it. My parents became my greatest supporters.

In keeping fit for cricket, I was not able to engage in any special course of exercises – there were no facilities anywhere. I did possess a pair of chest expanders, but Jimmy Iremonger made me give them away for fear I pulled a chest muscle.

Every night in the winter months I walked miles and miles. A local cricketing pal, Len Varnum, kept me company as we roamed all over the place, not knowing or caring where we went just so long as we walked. A man is lucky to have a friend who will help him like that.

Half-way through the 1925 season, when I was twenty, I got my real start in county cricket, against Yorkshire at Sheffield.

Herbert Sutcliffe faced up to me. Or rather, I faced up to him. He looked surprised at the speed of my first ball as it went past him. The second came off his bat and flew into the safe hands of my skipper, Arthur Carr, at slip.

It was a big thrill. Yorkshire's great opening batsman had returned from triumph in Australia where in seven Test innings he had made 59 and 115 (his first Test) and 176, 127, 33, 59 and 143.

The Nottingham *Evening Post* cricket correspondent said about this match in retrospect a year later:

I remember asking Whysall, 'What of this youth Larwood?' 'You will see,' replied the Notts batsman. 'We have found the best fast bowler for many years.' That was before Larwood bowled, and when I saw him I nearly laughed. It shows how careful one should be. Larwood didn't seem strong enough to bowl even medium pace — and now he is the world's best fast bowler.

Mr Carr, my Notts skipper, who was to captain England in four out of the five Tests against Australia the following year, wrote later about my early days with Notts:

I shall always remember 'Loll' (that's what we all call him) bowling at the nets for the first time. I asked who he was and was told his name was Larwood. Little did I think then that he was to become the present day finest fast bowler in the world. He was a tiny little fellow, very polite, serious, most retiring, but with both eyes and ears wide open.

I never thought he would become what he is as he was so small, and although he put the devil into his bowling, I was afraid he would never last in county cricket.

When he did come into the side, I used to bowl him four or five overs, but now I have known him to bowl an hour and a half on end. In fact in 1932 he bowled through the two innings to Leicester without a rest, an amazing performance.

When 'Loll' first played for Notts, whenever he hit the stumps, a broad smile came across his face which he tried to conceal. It would not interest him if somebody was *caught* off his bowling!

After taking Sutcliffe's wicket and two others in the Yorkshire game, I had a permanent place in the Notts side. I believed I had reached the top. All I wanted to do was keep my place, and I prayed I'd be good enough. My skill was hard-won, and each new season when I took up the ball at the nets I was terrified I might have lost it.

I'll never forget my first county 50. It happened in the return fixture against Northants in 1925, two months after I won my cap and blazer – in those two months I had taken 52 wickets at less than 22 runs each.

I went on to make 70 in the match, figuring with W. Payton in an eighth-wicket partnership of 151 in an hour and 50 minutes.

Almost 5,000 people applauded and cheered me when I got to 50. But out in the middle I heard one voice above the others. An uncle, excited at my first batting success, jumped up and bawled out, 'Hoo-bloody-ray!'

I echoed his sentiment quietly to myself.

The pony pit-boy had come a long way.

CHAPTER FOUR
Inside an England Cap

TO BE A GENTLEMAN in England in 1926 was one thing. To be
a gentleman *and* a cricketer meant you were in a class of
your own. Cricket, 'the meadow game with the beautiful
name', was still very much a gentleman's game, and one in
which he wore power and privilege like a cloak.

The amateurs, almost a thing of the past today, were still
gracing the creases then. England had many young chaps
with private incomes and nothing to do. Fathers had their
sons learn – *learn*, not taught – cricket to develop character
and qualities of manhood. For them cricket was very much
a noble pastime.

The war and its aftermath changed all that. Now they
have to work for a living. Even dukes have to find employ-
ment of some sort in these days. Some dukes, anyway.

Lord Hawke, president of the Marylebone Cricket Club
just before 1920, pointed to the difference in social status
between amateurs and professionals when he declared
publicly, 'I hope I will never live to see the day when a
professional captains England.'

It was nothing unusual, though, for some amateur Test
captains to have to seek the advice of professionals during a
game, it being obvious that they themselves were hardly
equal to the occasion.

The class barrier preventing professionals captaining
England, going right back to 1877 when J. Lillywhite led the
first English Test team in Australia, was to be broken in
1952 when Len Hutton was appointed captain of the
English side. Tradition went over the Lord's balcony as a
result of this change. But many traditionalists, even some

within the inner circle at Lord's, regarded it as a retrograde step, and Hutton had to fight off an attempt to dethrone him.

The fears of the poobahs were unfounded, however, for Hutton led the English Test team in the same dignified way as had the amateurs before him. And his team in 1953 won the Ashes, which Australia had held since 1934, and held on to them in Australia a year later.

In 1926, as in the year before, the professional treated the amateur with deference. There was no option. Cricket was your job, your livelihood. It was his pastime. The respect for one's 'betters' was even more pronounced if the professional happened to come from a working-class home. You were expected to call an amateur 'MR', and did. The captain, though, was usually 'Skipper'.

It was a new experience for me to be thrown on to the fringe of a class-conscious society. I was always conscious of the division, but it never worried me. I had my own standards, and I didn't worry about anybody else.

I don't think the amateurs actually looked down on the professionals. If there *was* any feeling between the two, it was caused by cricket administrators. They were the ones who insisted on discrimination, such as calling the professionals by their surname. Out in the middle, we were all equal. I showed my annoyance with anybody who dropped my catches, pro or amateur.

But equality ended as the team left the field. The amateurs went through one gate, the pros through another. We even used different dressing-rooms. We usually kept apart when having a noggin or two of ale, too. We pros didn't mind because it meant we could talk more freely. The presence of the captain, always an amateur, tended to put a damper on conversation if he happened to be among a group of pros off the field.

I took every man as I found him, no matter what his background. But to me some of the greatest gentlemen were to be found among the pros. Jack Hobbs was one. As I got to know him over the years, while privileged to watch and challenge his peerless batting, I came to understand that he was incapable of anything paltry or mean.

I shall always believe Jack Hobbs was the man who gave me the break of my life. In 1926 he was without doubt still the world's greatest batsman. In a game between Notts and Surrey at Trent Bridge, I bowled Jack cheaply with one that fizzed back from the off. It was a feat for any bowler to break Jack's wicket once.

Jack said it was a fluke when the press asked him how it happened. In the second innings, his reputation and skill brought out the best in me, and I bowled him early again with the same ball. Most newspapers again branded it a fluke for an unknown youth to twice humble the Master. But Jack was silent the second time.

That was when I entertained thoughts for the first time that I might be considered for Test selection. The Australians had arrived in England to defend the Ashes which, allowing for the intervention of World War I, they'd held since 1912.

The first Test came and went, and I didn't get a mention. Played at Nottingham, it was washed out after 17 overs.

England had so many good fast bowlers at that time that I didn't expect to be picked, and so I wasn't unduly disappointed. I knew I was pretty fast, but there were some bowlers around at the time who might have been faster.

Every county had at least one good fast bowler. Some had two: bowlers like Nobby Clark, the Northants left-hander, Maurice Nichols of Essex, and Fred Root, the left-arm swing bowler from Worcestershire. There were many others.

When Arthur Carr came up to me at the Trent Bridge nets one morning in mid June before the second Test and quietly told me I was to play for England at Lord's, I was overwhelmed. Carr wrote later:

When the selection committee picked him to play for England under self in 1926, I told him.

He replied quietly, 'Surely Skipper, I am not good enough to play for England?' He had always been so modest.

From the coal-seams near Nuncargate to the Holy of Holies

in three years was more than I had dared to hope for.

Jack Hobbs was on the MCC selection committee and, although he never told me, I know he had a lot to do with my rapid rise to Test cricket. How else could an obscure youth represent England in the greatest of national games without somebody to sing his praises in the cloistered corridors of Lord's? It would have been so easy for a batsman of his fame and standing to ignore his double dismissal at the hands of a boy, letting his public think it was just one of those things that happen to everybody. But Jack was a sportsman in the finest sense.

When I got my head inside an England cap I was twenty-one, 5 feet 7½ inches high and weighed well under 11 stone.

Coming face to face at cricket headquarters with giants like Jack Gregory, whom I venerated, Warren Bardsley and Charles McCartney was the stuff that dreams are made of. King George V and 30,000 of his subjects were there to top it off.

Bardsley, great opening left-hander that he was, made 173 not out in this match. The King congratulated him, and I met His Majesty when both teams were presented. Bardsley, at forty-one, was on his fourth tour of England. But he hooked me and pasted me to the boundary. So did McCartney, but Sutcliffe caught him for 39 in slips off me, and I bowled Gregory as he tried to hit me out of the ground. My figures were 2 for 99 and 1 for 37. The wicket was felt-like and even-paced and gave the bowlers little chance. The match was drawn, Hobbs making 119 and Hendren 127 not out. One paper summed it up well: 'On the day it was good bowling, without being quite subtle enough to nonplus the Australians.'

A report of that match by Frank Thorogood in the *Daily News*, dated Monday, 28 June 1926, had an interesting reference. It said:

On the whole Larwood came out of the ordeal well after bowling short in his first spell, and Root responded gamely to the frequent calls made upon him, although *the Australians generally contrived to find a way out of his leg traps.*

Twice in one over Bardsley hit the Notts man (Larwood) to the boundary and McCartney took 11 in the next with two 4's and a 3. But the frequent change in bowling had a disturbing effect on the pair, although *the wiles of Root with his leg side army of men were resisted.*

'Plum' Warner, in his book, *The Fight for the Ashes in 1926,* had a word to say about Root's bowling in that game. He wrote:

The wicket was not difficult. It was not exactly plumb, for there was some moisture on it, but Root did not owe his success to anything in the state of the pitch.

It was Root's last minute in-swerve, combined with a most accurate length, which gave him his fine analysis.

He had four short-legs close in, a mid-on, and a square-leg: and the batsmen seemed immobilized. There was always the shadow of these four brave men – 'the suicide club', as someone called them – across the minds of the batsmen.

For Root I have a great admiration. Strong in build, a lion in heart, he can literally bowl all day.

Some people describe him as a 'mystery' bowler, but there is little or no mystery about his methods which have been well known to cricketers all over England for some years.

Larwood and Geary also bowled well. The wicket was on the slow side for a bowler of Larwood's pace, but in spite of that he made the ball swing away sharply from the batsmen at the last moment. Three times he beat McCartney with a delivery of this description, and with his nice action and not over-lengthy run he made a good impression.

A week before the third Test at Leeds, where McCartney made a hundred before lunch, I met the Australians again when they played Notts. I was fresh from taking a hat-trick at Cambridge and had been presented with the inscribed ball by my skipper.

I was nowhere near as fast then as I was to become later. My run-up was still imperfect, causing a waste of energy. To make the ball fly I had to drop it short, and I dropped it short in this match.

Bardsley once more showed what he could do to fast

bowling by hooking me vigorously. I was glad he wasn't younger, and I learned then that to bowl on his leg or middle stump even at that age was to give runs away. He had scored over 2,000 runs on each of his three English tours before. He got 87 before I bowled him, finishing with 3 for 88 off 27 overs. Woodfull, maintaining his reputation as the unbowlable, carried his bat for 102.

An incident happened in this match in the dismissal of Johnny Taylor which will give some idea of my speed at this time. Johnny edged one from me between Staples at first slip and Whysall at second. They both dived for the ball, Staples catching it with Whysall's hand ending up behind his and taking the jar. Although Whysall's hand didn't touch the ball, it was bruised all over.

The selectors passed me over for the third Test and the fourth at Old Trafford. I was on the ground for each match, but there was rain about, the pitch was soft on both occasions, and other bowlers were preferred. Both matches were drawn, and when I came into the side for the last Test at the Oval, the stage was set for a cliff-hanger of a game to decide the Ashes. The previous Tests had been played over three days, but this was to be a fight to the finish.

Wilfred Rhodes, who first played for England in 1899, was brought out of Test retirement for the match. Rhodes was then forty-eight. He and I were to rout Australia in the last innings.

Knowing what it meant to be cut off from the thing dearest to my heart, I put so much devil into my bowling in that match, in case I never got another chance, that I made Herbert Strudwick stand further back from the stumps than he'd ever stood before. It was the last Test appearance of Surrey's stylish keeper.

Arthur Carr, who had captained England in the four Tests up to then, and done so much to weld the team into a fighting combination, was dropped in favour of the Kent amateur, A. P. F. Chapman. In fairness, Carr was out of form and not yet recovered from a recent illness.

A tattered old MCC flag taken to Australia for the victory tours of 1903–04 and 1911–12 flew from the Pavilion flagstaff for the match, and everybody hoped it would be a good omen.

England's first innings notched 280, Mailey getting 6 wickets. I made a blob. Australia scored 302 in reply, Tate taking 3 for 40. I took 3 for 82. My victims were Bardsley, Tommy Andrews and Collins.

The ball that bowled Andrews caused plenty of comment among the Australians. Everybody else talked about it too. In the irritating style of so many batsmen of the time, who lifted their bats and padded up to anything outside the off stump from a fast bowler, Tommy gracefully lifted his willow to let the ball go past. It uprooted his off stump.

Andrews claimed there must have been a piece of dirt or something on the pitch. You don't get pieces of foreign dirt on Test wickets. It was my break-back, the ball I got Hobbs with twice in the same match. I was trying to bowl an in-swinger, but as I cut my second index finger to the right and whipped my hand down my right thigh instead of following through in an arc to the left for the conventional out-swinger, the ball would cut back at speed like an off-break, sometimes as much as 6 inches. Try as I might I could never bowl the in-swinger.

Plum Warner wrote:

The ball with which he bowled Andrews will long be remembered. That particular delivery brought back memories of the palmy days of fast bowling. It would have done credit to a Lockwood or a Richardson, for it came back 5 inches, making rare pace off the ground, kept low and sent Andrews' off-stump flying.

England got going in the second innings on a wicket that was a bad one. Poor tactics by the Australians let them down. A. J. Richardson, not to be confused with Victor Richardson of a couple of years later, was allowed to bowl long spells round the wicket with several fielders in the short-leg area. Hobbs and Sutcliffe simply tided over the period when the wicket was helping the bowlers, and both went on to make a century, Hobbs scoring 100 and Sutcliffe 161. England's total was 436.

Another tactical error was made when McCartney, their only left-hander, bowled over the wicket on an ideal left-hander's pitch. Whenever his spin, pitching on the wicket, beat the bat, it missed the stumps. His bowling was good, narrowly missing a wicket several times, but it was an outstanding example of a left-hander throwing away a rare gift. If he had bowled round the wicket and Richardson over, Australia would probably have won.

The result might have also been different if the Australians had appealed in the first over. England had a lucky break second ball when Mailey opened to Hobbs. A googly hit the batsman on the pad, but there was no appeal. Umpire Frank Chester told us later he had actually begun to raise his finger but pulled it back when nobody asked a question. His opinion was the ball would have taken Hobbs's middle stump. The Australians realized their mistake too late.

As it was, Australia was set the task of making 415 to win. Towards the end of England's second innings, about midday, rain fell on the fourth day followed by a hot August sun. The Australians erred by using the heavy roller when they did. The intention was to bring up as much moisture as possible from the turf to deaden our fast bowling and stop the slow bowlers from being effective. The roller was put on too late, bringing up just enough moisture to make the top 'cakey', with firm soil underneath. I was able to make the ball kick sharply, and Rhodes found he could turn it quickly. It was the only Test wicket in that season where a fast bowler had a chance, although I did not think it was a particularly difficult wicket for batsmen.

The Australians began their task at 3.30, but it was all over soon after 6. With one run on the board, I had Woodfull, even then a heart-breaking defender, caught in the gully by Geary for a duck. Rhodes worried Ponsford and Collins out, and I had McCartney and Andrews caught. I finished the innings with 3 for 34 off 14 overs, Rhodes got 4 for 44 and Tate, Geary and G. T. S. Stevens a wicket apiece.

London newspapers were filled with stories of the 'glorious victory', and Clem Hill in an article said the match was 'deservedly and gloriously won'.

A report in the *Morning Post* of 19 August shows the enthusiasm for cricket in the England of 1926:

Memorable moments crowded one upon the other outside the *Morning Post* building yesterday. But the most memorable moment of all, the thrilling climax of a four days' vigil, by the great throng of cricket enthusiasts who have lined Aldwych and the Strand watching the sensational serial unfolded by figures on the *Morning Post* scoreboard, came just after six o'clock, when the scoreboard swung inside for a second, to reappear with the fateful figures announcing England's victory.

Even as the board turned in the crowd sensed the news. A mighty cheer rang out, to swell and set the echoes rolling down the Strand to the west, down Fleet Street to the east, and to the north up Kingsway.

At noon, though play had not yet commenced, thousands were lining up. When the board showed that Rhodes and Tate were winning their way towards the fourth century enthusiasm grew apace. The appearance of the figures brought a cheer that drew men and women and boys and girls from every adjacent area. When, at 1 o'clock, the board showed 422, putting England 400 ahead of the Australians' total, there was another demonstration. And then, as an anti-climax, the sombre notice: 'Rain stopped play.'

The announcement that the wicket was being inspected, and that play was to recommence, sent the contingent of small boys into chattering delight. The fall of Strudwick, with the signal that England were all out for 436, served but to heighten the anticipation. 'Can Larwood, Tate and Rhodes go through the Australians on the drying wicket?' That was the general question. 'Of course they can.' That was the unanimous answer.

Confirmation came quickly – and sensationally. Within a minute of Geary holding that express from Woodfull's bat the thousands outside the *Morning Post* building were shouting, skipping, laughing, cheering, and shaking hands with each other.

When McCartney's name followed with the magic signal 'out' against it, the delighted cheers brought hundreds more from Long Acre to the scene. Thence, as the names of Bardsley, Ponsford, Collins, Andrews, Gregory and Richardson followed in succession into the limbo of the dismissed, excitement was unchecked.

England had but a few minutes to wait for the custody of the 'Ashes'. And yet – the crowd was impatient, for the Australians were not quite all out, and matches had gone astray before when all had seemed set for victory.

But when, after a quarter to six, Oldfield and Grimmett were separated, the magic moment was manifestly moving nearer. All was set for a great scene.

And then – at last – just after six o'clock the board swung in and reappeared: Australia, 125 – 10 – 6.

A roar, a furore, a gay pandemonium, a massed expression of heartfelt joy. There were cheers for everybody.

The *Daily Mirror's* report on the same day, gives another good account of the game:

Amazing scenes followed England's winning back of the Ashes, after five years, at the Oval yesterday.

Sensational though the final day's play was – Australia were skittled out for 125 runs – it was nothing to the scene that followed. Thousands of wildly excited men and women dashed on to the field while the players fled to the pavilion. Hobbs was captured and had to be rescued by a party of stalwart officials. . .

Larwood was obviously affected by the warmth of the reception given to him in recognition of his splendid bowling (I was weeping and thinking, This is the greatest moment of my life) and even Hobbs, so used to public applause, blushed with pleasure at his greeting. . .

The English team off the balcony, the crowd demanded the Australians, *but they could not at first be persuaded to leave the comfort of their baths.* Later they were given a reception that equalled that given to the victors.

England's team celebrated their victory in champagne, but the Australians, who are mostly teetotallers, *took cider*.

Tributes flew thick and fast for 'Demon Boy Larwood'. The *Leeds Mercury*: said 'Here is an England bowler in the making. At twenty-one he is too young for Test cricket. In a few years he should have built up the strength for the job; for they do not breed weaklings beneath the slag heaps of his county.'

Gilbert Jessop, former big-hitting Test batsman: 'Larwood kept up his pace until the end; and in him is much hope for the future.'

Daily Herald: 'We have got a genuine good fast bowler at last in Larwood – the diminutive dynamic youth from Nottingham Town who has been dubbed the "Jimmie Wilde of cricket".'

Daily Telegraph: 'Rhodes and Larwood, the veteran and the stripling, broke down the defences of the crack Australian batsmen in their second innings in a style that will make Sydney, Melbourne and Adelaide gasp with astonishment. The ball can still beat the bat when the pitch is helping.'

Plum Warner, who captained England on the 1903–04 tour of Australia: 'The youngest member of the eleven, Larwood, of Notts, took six wickets in the match for 116 runs, and fielded well. He should have a big future before him, but he must guard against bowling just short of length. He is small in stature but great in endeavour, and the rest is in his hands.'

Daily Sketch cricket writer, L. V. Manning: 'Larwood's bowling was the fastest we have seen since Gregory in 1921. Moreover, it was pace intelligently reinforced by length and direction. Not for years have we been able to enjoy the spectacle of Australian batsmen ducking their heads.'

Before the Australians left England, I played against them once more in an England eleven at the Folkestone festival. Douglas Jardine kept wicket to me on a green-looking wicket. I finished with 7 for 95 off 26 overs, taking the wickets of Woodfull, Ponsford, Collins, Bardsley, Ryder, Hendry and Oldfield.

I remember well how the ageing Bardsley and Hunter (Stork) Hendry attacked my steep-rising balls in that match. They hooked kickers to the leg boundary, Bardsley making 55 and Hendry 81.

A banquet was held for the Australians after the match to honour cricket and Empire, and those present included Earl Beauchamp, Lord Warden of the Cinque Ports, Lord Harris, Viscount Folkestone and Mr Warner.

Mr Sydney Smith, Australian team manager, said in his response to the toast to his team that Australia had been beaten fairly and squarely by the better team, and they were not squealing about it.

Referring to the sports ground provided by the Folkestone Corporation, Mr Smith remarked that if other municipalities took the trouble to provide such fine grounds, England would be able to provide more cricketers.

'It is on the cricket fields of England and Australia that the characters of men who have the destiny of a nation in their hands are moulded,' he said.

'I feel sure that what cricket has done for England and Australia has been for the good of the Empire as a whole.'

Cricket was indeed *king*.

Bodyline was yet to come.

CHAPTER FIVE

Façade of Savagery

FAST BOWLERS have a sense of humour all their own. They are a breed apart and need a certain brand of humour to sustain them in their heavy work.

The man of speed, the workhorse of cricket, puts more physical effort into his game than any other player. In a day's play he runs miles, tears up to the crease, disregarding the risks of sprains, torn muscles, hernia and other injuries; and at best he finishes the day bone-tired and foot-sore. His rewards are fewer than for batsmen and, usually, other bowlers.

His brains are in his boots, for he can bowl flat out for only six overs and then has to slow up. A batsman merely has to weather the first few torrid overs, then score off the bowler's energy, using the pace of the ball to score runs through cutting and glancing.

But the sound and sight of a flying stump is enough to restoke a fast bowler's inward fires when they are waning. At other times his system is recharged with energy when the batsman bravely goes across the line of flight but suddenly bends at right angles as the break-back or swing surprises him, the ball shaving his stumps. The batsman has been morally bowled, and the bowler's tail is up once more.

Often, however, the fast bowler's light and shade comes in incidental moments.

. I remember at the Trent Bridge nets in the early season when Bill Voce and I were giving the batsmen a work-out. Bill came from the mines to be a slow bowler with Notts in 1927 but soon switched to speed.

The batsmen used to hate facing us after lunch. That was the danger time. We'd go to the local pub for our midday break and have a few pints. Feeling no pain when we returned we'd bet each other half a crown who would be the first to crack a batsman in the ribs? The wager was made to pep us up. We'd give it to them full blast and every batsman knew it. They reckoned it was murder until the money changed hands.

An Indian touring team which played Notts had among its batsmen a Sikh named Lal Singh. He was a classy bat, and he could hook. He wore a turban which intrigued us.

We got talking about it one night during the match and Sam Staples said to me: 'I'll bet you a packet of smokes, Loll, you can't knock his turban off.'

That did it. Next day in came Lal Singh, and the field settled down. I moved in on tip-toe and dropped him one short, Lal Singh moved into line correctly to hook, missed . . . and his turban went spinning into first slip. He wasn't hurt, and I would never have bowled to him like that if he hadn't been a good batsman.

In a Test at Lord's in 1928 that splendid West Indies personality, Leary Constantine, developed tremendous speed against England's batsmen in our first innings. Frank Chester, when I took my first spell after a few overs, asked me what was wrong with me. 'I thought you were fast, but Leary is yards faster than you today,' he said.

When I bowled again a little later I thought of what Chester had said. Uncertain whether he was serious, I though I'd make sure. One of my balls knocked the peak of F. R. Martin's cap sideways. Another struck him on the forehead – Patsy Hendren rushed forward to help him but to everybody's relief he regained his feet at once and said, 'I'm all right, Patsy.'

George Challenor, Martin's partner, also had his cap creased and turned almost back to front by a flyer.

Frank Chester wrote in his book, *How's That*!: 'This was Larwood at his fastest; it seemed to be that the moment the ball left his hand it was at the opposite end of the pitch.'

It had always been the fast bowler's time-honoured right to test the batsman's pluck with sharp-rising balls. Just as this was the accepted thing, it was the batsman's *riposte* to hit bumpers to the boundary, to help himself to fours and put a stop to the speed merchant's nonsense. If he could.

Even after my successful Test debut in 1926, Arthur Carr often cautioned me not to bowl short at some batsmen. It was just asking to be hit. Jardine could hook effectively and so could Maurice Leyland, Wally Hammond, Ernest Tyldesley, Sutcliffe and Percy Holmes. Patsy Hendren was the best hooker I've seen in my life, and Les Ames was also a fine exponent of the shot, but there were lots of others who would crack you to the boundary, almost greedily. Most of the Australians in 1926 were good hookers.

George Gunn handled fast bowling better than any batsman I knew. He was a member of the family which for three generations had represented Nottinghamshire since 1880.

The only instance I know of a father and son making hundreds in the same first-class innings was against War- wickshire when George made 183 and George Junior 100 not out.

George made 119 in his first Test appearance against Australia at Sydney, in 1907. And he was up against Tibby Cotter at his frightening best.

George would move down the pitch to fast bowlers, cutting and hooking and taking the sting out of the attack.

In a county match one day he came back to the pavilion after a characteristic slamming knock against the pace men. Someone said to him: 'Gee, George, you love fast bowling.'

'Do I?' said George, taking off his pads. 'Nobody likes it, but some play it better than others.'

And George was right.

You can't afford to make a mistake against the men who are frighteningly fast. If you do, they'll remove your top set or break your arm. They make you feel that if you miss they'll put a hole in you.

It used to be said among old-timers that if Worcestershire fast bowler W. B. Burns hit you he'd pin you to the sight-screen. If legend hasn't been coloured too much by time, scared batsmen used to retreat hurriedly to leg when he reached the crease to let go. Burns was killed in World War I.

Even in the days of the last century, when wickets mostly favoured the bowler, batsmen had their courage put to the test with kickers – uncertain kickers. That bearded, barrel-bellied patriarch of the game, the late W. G. Grace, wrote in his book *Cricket* of a torrid time he and Mr C. E. Green of Essex had against flyers:

I can recall one match at Lord's, MCC and Ground *v.* Yorkshire in 1870, when he (Mr Green) stood up to Emmett and Freeman, on one of the roughest bumpiest wickets we had now and then on that ground twenty years ago. About every third or fourth ball kicked badly, and we were hit all over the body and had to dodge an occasional one with our heads.

Shooters were pretty common on the same wicket, and what with playing one ball and dodging another we had a lively and unenviable time of it.

The old Australian cricketer J. W. Trumble wrote in the Melbourne *Argus* that, facing C. T. B. Turner and J. J. Ferris (who were known at times to bowl unchanged for Australia) on a pig of a wicket, he was hit twenty times all over the body by quick-rising balls, while contending with close-in fieldsmen. Feeling at the time was that you had to take the rough with the smooth.

F. R. Spofforth, the original 'Demon', at times gave up fast bowling on the turf wickets of his day simply because short-pitched deliveries which didn't rise enough to frighten 'em were looked upon as rubbish and heavily punished.

Ernest Jones, the South Australian fast bowler who rocked Englishmen late last century with sheer speed, was nicknamed 'Jonah' because he was considered a whale of a bowler. He usually had the ball round the batsmen's ears.

On his first visit to England in 1896, he is credited with whizzing one through Dr Grace's beard after thoroughly bruising his chest with direct hits.

C. B. Fry's story was that Grace rumbled, 'What!' through his whiskers, and Australian captain Harry Trott, not wishing to upset the good doctor, said to Jones, 'Steady, Jonah!'

Jones apologized: 'Sorry, doc, she slipped.'

Jones in that innings took 7 for 84, his victims including Grace, F. S. Jackson (who had two ribs broken but struggled on to make 93), Fry, 'Ranji', Shrewsbury and William Gunn.

Two players deliberately deflected the ball into the slips and were on their way even before it was caught, deciding they would rather live to bat another day.

I remember something similar happening one day when Notts played Leicester. Hayden Smith, Leicester's fast bowler, had been making them fly at our batsmen and when he came in No. 10 one of our lads said, 'Give him one, Loll.'

I dropped him one short outside the off, and it reared past his head. The second, on his stumps, flew off his bat down towards gully. It landed a yard short of Sam Staples who scooped up a bump ball.

As Smith walked out, Sam shouted, 'Hayden, I didn't catch it! I didn't catch it!'

'You —— well did!' Smith called back and kept walking.

When I first went to Trent Bridge, they were still talking about the terrifying speed of Albert (Tibby) Cotter, the human catapult who was reputedly a menace with the ball even when a boy in short pants playing for Forest Lodge public school in Sydney.

When he came into the game in Australia, Trumper, Noble, Duff, Hopkins, Syd and Charles Gregory were all in their prime, with colts like Bardsley, McCartney and Kelleway looming up behind.

Cotter was picked for Australia against England in the fourth Test in Sydney in 1904 at the age of twenty-one, the youngest fast bowler to win Australian colours since Sammy Woods in 1888. Ernie Jones had finished his career by riding his bicycle into a water-cart and breaking his arm.

Although the returning Englishmen reported that Australia had unearthed a new pace bowler, nobody was prepared for the Cotter who demoralized English players in 1905 (he took 8 for 65 in the last Test). At Worcester he so unnerved the county team that he took 12 wickets for 34 in one day. He bagged 124 wickets on the tour, leaving behind many a set of bruised ribs. The Sydney Express, as they called him, was described on all sides as terrifying, his deliveries frequently playing about the ears.

Cotter won several Tests with his bowling and big hitting. And in a club game in Sydney he once hit 121 for Glebe in 64 minutes and for New South Wales against Victoria scored 68 in 20 minutes.

No cricket enthusiasts were surprised when Tibby was mentioned in despatches for gallantry in World War I in bringing wounded out under heavy Turkish fire.

In March 1916, when the war was at its height, a cluster of troops on leave renewed memories of more peaceful days when they gathered at the Gezireh Sports Club, Cairo, to watch a cricket match. The game was between a team of English troops and AIF members. Some of the Australians were from the small headquarters staff left in Egypt after the Gallipoli evacuation, the rest were light-horsemen training for the campaign which eventually was to beat the Turks in Palestine.

The odds were on the Tommies. Several had played for English counties and their captain, Colonel J. W. H. T. Douglas, was the celebrated 'Johnny' Douglas who had led England to victory against Australia and South Africa.

Expecting an easy win, the Englishmen weren't prepared for the shock they got from a big and powerfully built light-horseman who was brought in from the Suez Canal and dressed for the match simply by discarding hat, shirt and leggings.

Apologizing for being a bit out of practice, the Australian

skittled the Tommies with short-pitched bumpers, yorkers that knocked bats out of some hands, full tosses which broke a couple of stumps and occasional good-length balls. Most were out before scoring. He then pasted the bowling all over the field before retiring to catch a train back to Suez.

A bullet ended Tibby Cotter's life. About eighteen months later, on 20 October 1917, he was shot through the head at Beersheba by a Turkish soldier and was the first Australian international cricketer to be killed in war.

From the AIF team came Jack Gregory, one of the most ferocious of all fast bowlers. With smooth-moving Ted McDonald, they caused heavy casualties among batsmen in the 1921 tour of England, with usually three men posted on the leg side.

In the first Test at Trent Bridge, Gregory knocked out Ernest Tyldesley and bowled him with the one ball, which hit the wicket off Ernie's head. At the Oval in the last match, Tyldesley attempted a hook off McDonald and was hit on the jaw. In the second match at Lord's, Frank Woolley earned admiration by going on to score 93 and 95 after Gregory had hit him early in the ribs and on the shoulder with bumpers. Lord Tennyson got several in the ribs. In the first three Tests these terrible two took 39 wickets.

Gregory had hit Strudwick in the second Test in Melbourne in 1920 three times over the heart with successive balls.

Strudwick said what every battered Test cricketer before him had said: 'I do not believe for a moment that he tried to.'

Gregory bowling was the essence of savagery, his great kangaroo leap at the last instant presenting an awesome sight to any batsman. Off the field you could not meet a more friendly and amiable chap.

Fast bowling has always been dangerous. It was dangerous long before I came on the scene. Every batsman has known that, even George Gunn, who scored a century on his fiftieth birthday. A short ball from Surrey fast bowler Alf Gover hit him on the head causing his retirement from first-class cricket. And he could really play fast bowling.

Cricket is a batsman's game. For the sake of the public it is essential it should remain so, although that is no consolation to the man bowling his heart out. Covered wickets and nearly all the new laws over the years have favoured the batsman, making the fast bowler's task more burdensome. When somebody says, 'It's a perfect wicket', they mean perfect for the batsman, not the bowler. And no batsman apologizes when he hits you to the boundary.

The fast bowler's attack is an elemental physical attack, based on force rather than subtlety. He tries to batter his way through the batsmen's defences, giving him time for only a flicking, often involuntary stroke. That is why he is so fascinating to watch. But if he can't pierce the defences, and the batsman will not make any shots and give the bowler a chance, he is at a loss. Purely defensive batting reduces the speed bowler to panting futility.

That is why he must drop a few short. In doing so, he puts the dynamite into cricket. Every fast bowler in history has done that. And when he does drop one short, everybody knows it is a ball intended to intimidate, to unsettle, to test the batsman's combination of skill and nerve. When the fast bowler is no longer permitted to make the ball rear at the batsman, cricket can no longer be regarded as a manly game.

Although fast bowling invariably tends to become mechanical, the best fast bowling has more of method than of madness in it. It is not merely a matter of hurling the ball down at the best pace muscle can command at the best length practice can ensure. Pace without control holds little terror for class batsmen on wickets mostly made to their liking.

It is not enough for the fast bowler to use his pace blindly in sheer exuberance of spirit, even when his attack is at its ferocious peak. He must control his talents if he is to succeed. In bowling there is an artistry of speed no less than an artistry of spin.

I believe that by 1928, after perfecting my run and delivery, I had achieved almost complete control of the ball.

It was said of me that I could drop it on a threepenny-bit, but that, of course, was an exaggeration. However, I achieved the nearest thing to pin-point precision in landing in the target area balls that, on general agreement, almost outstripped the eye in speed.

A short-leg fieldsman could stand a yard and a half from the edge of the bat without fear of my ever sending down a loose ball to the batsman who was so close he could reach out and touch him. Percy Chapman proved that in 1928 when he breathed down the necks of Australians to my bowling.

Any onlooker, to whom I was unknown, watching me casually in the field, would not have had an inkling of my speed. I was not big like the fast bowler traditionally is nor was I even of average height. As for my expression, I doubt whether I looked remotely hostile. But perhaps the spectator realized that in the final aggressive flurry of my delivery, I hated the batsman.

When I gripped the ball I loved the game but hated the batsman.

CHAPTER SIX

The Melbourne 'Incident'

I DIDN'T WANT ANY FUSS. I've never been one for show. And so there were only three spectators at this 'match'. My bride was Lois Cynthia Bird, a charming girl of twenty, from the Nottinghamshire village of Huthwaite.

Nobody outside our families knew the wedding was taking place, and we were married at Basford registry office. I swore the registrar to secrecy because the whole district would have been there had it become known. The three present were Miss Irene Bird, my bride's sister, Miss Vera Randall, who attended Lois, and Bill Anthony, the best man.

After the wedding we went to my parents' home in Nuncargate for a family party and wedding breakfast. A few of our personal friends dropped in to congratulate us.

Our honeymoon was spent at Blackpool and, at the boarding house where we stayed, we read the story of our wedding, a full account, in one of the Sunday newspapers. Somebody recognized us, and everybody did what we didn't want: they made a fuss. But really we didn't mind.

That was in September 1927. In the previous season I had finished top of the county bowling averages with 96 wickets, taking 137 wickets in all matches. In the 1927 season, just ended, I was third in the England bowling averages with 100 wickets, although I'd twice been prevented from playing through injuries.

Lois and I bought a house at East Kirkby. My married career got off to a bad start because a cartilage I had displaced in my left knee towards the end of the season playing for the Rest against England was giving me a lot of trouble. I think the injury was due to bowling too long in one spell – about a dozen overs straight. I doubted in the off-season if I would ever be able to bowl again.

An operation was the only hope and, after I had it, I spent several weeks in a nursing home, going home on Christmas Eve.

In 1928 I played against the West Indies and in the season topped the England bowling averages with 138 wickets and at an average of 14 runs apiece. Towards the end of the year, the MCC picked me as the only fast bowler in the team to tour Australia, under the captaincy of Percy Chapman, the 'blond cavalier' of cricket.

I wasn't in the best of condition, my knee was still causing trouble, and so too was a thigh muscle. But a restful sea voyage did a lot to improve my condition.

An official booklet on the tour and its prospects said this about me in its comments on the English players:

A newcomer and likely to create something of a sensation. Though much under the average size of fast bowlers, he will be found quicker than anything met with in cricket today. The ball will jump at the least provocation.

Harold has had spells of rest this past season through thigh trouble but the sea voyage should have got him thoroughly fit. Has the confidence of the whole British nation, which believes him to be the best fast bowler in the world. Will do his bit with the bat and is an excellent field at short leg or mid-off. Age 24 and stands 5 ft 7 in. Was once a lad in the coal pit.

I was off to a good start, but the hard Australian wickets made my feet sore. The hard dry turf took the sheen off the ball at what I regarded as an alarming rate, and I was able to do less with the ball than in England. But there was one major difference from previous experience – I could get the ball up from a good length. Instead of having to pitch it a little short to make it fly, as in England, I found I could make it whip off the pitch moving up into the batsmen from a good length.

Early in the tour I took 7 for 51 against Victoria in Melbourne. I was hailed as the fastest bowler seen in Australia since the days of Tibby Cotter.

The *Daily Express* report of that match said, under the heading: 'Larwood Triumph at Melbourne – Great Batsmen Helpless':

Harold Larwood, the 24-year-old Notts miner, made cricket history at Melbourne yesterday when he took seven wickets for 51 runs for the MCC in the match against Victoria, the strongest batting side of all the Australian states.

He did not take a wicket in the match against South Australia a few days earlier, and the prophets of disaster who are always ready to declare that everything is wrong with English cricket made haste to predict that he would be a failure in Australia, and that the Test matches were lost already. Yesterday Larwood proved that he had only been studying the conditions.

He was irresistible. He bowled as England knows that he can bowl, and gave Australia, the home of fast bowlers, a demonstration of how utterly unplayable a ball can be. He took the wickets of all the best batsmen in the Victorian team and hit the stumps four times – on more than one occasion with balls which completely baffled the batsmen.

The Australian opinion of his performance is shown by the glum comment of W. M. Woodfull, the only batsman of note to withstand him. If, as he suggests, Larwood is not yet bowling at his fastest, what will happen when he begins to bowl in earnest?

Writing in the Melbourne *Sun*, Woodfull said batsmen could anticipate trouble when Larwood, showing old-time accuracy, worked up to top pace.

One or two incidents occurred during the game. I learned later that Bill Ponsford remarked to some of the Australians watching us practise at the nets that I didn't appear to be so fast.

As Ponsford returned to the pavilion after I dismissed him cheaply in that match, 'Stork' Hendry, the next batsman in, said to him: 'He must be a bit faster than you think, Ponny.'

We were all waiting for Hendry to come in. He had written several controversial articles, suggesting that I was no different from any other fast bowler, and I could be easily hit. Stork had been telling the Australian batsmen that as soon as I gave him a bumper he'd hook me to the fence. I didn't know this at the time, but he told me of this years later. I sensed his attitude, because he'd shown a relish for short stuff in England two years before and had to live up to those articles.

This, then, was the situation when he came in. In the first over, I dropped him one short. Stork shaped to hook, missed, and the ball hit him over the heart. He went down, and we were condemned for not going to his aid immediately. The fact was that Stork regained his feet quickly. We would have helped him if he had stayed down and looked hurt. Stork never held that against me although for two days he had the stitch markings of the ball clearly imprinted on his chest. He always said it was his fault, and I admired him for being a red-blooded sportsman.

I think it was in this match that Douglas Jardine first came to grips with the Australian barracker. They regarded his Harlequin cap as an object of great amusement. The official tour booklet said of him: 'Never known to smile on the field, but he has a fund of dry humour. Old Oxford boy.'

Jardine was nearing his century, and the crowd had been very patient. As the players walked off for afternoon tea, Stork Hendry complimented Jardine for 'a hell of a good performance'. The Surrey amateur thought it had been a bit slow, and they chatted in a friendly way. After tea Jardine got his century but continued to bat slowly and the crowd started.

'Get a go on, you mug,' they yelled.

From the slips Hendry said to Jardine: 'The wolves are out.'

Jardine said something indicating that he didn't have much regard for Australians and Hendry retorted: 'If that's your attitude you can go to ——!' They didn't exchange another word on the tour.

In Launceston against Tasmania I bowled G. P. Martin with a ball which knocked one of the bails 66 yards, almost to the sight screen. That was just over a yard short of the record for a first-class match, held by R. D. Burrows (Worcestershire) who, against Lancashire at Manchester in 1911, sent a bail 67 yards 6 inches.

The opening Test in this series was the first ever to be played in Queensland, at the Exhibition Ground in Brisbane. It was like playing a match in Aden or the Sahara. But it was a happy event for me.

I scored 70 runs (clumping one six) in the first innings, setting a record eighth-wicket partnership of 124 runs with Patsy Hendren (169), and took 6 for 32. At one stage I had 3 for 9 from 5 overs. My victims were Woodfull, Ponsford, Hendry, Kelleway, Ryder and Ironmonger. Australia was bundled out for 122 in reply to England's 521. In the second innings, I scored 37 runs and took 2 for 30, thus becoming the only English player to score 100 or more runs and capture 8 wickets against Australia in one match. I also took 4 catches. England won the game by a record margin of 675 runs, one of the most crushing defeats in Test history.

Barrackers cut loose in the match, calling out at anything and anybody. I was surprised to find they barracked even their own players. Jardine, with his colourful headgear, came in for a lot of attention, one full-throated character dubbing him 'Rainbow' and yelling every now and then during the innings of the England captain: 'When are yer goin' to get a move on, Rainbow?'

The match saw the introduction to Test cricket of the New South Wales colt, Don Bradman, and England's Wally Hammond. Bradman scored only 18 and a single and was dropped for the next game. Two mainstays of Australian all-round cricket, Charlie Kelleway and Jack Gregory, had their last games here. Both went out in sad circumstances. Kelleway became ill and Gregory, at the age of 33, injured his knee. The 6 foot 3½ inch giant, who brought the ball down from more than 7 feet and made it bounce fast and high, broke down when bowling to me in the first innings when I was on 34.

I cocked up a rising delivery from my glove. Making a great effort to take a catch, Jack fell full length on the pitch. He just managed to touch the ball but couldn't hold it. There were tears in his eyes, not from the pain of his injury, but from the realization that he could no longer play the game he loved.

I felt wretched about it. I wished he had caught the ball and not fallen. He was one of my favourites. When still a boy, I dreamed of his exploits. In twenty-one Tests against England and three against South Africa, Jack Gregory took 85 wickets. Probably the most deadly burst by a fast bowler this century was his 3 for none in two overs at Trent Bridge in 1921.

Wilfred Rhodes wrote about the match in the Nottingham *Evening Post*:

At the Oval in 1926 I had Larwood in the gully to me – he was fielding close in — and he was not worried in the slightest. He was a calm, cool, self-possessed young man and he made himself just as much at home as he would have done in a match that was of no consequence.

Larwood has always been a fighter. He has always had to 'bowl uphill' because of his size and yet he has persevered and come out triumphant.

Surrey captain, P. G. H. Fender, cabled to London that Ponsford drew away from the ball with which I took his off stump in the third over.

Before the Sydney Test I was sent this poem from a Mr D. McMahon:

> O, Lord, give us the skill to smite
> Larwood and Tate to left and right.
> In this, our blackest hour of need,
> Make of Jack Hobbs a broken reed.
> Oh help! Oh help us do our best
> 'Gainst Chapman in the coming Test.
> Grant that our bats may trounce and flail
> This lion from its head to its tail.

O, Lord, our help in ages past
Send us a bowler straight and fast.

The second Test, which England won by 8 wickets, was notable for two reasons – the 'Kippax incident' and an injury to Ponsford.

When Ponsford came in lower in the batting order, second wicket down, I was brought on for his special pleasure, as one paper said. The Sydney *Daily Guardian* reported, under the heading of 'Larwood puts Final Hoodoo on Ponsford': 'What a tragic story has been the three meetings of Ponsford and Larwood at Brisbane and Sydney. First he was clean bowled for two; then he was caught behind for six; and yesterday with five against his name, a ball from the express bowler rose high and caught the back of his left hand.' Unfortunately for Australia, Ponsford had a broken hand and was out for a month.

The dismissal of Kippax, whom Australians knew as a sportsman and a gentleman, caused an explosion from an angry mob on the Sydney Cricket Ground Hill, the worst demonstration there since hooting stopped a Test match in 1903 for half an hour when a doubtful run-out decision went against Clem Hill. The Kippax incident is today just as lively an argument as it was then.

Kippax was given out by the square-leg umpire on a second appeal, bowled Geary, and not by the umpire at the bowler's end, George Hele. A bail had been dislodged and Hele apparently was convinced the ball came off the pads of the wicketkeeper, George Duckworth, and rebounded on to the stumps.

I didn't have a clue what really happened, and I don't think Alan Kippax did, either. But other players at close quarters thought the ball hit Kippax's left pad and curled on to the stumps. They sat down on the ground, convinced that the batsman was out.

Meanwhile, George Hele called 'over' and walked away to take up his position at square leg for the next over. Kippax stood rooted to the spot; some of the fielders still lay on the grass waiting for him to walk to the pavilion; and several of the England players told Kippax he was out.

The Hill mob came in fast. They started to jeer. Eventually a number of fieldsmen appealed to umpire Elder, at square leg, and he ruled that Kippax was out – bowled. I'd never heard anything like the demonstration that followed.

A check with Rule 47 of the laws of cricket indicates that Kippax had some reason for his attitude and the *Year Book* of the New South Wales Cricket Association later held that a bowled decision by a square-leg umpire was unconstitutional. The Hill was right, though it is doubtful whether they saw exactly what happened. They sensed rather than saw.

The letter-writers were busy after that, most of them signing their names. One bluntly asked Chapman: 'How much did you pay Umpire Elder for this job?'

I received one from a Mr H. Martin, of Rozelle, dated 16 December 1928. Mr Martin said he had watched all the Englishmen in Sydney from the time of Shrewsbury and Gunn and had always found it a pleasure:

But I want to refer to the incident on Friday when you injured Ponsford to such an extent, and I think, purposely.

Why didn't you go and sympathize with him instead of stretching yourself out on the grass? I suppose you have heard as well as others why people thought it was done, but Ponsford was quite right in saying you are not unplayable. I think you think that yourself. You get a swelled head. You might be better when you leave your mother's apron strings. . . Until you learn to take a curb on yourself you will do no good. Also, the affair with Kippax was doubtful and the batsman should have got the benefit. Wishing you all the Compliments of the Season.

I didn't know Ponsford's hand was broken at the time. Besides, several players had moved over to him. A fast bowler has to work hard for his wickets, and if he shows any sympathy, he's finished. He can't afford to have any friends when he's bowling. He must keep up his façade of aggression. If he walks up to the batsman and apologizes every time he accidentally hits him, although it's the batsman's

fault and a natural hazard of the game, he restores the
batsman's confidence. It's a different matter when an injury
is obviously serious.

One other thing about that Test will always live in my
memory. It was known generally that the appearance of
Jack Hobbs would be his last in Sydney. The crowd gave
him the most warm-hearted applause I've ever heard, insist-
ing that he walk once around the arena while everybody
stood. An unassuming man, Jack was clearly embarrassed
and blushed hotly.

England retained the Ashes in the third Test in
Melbourne, Hobbs and Sutcliffe giving a brilliant display of
sticky wicket playing when England was set 332 to win. We
should not have reached 50, but with covered wickets
giving the Australian bowlers little experience of wet
wickets in addition to facing the world's two greatest batsmen on gluepots, England came from behind. Hammond
later got 200. Bradman made 123 for Australia. I finished
with 3 for 127 and 1 for 37.

In the fourth Test, which England won by 12 runs, the
twenty-year-old Sydney batsman, Archie Jackson, made his
debut, going on to score a stylish 164. Bradman made 40
and 58. Hammond made two centuries, 119 not out, and
177.

Arthur Mailey reported on the match in the Adelaide
Advertiser, dated 5 February 1929. He said:

Yesterday he (Jackson) batted like one inspired. Larwood tried
off-theory, and Jackson cover-drove and back-cut him with the
greatest of ease. Then a strong leg field was set for the fast
bowler, who began his famous leg theory. But the young
Balmain batsman glanced the ball through the field with fine
accuracy. All theories and all bowlers were alike to him.

Mailey also said:

Larwood also appeared to feel the strain more than the other
bowlers, and is now probably convinced that fast bowling in
Australia – like measles – is something to be avoided. We
found him during the latter part of the day cutting half a dozen
yards off his run to the wicket, and hoping that one of the

willy-willies – or whatever they call those spiral winds which were screwing round the oval – would pick him up and put him under a shady tree.

Bradman showed unorthodox class in the fifth Test and, mainly due to his 123 and Woodfull's 102, Australia won its first match, beating England by 5 wickets. Bradman showed a keen eye and jumped down the pitch to meet the bowling in refreshing style, generally looking brilliant but risky and often wielding a cross-bat.

Before the final Test, in the return game at Melbourne with Victoria, there was trouble and plenty shown – the crowd resented the action of Chapman in bringing me on to bowl (I was tired anyway) at Ironmonger, the batting 'rabbit' of the team.

The Nottingham *Evening Post*, no doubt because I was involved, published a full account of the incident. It read:

Any glory attaching to a wonderful batting display, which realized a not out 275 for Woodfull, was completely obscured today by the unprecedented and unaccountable attitude of the Melbourne crowd.

At the second stage of the match, one of the blackest pages in the history of Anglo-Australian cricket was written by the concerted efforts of a section of the spectators. . .

The incident occurred just before tea. The last Australian, Ironmonger, came out to bat, the score being 560 for 9 wickets. Chapman put Larwood on to bowl and immediately the Notts player was given the ball the crowd became most unmannerly.

They booed and jeered him with such obviously bad feeling that Chapman, realizing that this barracking business had reached an unbearable climax, told the fieldsmen to cease play.

The chorus of jibes and catcalls continuing, the field sat down on the grass until the cloud had passed over. Instead, however, it developed into a veritable storm.

Woodfull, the hero of the match, walked over and appealed in vain to the crowd to behave themselves. Then came a lull, and Larwood picked up the ball and the field stood up for play. But this was only the signal for a renewed outbreak.

Three times Chapman attempted to re-start the game and each time the crowd sank lower into the mire of bad feeling.

Both Woodfull and Chapman walked over to the alleged sportsmen and entreated them to conduct themselves with more propriety.

Chapman beseeched them to 'act like sportsmen', but not even England's captain could bring them to see what churls they were. Chapman was refused a hearing. He went among them like the gallant figure he is, but it was all in vain.

Finally Ryder, the Victorian captain, said that to save further trouble the tea interval would be taken.

Chapman walked in through the pavilion enclosure to a mixed reception. The cheerers, though in the preponderance, were not numerous enough to drown the booers.

The climax was reached when a spectator rushed up and uttered an offensive epithet, which was addressed to Chapman.

Finally the Englishmen disappeared into the pavilion, and the crowd was left to an empty field – as they deserved to be. The tourists were very much upset at the disgusting scene.

The crowd's behaviour was all the more ill-timed, as when it occurred Victoria had kept the Englishmen fielding in a sweltering heat for the best part of two days.

They had everything to congratulate themselves upon, but instead preferred to be miserably ungenerous.

Regarding the incident, Mr F. C. Toone, the English manager said, 'We must always remember that the game of cricket calls for the exercise of the highest character, and greatest traditions. With that in view I am confident there will be no recurrence of today's incident.

I didn't know what hit me when I struck the Aussie barrackers. I took it personally. It upset me and definitely put me off when they counted me out and called out personal remarks.

I didn't understand the Australian character. Especially

when, two days after the experience, they stood and cheered me when I went in to bat.

Had I, on this day in question, been butchered to make a Roman holiday?

CHAPTER SEVEN

The Don's Luckiest Day

I REMEMBER THE DAY 'Dodge' Whysall was laid to rest. Dodge was a great Notts and England batsman and a good friend. He was only eighteen when he began to play for the little club of Nuncargate.

Dodge was the best of fellows and a cricketer from the cradle. Nothing ever flustered him, and the tighter the corner, the better he played. In his last five years with Notts, he scored 10,800 runs.

Dodge died on Armistice Day, Tuesday, 11 November 1930. He slipped and fell a week before at a dance, grazed an elbow, and thought nothing of it. But septicaemia set in and specialists at Nottingham General Hospital were unable to prevent Dodge's innings finally coming to a close.

Eight of us from the Notts club bore his coffin through the streets of Mansfield. They were lined with sympathetic townsfolk. I'll never forget the scene at the cemetery. Members of the Notts committee had edged the grave with green foliage and yellow roses, the club's colours. At the head of the grave rested a floral tribute arranged by Dodge's playing mates. It represented a broken wicket on a green pitch made of asparagus fern. Framing this were white carnations, orchids and golden roses.

I think all of us wept as the coffin was lowered. I know I did. But before it sank from sight I saw the most touching thing in my life. Mrs Carr, on behalf of Arthur Carr, who was captaining the MCC team in Africa, moved forward and laid on the coffin Whysall's blue county cap.

Bill Woodfull was one of hundreds who sent tributes. So, too, was an anonymous boy who wrote to Dodge's widow telling her Dodge had once stopped and willingly obliged him with an autograph, although he had been in a great hurry at the time. The lad, signing himself 'Leicester Autograph Hunter', was moved to write 'The last ball is bowled, the game of life is o'er.'

I remember 1930 for another reason: Donald George Bradman. He hit us like a tornado and, mainly through his batting, Australia regained the Ashes. He was a different Don from the one I had met in Australia, more calculating and assured now, taking fewer risks on the slower wickets; he was impregnable.

Bill Woodfull led the Australian side containing many newcomers. Only four had been to England before. On paper both teams appeared equal, but Bradman made the difference when he got going.

And it didn't take him long. Within a week of stepping off the deck of the *Nairana*, he hit up 236 against Worcester, beating a record that had stood since 1882, and followed this with 185 not out at Leicester.

Don showed a preference for shots off the back foot, and the slow-paced English wickets suited him admirably. He became the first Australian to score 1,000 runs before the end of May. Don apparently was a little lucky to make it because it was the last day of the month and when Hampshire won the toss their captain elected to bat. But Clarrie Grimmett gave the batsmen plenty of walking to do, and Don opened with Archie Jackson, hitting up the 1,000 just before rain drove players from the field. It was a great effort.

Bradman finished up with 974 runs in the Tests, a record that still stands. His total of 2,960 runs in all matches also remains a record for an Australian in England.

In the first Test I took 1 for 12 off 15 overs and 1 for 9 off 5 overs. As can be seen from the figures, I was treated with respect but didn't have any great penetration. I developed tonsillitis during the game and was not available for the second Test at Lord's. I also had other trouble and began a series of visits to the dentist, who said I'd not be fit again until I had some teeth removed.

After I became ill, in the second innings, Maurice Tate took over the burden of attack, sending down 50 overs, off which only 69 runs were scored. England ran out a winner in the first Test, Australia winning the second and fifth with the other two being drawn.

Duleepsinhji, a delicate artist with the bat if ever I saw one, made a century in his first Test at Lord's, getting 173 before Grimmett had him. Bradman made 254 in the first innings, and with Woodfull (155) put on 251 for the second wicket. Australia made a total of 729. Bradman's score was the highest in a Test in England.

I came back in the third Test at Leeds and took a merciless pasting from the Don. In that game he scored a hundred before lunch, went to 309 at the end of the day and next day took his total to 334, overshadowing his score of a week or so before and setting a new world record for a Test. I finished the innings with 1 for 139 out of a total of 566.

Something happened in that innings of Don's which has never before been made known publicly. Even before he had scored I had him caught behind the wicket. There is no doubt in my mind he was palpably out. Everyone around the wicket appealed, even Jack Hobbs, the fairest man I ever met on a cricket field. That would have been two down for one run, as I had just caught Archie Jackson off Maurice Tate.

I've never moaned about it because I've always believed you have to take the rough with the smooth, and the umpire gave his decision. Any member of the English team, like Wally Hammond, Herbert Sutcliffe, or George Duckworth, could confirm that Don snicked the ball but was given the benefit by the umpire.

After his mammoth innings, Don received a cheque for £1,000 from an Australian philanthropist, Mr A. E. Whitelaw, 'as a token of his admiration'.

I was dropped from the fourth Test.

Maurice Nichols was given a chance in my place and managed 2 for 33.

Back in favour for the fifth Test at the Oval, I took

another trouncing from Don, finishing Australia's only innings with 1 for 132 off 48 overs. The wicket I took was Don's. He made 232, going his own sweet way.

Don mentioned in his book, *Farewell to Cricket*, that in this match he was given out caught behind off me when he did not touch the ball. 'It swung away slightly as I played at it,' said Don. 'Noticing the swing I turned my bat at the last moment and I was amazed when Larwood appealed (he was the only one who did) and more amazed still when the umpire gave me out.'

It about sums up Don's attitude on the tour. Most players were satisfied with a century, but not Don. When he got his first hundred, he settled down for another as if he had just come in. And then another.

I can only say regarding the catch in question that Don could be right. I wouldn't deny it, but at the same time I can't say he is correct. I don't think I would have appealed unless I thought he had given a chance, but, honestly, I can't remember. I was never one to bluff on these occasions, but at the same time I expected a man to leave the crease when he was out. The fact that I was the only one to appeal doesn't mean a great deal. It was the practice in England for only the bowler and those close around the wicket in a position to see or hear to appeal. I was amazed to find in Australia that even fieldsmen near the fence appealed. Most of the Aussies played the game hard.

Frank Chester said in his book: 'Larwood's nature seemed to be quite unassociated with the dynamite released from his right arm. He was the cricket gentleman of all times. When I handed him his cap at the end of an over he invariably said "Thank you". His appeals were always justified and if it was not out he would turn to the umpire and say "Sorry".'

There seemed to be no answer to Bradman's batting in 1930. He did all the things you didn't want him to. You could bowl on the off, trying to get him to lift one or give a catch behind, and he'd pull you hard to the leg fence. He had the quickest eye of any batsman I ever met. There seemed only one way to get him out – tire him out. But he never seemed to tire. His stamina and concentration were extraordinary.

Don was cruel the way he flogged you. He seemed to have a computer-type approach, never giving anything away and always able to go his own inexorable way. He jumped down the pitch to the bowler just when he felt like it, which was most of the time.

Nobody watching the majority of 'pat-ball' batsmen of today can have any idea what Don was like. Good-length stuff went to the boundary like a bullet. He used all the shots in the book, and a few that weren't. He used to lean back and cut you or move into position for a leg shot even before the ball was delivered.

But we took it all as part of the day's work. There seemed always a hope bowling to Don because he made shots, although it became frustrating because the chance seemed as though it would never come. Don didn't break my heart in 1930 – he just made me very, very tired. He was the most challenging batsman I ever bowled to.

Plum Warner told reporters privately that Don was the only batsman he had seen who could square cut me from right over the stumps. The ball could not be seen till it rebounded off the pickets. That's how Warner described it, and he was right.

Apart from giving the bowlers a headache, Don caused a flutter among the august rulers at Lord's. Still only twenty-three, and with the prospect of years of cricket ahead of him, Don had humbled England's bowlers, and there seemed little chance of regaining the Ashes, which had been so hard-won, while he was around.

Plum Warner, by now well entrenched at Lord's as an administrator and grand patron of the game ('The Prime Minister of English Cricket') , wrote for all England to see: 'Bradman has blunted England's best bowling force, Larwood. Is there a better bowler we can launch against him?'

There was just a faint chance though that Don was fallible after all. In the match at the Oval came a sign of a possible chink in his armour. A drop of rain had fallen and for about half an hour while the sun dried out the pitch; it gave the bowler an opportunity. It was the only Test wicket in the series where this had occurred.

I was able to make the ball rear on the Oval wicket while Bradman and Archie Jackson were batting. Good-length balls were jumping up around the chest and shoulders. Noticing the response from the wicket, I bowled as hard as I could. There is nothing more heartening for the bowler than to get a little lift from the wicket. It's like icy champagne to the palate. The ball popped sharply as I hurled myself into each delivery. I pinked Archie several times. He took it like a man and stood up to me, playing the game of his life.

Don didn't like the balls rising on his body. He was hit once or twice, but the real significance in his play during the duel was that he kept drawing away. It wasn't all that obvious to me at first because I was mainly concerned with getting the ball up off a length, but I began to notice that he flinched. Others saw it too and talked about it after the match. I thought Bradman was a bit frightened of the ball that got up sharply. I may have been wrong but that was my impression. I wasn't dropping them short – the ball was popping from a good length.

Don quotes a London paper report: 'The dangerous wicket helped the bowlers, who made the ball fly, Larwood being particularly vicious. Frequently the lads, after being hit, writhed in pain, but bruised and battered from head to toe, they carried on. Certainly it was a wonderful display of courage to withstand such a terrific onslaught.' I don't think they were bruised to that extent, but certainly they took a few knocks. Archie received most of them.

The two batsmen weathered the torrid half-hour or so and the wicket reverted to being a comfortable rug for them. That half-hour meant more than a brief but rough period for the batsmen.

In my sharp-rising balls was embodied a silent protest from every bowler in England at the over-preparedness of English wickets. Groundsmen for several years had been experimenting with marling, fertilizers, and so on, to perfect the wickets. They produced beautiful wickets but only for the batsmen. The bowler didn't have a chance unless the batsmen lost interest or made some elementary mistake, something you can't expect from a first-class player.

Even in the 1963 Australian Test series against England there were obvious signs of over-prepared wickets. For England to make 4 for 381 on the last day of the match, at the Oval, suggests this was very much a batsman's wicket. Those thousands who stood sheltering under topcoats and umbrellas, hoping vainly for rain to stop long enough to give England the chance to pull off a last Test victory and level the series, deserve better-balanced wickets. Draws because of dull wickets are not good enough for them.

To bowl short of a length on those wickets was simply to make the ball stand up and ask to be hit. It was as simple as that. That's why Bradman, with his naturally quick eye and snappy footwork, was able to stand back to good-length balls, having been accustomed to the faster and concrete-like wickets in Australia, and hit them at will all round the wicket.

The situation was already desperate. Fast bowlers, unable to take wickets with normal good-length bowling, had already resorted to other methods. They were all complaining because of the absolutely docile wickets.

Every left-hander was using leg theory, Bill Voce repeatedly. Fred Root had been bowling leg theory for at least five or six years. He used to get a ball swinging in sharply up around the thighs or ribs to a packed leg field, usually of six men. Nobby Clark of Northants was another who used leg theory in almost every match. He got the ball up high.

The reason was simple: it was to induce the batsman to play at a rising ball in the hope that he would pop up a catch or mis-hit when making an attacking stroke. As the ball was directed at the leg stump, it was in line with the batsman's body, so he could hardly ignore it.

Root bowled like this to Bardsley, McCartney and other Australian batsmen in 1926, and although it gave them some anxious moments and several knocks, they had little trouble in smacking him through the coterie of crouching fieldsmen. They could hook and weren't afraid to hook. They took the bowler on regardless of hits on the thighs and ribs.

I remember an incident when the Australians played Notts on that 1930 tour. Several of them expressed misgivings at what sort of treatment they might receive at the hands of Bill Voce. As one of the Australians said later privately to a correspondent: 'It wasn't Larwood we were worried about, it was Voce. We weren't thinking of Larwood at that stage.' Stan McCabe and Vic Richardson made runs in the match against Voce, who wasn't picked in any of the 1930 Tests.

I hadn't bowled leg theory in England. If I did, it was only to try it out as an experiment. I found that, despite the tremendous strain of bowling on unresponsive pitches, I could take a reasonable number of wickets through swing and break-back, combined with sheer speed. My county figures, even after 1932, will bear that out.

When I used leg theory in the Adelaide Test in 1928 against Jackson and Bradman, I had five or six men on the leg. I bowled rising balls on the leg stump. It was a desperation move to dislodge the batsmen who were on top in hot and exhausting conditions. They both seemed to play it well enough.

Leg theory was the bowler's revolt against wickets that didn't give him a chance. The dice were loaded against him another way, too. Under rules then existing, he couldn't take a wicket with a ball that hit the pads from outside the off stump. A bowler with an off-field setting would put one down just outside the off stump, challenging the batsman to make a stroke and give him a chance of taking his wicket, only to see him pad up and prettily wave his bat in the air, letting the ball pass or hit his pads. At the same time the wickets were so slow that batsmen had a tendency to play to leg balls that were pitched even on the wicket. This is what encouraged bowlers to set their leg trap.

Conditions like these caused several incidents in county

matches at the time. I remember there was trouble in 1930 in a match between Notts and Somerset. Bill Voce put down a long spell of leg theory. An amateur named Case was felled by a flier, dropped his bat and was so groggy when he walked out that he picked up a stump instead of his bat.

The last couple of Somerset batsmen in made their own form of protest. One, a right-hander, faced up with a left-hand stance and was promptly bowled. The last man walked away from the wicket without a ball being bowled to him.

The writing was on the wall, and it was time for cricket administrators to step in. The bowlers' plight was aired in English newspapers, but nobody in authority seemed to take any notice.

That indefinable quality that provides a balance between bat and ball was clearly disturbed. The bat had too many advantages. Groundsmen had done their work too well.

Balance in a game of cricket when the players of both teams are more or less of the same standard depends on the state of the wicket. A fast bowler's only chance at that time was to strike a wicket on which rain had fallen. When the sun settled on it, the wicket showed life.

Occasionally I found a wicket that responded without rain, but not often. It made all the difference to the match. You could tempt a batsman to make shots, knowing you had a chance to take his wicket. The match lived if the batsmen accepted your challenge and attacked the ball. Most batsmen played the game in this way, and there were quite a few of them who attacked the ball as if they hated it. But there was no challenge on dead wickets. The batsman had it all his own way.

The arrival of Bradman made the difference. His genius as a run-scoring machine put this imbalance in cricket up in lights for everybody to see.

CHAPTER EIGHT

Just a Little Night Out

I WAS A WORRIED MAN when I went to the nets at Trent Bridge in the spring of 1932. I always felt this way at the beginning of a season. I feared I might have lost it.

By now I had a family and responsibilities. Cricket was my livelihood, along with a chicken farm I was developing. If I lost my knack for bowling fast, there seemed little alternative to going back down the mine. Perhaps some other job would be offered to me, and I wasn't afraid of work. But mine work was the thing I was qualified for outside of bowling. There was a good deal of unemployment in England, and jobs were scarce. A man couldn't expect too much. But at the nets I was glad to find the old speed and control were still there. I settled straight in to my old rhythm.

There was to be a tour of Australia later that year, and I hoped I would be chosen. It was my only chance of making a bit of money. Playing cricket as a professional gave you just enough to make a good living. We were paid £9 a match and, with representative matches, it usually worked out at a little more than £400 a season.

In the 1932 English season I was to make my greatest impact so far on county cricket. I took 162 wickets – 24 more than my previous best – to head the England bowling averages at 12 runs a wicket.

In the 1928 season I had again headed the averages with 138 wickets (14 runs apiece), but in 1929 finished twenty-fifth with 117 wickets (21 runs). In 1930 I was fourth with 99 wickets (16 runs apiece), and in 1931 came back to first place with 129 wickets at 12 runs apiece.

I knew I was in the running for the Australian tour on my averages alone. But I really didn't expect to be chosen because my bowling had met with limited success in Australia in 1928, and Bradman had flogged me in 1930. In the five Tests I had taken 18 wickets for an average of 40 runs. I took a wicket every 88 balls. Very few forcing shots were made off me in that tour, and I would estimate that close to 75 per cent of the fours hit off me came from snicks or mis-hits. But my performance didn't look all that good on paper.

One reason for my poor analysis in Australia was that after two or three overs I couldn't swing the ball at all. My away swinger, the only one I could bowl, would not work when the shine wore off quickly on the glazed surfaces of Australian wickets. In England, in the heavier atmosphere, I could swing all day, right up to the 200 runs mark. I found that in Australia I was just plain up and down after about three overs, or perhaps four, and it was useless having slips. Even a great surge of speed is not enough to dislodge first-class batsmen if the ball isn't doing a little something.

I feared I would not be picked also because there was such a crop of good fast bowlers in England at the time. There were so many talented players about that most cricketers could never be certain of selection. These days a Test team more or less picks itself.

Apart from Nichols and Bill Voce at the time, there was the big, bespectacled Yorkshireman Bill Bowes, who first played for the MCC in 1929 and was really dangerous in English conditions. Gubby Allen, the Cambridge and Gloucestershire amateur, was another with strong claims. Apart from Nobby Clark, there was Ken Farnes, the 6 foot 4 inch Essex and Cambridge amateur who could get the ball up in a hurry. I felt I would miss out should only one fast bowler be chosen as in 1928, but thought that two would go this time, thus giving me a chance.

When the 1932 Test trials were announced, my name was missing from the English side. I was chosen for the Rest. Arthur Carr, my skipper, told me he thought it was an insult to my ability not to be picked for England. He urged me not to play, offering to pay me out of his own pocket the full allowance I would have received for appearing in the match. But I played for the Rest and was very relieved to find myself in the touring team for my second visit to Australia.

The captain was D. R. Jardine and the joint managers P. F. Warner and R. C. N. Palairet. The other members of the touring team were G. O. Allen, F. R. Brown, K. S. Duleepsinhji, The Nawab of Pataudi, R. E. S. Wyatt, L. Ames, G. Duckworth, W. R. Hammond, M. Leyland, T. B. Mitchell, E. Paynter, H. Sutcliffe, M. W. Tate, H. Verity and W. Voce.

Jardine was a member of the selection committee. The complete selection committee for the 1932 tour was Lord Hawke, chairman; Peter Perrin, an Essex official; T. A. Higson, a Lancashire official; D.R. Jardine, of Surrey, and P. F. Warner.

The MCC obviously considered Jardine an ideal choice to captain England in a bid to regain the Ashes. He was a blue-blood amateur who had obtained his Blue for Oxford as a freshman in 1920. His father, M. R. Jardine, had captained Oxford in 1891. In his first full year with Oxford, Douglas Jardine headed the batting averages, scoring 746 runs.

A polished and correct player, he hit many centuries for Surrey and in other matches, such as the Gentlemen *v.* Players. In 1927 he scored 120 for The Harlequins *v.* Oxford University in the annual game. He played in two of the three Tests against the West Indies in 1928 and, in that year, finished second (1,168 runs, average 61.88) to Hammond in the Australian tour figures, beginning the tour in brilliantly consistent form. He also captained England against New Zealand in the 1931 Tests.

A dour fighter, Jardine was one of the most classically correct batsmen I had ever seen. Nobody ever played a rising ball better, with the elbow pointing straight down the wicket in copybook style.

Jardine was born in Bombay on 23 October 1900, of

Scottish parents. By profession he was a solicitor, in London, and in a pretty big way. He was legal adviser to several London banks. Most of his legal work was concerned with the more lucrative aspects of the profession, such as conveyancing and probate.

As his selection to captain England was to have such a profound impact on the cricketing world, Jardine's background is significant. A man of contrasts generally looked upon as an upper-class Englishman, he regarded himself to be more of a Scotsman than an Englishman.

Although born in India of a distinguished colonial family – his grandfather was a judge and his father a lawyer there – he spent little of his childhood in India. He was an only child and went to school in England, to a preparatory school called Horris Hill in Newbury and then to Winchester College, one of England's most exclusive schools, where the code was of the stiff upper lip. Jardine's upbringing tended to be lonely, and he emerged a somewhat complex, introverted character.

Even at the tender age when he attended Winchester, Jardine showed some of the character traits which were later to cause an international furore. He is remembered at fourteen arriving at Winchester and having 'a somewhat unusual air; he was mature, tall and determined, clearly a new man who must be treated with respect'. He showed an intransigence through a lofty belief in himself.

Jardine's sporting days at school were notable for his leadership rather than his natural talent. He was a stickler for the rules of cricket, and for playing to the very margin of the game's code. He developed his ability by practice and dedication and at Winchester won his white flannels – the equivalent of a first XI cap – at the age of sixteen. At nineteen he led his school to victory over Eton and played for a public schools' side against the MCC at Lord's. He read law at Oxford, where many regarded him as 'difficult', and later joined a London solicitor's office. He also joined Surrey County Cricket Club, quickly establishing himself as a sound middle-order defensive batsman.

Jardine was outstanding at almost everything he did. A

fine shot with both rifle and shotgun, he spent a great deal of time stalking game in Perthshire on the estates of family and friends. He and his wife spent their honeymoon in Africa big-game shooting.

When the MCC appointed Jardine to captain England in April 1931, against New Zealand in the Tests, the die was cast for the game of cricket to be embroiled in its most vicious and acrimonious feud. As news of his appointment reached Winchester College, the great Yorkshire coach Rockley Wilson remarked that Douglas Jardine would make a fine skipper, 'but he might lose us a Dominion'.

Interestingly, the man who pushed Jardine's promotion was Plum Warner, a former England captain and then an influential member of the MCC's selection committee.

In recommending Jardine, Warner chose to overlook two vital clues which at the time might have forewarned Lord's of danger ahead. Firstly, although Jardine gained a freshman's blue for cricket at Oxford, and played three times in the varsity match, he was never asked to lead his university. Later there were some who said this was due to his brusque treatment of those under him at Oxford.

Secondly, Jardine was certainly not a popular figure on the 1928–29 tour of Australia, a fact which Warner acknowledged later when he wrote: 'Jardine had neither understood nor been understood by the Australians. He was not simpatico to them, nor they to him.'

Clearly Warner was motivated by a belief that only a man of Jardine's iron-willed determination could achieve the impossible by beating an Australian side which included the legendary young Bradman.

Warner's attitude of the time was shown in a book he wrote several years later, in which he revealed his personal promotion of Jardine. Warner said:

When in 1931 I came into closer contact with Jardine, I realized – it was easy to do – that here was a man who was a thorough student of the game of cricket, keen and competent, one who had thought much and pondered deeply over the tactics and strategy of the game and, incidentally, a stern critic of his own cricketing abilities.

The coming tour appeared to him in the light of a crusade, and it was certain that he would put his whole soul and endeavour into the work in front of him. Backed by my colleagues, I recommended him to the MCC committee in an appreciation of the situation which is, no doubt, in the archives of Lord's.

Warner was also to write of Jardine, in a personal letter after the 1932–33 tour: 'He is a queer fellow. When he sees a cricket ground with an Australian on it, he goes mad. He rose to his present position on my shoulders and of his attitude to me I do not care to speak.'

Of course, many of these historical facts were not to emerge until later. I knew little about Jardine. We were worlds apart: he was the English gentleman, a man of classically correct background, an intellectual who would become a student of Hindu philosophy, the representative of the establishment; I was just a young man from the pit face trying to make a living and grateful for the opportunity of playing for England.

Not long after England's team had been announced Notts came to London for a match. I think it was against Surrey. During the game Arthur Carr came up to me and said something like this: 'Loll, one or two of us are going out tonight for a little dinner. I'd like you to come along as my guest. I've asked "Tangy" (Voce) as well.'

It was more or less an order coming from the Skipper, and it was nothing unusual. He was a very generous fellow and would often stand us a drink and invite us to go on little outings.

After the match we went to the Piccadilly Hotel. Jardine came too. I don't think I was surprised by his presence, because he and Arthur Carr got on well together. We all had a few drinks, then we went into the grill room for a meal.

Eventually we got round to discussing tactics for Australia. Jardine and Carr were doing most of the talking. I didn't contribute much to the conversation, nor did Bill

Voce. We were professionals. At least, that's how I felt.

Leg theory was mentioned. I could see what they had in mind. Bradman was the big problem. He was the key man in Australia and Jardine wanted to curb his run-getting.

They spoke about the Oval Test when Bradman drew away from me. There had been a lot of talk among cricketers about this match, and I had heard it said that Don could well have a weakness to fast-rising deliveries on the leg stump. Many people believed that to be so.

I told Jardine I thought Bradman had flinched, and he said he knew that. I don't know how he knew because he didn't play in the match, but he could have been watching it or perhaps someone had told him.

Jardine decided that Voce, being a left-handed natural in-swing bowler, should concentrate on Bradman's leg stump and bowl to his normal leg-theory field which he had been using in England for at least two years. It was felt that Voce, a big fellow of about 6 foot 3 inches, with a powerful action, would be able to get the ball up pretty well off a good length on the faster Australian wickets.

Then Jardine asked me if I could bowl leg theory.

I said: 'Well, Mr Jardine, there's this to be said. After about two overs it's useless trying to swing the new ball in Australia.'

Arthur Carr knew that I was very accurate, and he and Jardine kept asking us what we thought about everything.

Finally Jardine asked me if I thought I could bowl on the leg stump making the ball come up into the body all the time so that Bradman had to play his shots to leg.

'Yes, I think that can be done,' I said. 'It's better to rely on speed and accuracy than anything else when bowling to Bradman because he murders any loose stuff.'

We had a few drinks as we talked, and it was a very pleasant night.

It seemed that the leg theory Jardine wanted us to bowl in Australia was no different from that which English county teams had been accustomed to for years. It was the same thing that Fred Root bowled to Bardsley, McCartney and the other Australians in England in 1926, only in my case it would be faster.

I had bowled leg theory a few times, but only for short periods. Bill Voce had used it quite a lot, and I thought at the dinner that he would be much more successful than I in Australia.

There was some talk about F. R. Foster having bowled leg theory against Australia. Foster, to all accounts a magnificent fast-medium left-hander, routed Australia with S. F. Barnes in the 1911–12 tour there. Between them they took 66 wickets, Foster several times taking five or so wickets, bowling to a packed leg field. Foster bruised Victor Trumper badly, getting the ball up round the thigh and ribs.

Old-timers also talked of George Hirst, the thick-set Yorkshireman who went to Australia in 1904 and gave Australians a taste of leg theory. His best was 5 for 48 in Melbourne. I don't know whether he bowled it all the time in Australia, but from what I had heard he bowled a lot of it in England. Against Australia at Birmingham in 1909 he took 4 for 28 and 5 for 58.

At the dinner I didn't think we were breaking any fresh ground in deciding to bowl leg theory to Bradman. At the same time I had no doubt of its purpose: we thought Don was frightened of sharp-rising balls, and we reasoned that if he got a lot of them over the leg stump he would be put off his game and be intimidated, and eventually, having to direct his shots to the leg all the time, would give a catch to one of the onside fieldsmen.

Jardine made the observation that if leg theory unsettled Don and succeeded, it might well succeed against other Australian batsmen. I went along with the idea. I could see it was my only chance. I knew I couldn't swing the ball after two or three overs, and then I could see myself pounding down on the hard Australian wickets, panting and perspiring under a blazing sun and being hit all over the place by Bradman. He had pasted me two years ago when I could swing the ball. What would he do to me in Australia?

I also had a score to settle with him. He had got on top of

me. As a professional, any scheme that would keep him in check appealed to me a great deal.

I could have said at that dinner that I wouldn't bowl leg theory but, really, there was no reason why I should have felt that way. I could see it might give me a chance. Jardine seemed to think it would succeed and, after all, we were only going to try it. For all I knew Bradman might hit me all over the leg side. But it was worth the effort. That's where it all started as far as I was concerned. It was just an ordinary little night out.

It was after this dinner that Jardine apparently began to pop in to F. R. Foster's flat in St James to talk over leg theory field placings with him. I have no direct knowledge that Jardine ever did so, but it is a view widely believed, especially since Foster confirmed it later in an Australian weekly newspaper.

It has also been claimed that Jardine spent several days analysing diagrams of Australian batsmen's Test innings that had been compiled by Bill (Fergie) Ferguson, the famous scorer. I don't know anything about that. The only time leg theory was mentioned to me after that night out was on the voyage to Australia. I don't know of any discussions Jardine might have had with anybody else. It has been asserted that the form of attack which I used in Australia in 1932 was suggested to Jardine by somebody. It may have, but I don't know. I can only tell what I know.

George Duckworth, the Lancashire wicketkeeper who visited Australia in 1928 and 1932 and played in all the Tests in England in 1930, including that fateful one at the Oval, has been named in this connection.

George was as good as any captain. Often in a Test he'd chat to you after an over as you stood in the slips and offer various suggestions if he had noticed what he thought was a weakness in any batsman. Whether he saw Bradman flinching in that match, and later pointed it out to Jardine, I wouldn't know. He and Jardine were very friendly, but beyond that I cannot go. Archie Jackson told his friends that Duckworth was the first one to notice Don drawing away and mentioned it to Jardine.

Others have suggested that it was P. G. H. Fender, Jardine's county captain, who gave him the idea. The notion is intriguing, for Fender had a reputation as being one of England's greatest captains, a man who was a shrewd judge of human nature, who could recognize the moment of destiny when it arrived and do remarkable and unexpected things. Certainly he did a lot for Surrey with only a mediocre attack and between 1920 and 1930 there were many who claimed he was the ideal man to lead England.

As a captain against whom I played many times, I regard him as one of the greatest I ever came up against. His bowling looked very ordinary, but he was so clever and calculating that he used to 'think' batsmen out. I remember that he and Arthur Carr disliked each other intensely, possibly because they were rivals, and whenever they met Carr used to try to hit Fender out of the ground almost with every stroke.

Certainly Fender would have been motivated to try to prove Bradman a less sublime batsman than the rest of the world believed, and he was no doubt aware of the talk among English cricketers that Bradman, following the incident at the Oval, was afraid of the sudden and unexpected rising fast ball.

As a pressman in Australia covering the 1928–29 Tests for two London papers, and in a book later, Fender severely criticized the brilliant young newcomer. He suggested that Bradman was 'unwilling to learn', that he was brilliant but unsound. Fender wrote: 'One minute one would think him a grand player, and the next he would look like a schoolboy.'

The criticism stung Bradman. After his onslaught in England on the 1930 tour, Bradman mentioned the fact in a book on himself:

I hope for pardon when I say I had a particularly personal reason for looking forward to my first match against Surrey. Mr Fender, the Surrey captain, besides being a great captain of a great county, is also a leading critic of his country; and if I have not misunderstood him, he did not think too highly of my batting or my fielding.

In the Australians' traditional opening match against Surrey in 1930, with Fender as captain, Bradman cut loose, scoring 252 not out at the end of the day, deprived of taking his score higher only by rain washing out play. He went from 50 to 100 in less than an hour and from 100 to 200 in only eighty minutes. He is reported as saying on reaching the dressing-room: 'I wonder what Fender will have to say in the morning paper this time?'

Fender could not have enjoyed the experience of having to eat crow, of having his words of wisdom hurled back in his teeth right on his home ground as he neared the end of a distinguished career. Fender and Jardine were friends (Jardine replacing him as Surrey captain in March 1932), and with Fender's reputation as a tactician, there is absolutely no doubt that Jardine discussed his fast leg theory tactics with his old friend and skipper, even if the inspiration for those tactics did not originate with Fender.

For all I know, Fender may have been the first one to mention this possibility to Jardine, but even if he didn't I feel sure he played a leading role in exploring the potential of fast leg theory in discussions with Jardine. Fender denied the claim, but I don't think his disavowal could be taken seriously.

Arthur Carr pointed the finger towards Fender in the post-mortem that followed the bodyline tour when he said: 'He (Fender) gave me the tip that Jardine wanted to learn more about my two bowlers, Larwood and Voce, and proposed to ask the two bowlers and myself out to dinner to discuss things. We all went to the grill room at the Piccadilly Hotel.'

I had no knowledge of that. Carr did not discuss that aspect with me. The first I knew of any special tactics for the coming Australian tour was when Carr invited me to the grill room and Jardine brought up the subject.

Carr always maintained he did not mastermind the bodyline plot, as some Australians suspected, and I am inclined to believe him. But he played a part. Jardine certainly consulted him, as he was something of an authority on the subject of fast leg theory with Voce and me in his Notts team. He asked us occasionally to bowl in that style, although Bill Voce used the method more often than I. My bag of English wickets was always reasonable with orthodox fast bowling.

The prospect of unleashing a burst of fast leg theory against the Australians would not have been unpalatable to Carr. He came from a privileged background and shared a dislike of Australians with Jardine. He thought Australians played the game much harder than the English. I'm sure he subscribed to a belief popular among many Englishmen then that for too long English cricketers had played the role of gentlemen against the rugged Aussies who went all out to win Test matches. These people saw the appointment of the tough-minded Jardine to captain England as a welcome break with tradition.

Some Australian cricketers put the blame on V. W. Jupp, who was both a professional and amateur in his long career. Nine times he took 100 wickets and scored 1,000 runs (a record for an amateur in 1932), and as captain of Northants turned Nobby Clark loose to give the visiting Australians a taste of real leg theory in 1930.

There again, I can't say. I do know the members of the MCC selection committee must have been fully aware that the Australians in 1932 were in for a further taste of leg theory and the reason why, when Duleepsinhji dropped out, a fourth fast bowler in Bill Bowes was added to the MCC team a few days before we sailed. There had never been four speed merchants sent to Australia before.

In my opinion there was another man, generally excluded from these discussions, who had as much to do with bodyline being used against Australia as anybody; he was Plum Warner. He always gave the impression to outsiders that he was compelled to walk a diplomatic tight-rope and exercised no influence over the captain. But he never spoke against bodyline on that tour as far as I was concerned. Behind the dignified and affable English exterior there was a shrewd brain and dominating personality that would not hesitate to drive home any advantage. It was Warner who, after winning the toss and deciding to bat in a Test match at Sydney in 1904, changed his team by substituting a batsman, A. E. Knight, for a bowler. This move brought a change in the rules, making it compulsory for captains in future to exchange teams in writing before the toss.

Warner was also the captain of the MCC team in Australia in 1911–12 , before ill health forced him to hand over duties to 'Johnny Won't Hit Today' Douglas. That was the series in which F. R. Foster, probably the father of leg theory, used the theory with such good effect to enable England to regain the Ashes by a 4–1 margin. He took 32 wickets at 21.62 and, with the help of Sydney Barnes, demoralized the Australians. Foster kept the ball well up.

In helping to choose four fast bowlers, Warner must have known that Don Bradman and the other Australians were in for a taste of leg theory. His own admission later, that he saw in Jardine a man with the spirit of a crusader, indicated his own steely attitude towards winning.

For my own part, something that I was to write after the tour in a book called *Bodyline?* created some confusion on the issue of who was to be held responsible for hatching the bodyline plot. I said in that book:

Fast leg theory was born in the Test match at Kennington Oval in August 1930, unknown to anybody but myself. A spot of rain had fallen and the ball was popping. My great friend, the late Archie Jackson, stood up to me and got pinked once or twice in the process, and he never flinched.

With Bradman, it was different. It was because of that difference that I determined then and there that if I was again honoured with an invitation to go to Australia, I would not forget that difference.

The phrase 'unknown to anyone but myself' combined with the determination that I would not forget, could have been construed to mean that I alone dreamed up the idea of bodyline and kept the dark secret to myself. That wasn't so. I talked about Bradman flinching that day, and so did others. It was a talking point among some top cricketers after we drew attention to the supposed flaw in Bradman's play.

I thought from that incident that Bradman was frightened of the fast-rising delivery, and it set me thinking. I wondered if he might not be susceptible to balls that got up sharply, but I did not sit down then and there and work out tactics to beat him. I merely stored it away in my mind for the next time we might meet.

The thought that Bradman could be frightened of, or at least uneasy, about such deliveries, obviously became known to Jardine long before the team was picked for the 1932-33 tour. Who told him, I don't know.

All the intimate details of how bodyline came to be formulated will probably never be known, but history must accept the fact that Douglas Jardine is the man who seized upon an idea, shaped and moulded it and put it into effect.

Bodyline was not devised in England as some grand master plan for victory, worked out to the last detail; it was merely a scheme in Jardine's mind, which he thought might succeed, and I went along with the idea, believing it to be the only chance of dominating the brilliance of Don Bradman.

The first understanding I had of a mere thought being translated into action, into actual tactics, was when Jardine raised the subject with me in the grill room of the Piccadilly Hotel. That was the real beginning of it as far as I was concerned. It was a simple grill room tactical talk that was to split the Empire, something I could not imagine at the time in my wildest dreams.

The truth is that bodyline was probably an amalgam of several minds, beginning with my observation at the Oval that Bradman had drawn away from the sudden flyers; Jardine, hearing about this, saw the potential of a strategy that might succeed in curbing Bradman and, after various discussions, became the architect of it.

Jardine's reticence to talk about his tactics as the tour began, and his decision to hold back the bodyline attack until a crucial point in the tour, no doubt sprang from two reasons: he wasn't sure the plan would work, and he wanted to surprise the Australians as late as possible, just before the first Test.

It was to prove interesting on the tour to see who was *for* leg theory and who was *against* it, and where they stood after the tour.

CHAPTER NINE

Jardine versus the Press

'SARDINE', THEY CALLED HIM. And the Man in the Cap. And, of course, hundreds of less polite names.

I first met Douglas Jardine in 1927 in a county match and again at various times later under similar circumstances, but I don't think we exchanged more than half a dozen words. I know I was surprised at the first encounter because he came in to bat at about No. 5 or 6, and I expected him to be easy meat. But he proved himself a sound defender, and I thought he should have been higher up in the Surrey batting list.

Australians who played against Jardine for the first time when they met Oxford in 1923 claimed he was so withdrawn it seemed an effort for him to whisper 'two legs' to the umpire when he came in to bat. They said he didn't speak to any of them.

Even on the 1928 tour of Australia, Jardine and I had little to say to each other. He was friendly but, as was the custom, amateurs and professionals stayed away from one another, although on tour we used the same dressing-rooms.

Apart from that one night out, Jardine and I didn't have a great deal to say to each other until the 1932 touring team sailed for Australia in the *Orontes*. Jardine didn't give me the impression he was a snob, but I felt he preferred the company of men of intellect. It was a good trip out; we danced, joined in parties and played deck sports. Jardine was friendly enough with team members, but much of the time he kept to himself. I remember often seeing him sitting in a quiet corner reading Chaucer.

I took the opportunity of having a good rest and put my feet up because I knew how strenuous the tour would be. It wasn't until towards the end of the voyage when the *Orontes* approached Fremantle that I started to do any real exercise.

One of the many tall stories that began to circulate about the 1932 tour was that Jardine had his fast bowlers hard at work on deck practising leg theory against a single stump. I didn't need to be rehearsed to gain accuracy, and any cricket that was played was merely to keep the muscles supple and the eye in.

Leg theory was discussed by Jardine several times, and he outlined his method of attack to the other fast bowlers in general terms. I am certain that all the fast bowlers on that trip were aware that leg theory would be used in Australia in the hope that it worked. Jardine may have had talks on tactics with Hammond and Sutcliffe on the voyage, but I cannot be certain of that. I do know that every member of the team knew what our tactics would be simply as a matter of conversation, even if Jardine did not specifically mention them to every member. The subject of leg-theory bowling was often mentioned, but it occupied very little of our time. There were no team meetings on tactics, no outlining of field placings on blackboards, or anything like that. But everybody knew leg theory would be tried, and we were asked to keep it quiet when we arrived in Australia so that we could give Don Bradman and the other Australian batsmen a surprise.

On arrival in Perth the tour got off to a normal start, with officials trotting out the customary platitudes about the glory of the game, and so on. It was the same on every tour.

Jardine was to come to grips almost immediately with the gentlemen of the press and, as for us, he began to rule the team with a firm hand and made it known on all sides that he had only one purpose in mind – to win the Ashes.

Famous cricketers as a rule imprint their epitaph on the scoreboard, but Douglas Jardine was to leave a legacy far more complex and intriguing than a whole book of Test match statistics.

One of the first things Jardine did was to refuse a gift of a bottle of Scotch for each member of the team. The local agent of a firm of whisky distillers had called at the Palace Hotel in Perth, where we were staying, and made the offer to Ferguson, the scorer. Jardine told him he would not allow his team to accept the gift. England's team members were going to put fitness before all else.

Then came the first clash. Claude Corbett, the Sydney *Sun* representative, bowled up to Jardine in Perth, in the usually disarming way Australians have, and suggested to him that if the team selections were released each morning his journal, an afternoon paper, would be able to get a scoop. Jardine frowned, looked at Corbett for several seconds and said 'What damned rot! We didn't come here to provide scoops for yours or any other bally paper.'

Corbett sent off a story saying that he found Jardine rude and unco-operative. Somebody arranged a peace meeting between them in Jardine's bedroom, and over a glass of beer he agreed to forget the incident 'for the time being at any rate'.

It was a bad start for England's captain with the Australian pressmen, who didn't seem to understand him. Jardine, I think, regarded them with undisguised suspicion. He was a highly educated and cultured man, but I felt his austere approach was caused partly by shyness.

While in Perth Jardine indicated to us that he would not stand any nonsense. He confiscated Freddie Brown's golf clubs because he said his strokes were becoming like a golfer's. Press relations with Jardine went from bad to worse after the first match of the tour against Western Australia. We were about twenty minutes late on the field, and Claude Corbett promptly pointed out in the Sydney *Sun* that Bryant, the captain of the Western Australian team, under the laws of international cricket, could have claimed the match because of our tardiness.

The story got around among pressmen that Jardine was late because he had been shopping in Perth. I can't remember what the reason was and probably didn't know at the time. As a result, Jardine received a number of letters criticizing him for being discourteous to the waiting Australian crowd. When we were in Adelaide, he sent for Corbett and, in the presence of Plum Warner, told him that his explanation for our lateness was wrong and said he was very annoyed about it.

Jardine said, 'Mr Corbett, I have received a number of letters from Australians, abusive letters. These I disregard. I have also received a letter from an English friend of mine living in Australia. Of course, I shall reply to him. In view of what I have told you, is there anything you would like me to add to the letter as a comment from yourself?'

Corbett said, 'Yes, Mr Jardine. There *is* something you can add. You can tell him from me that my comment is this: You can go and get f——!'

Corbett's phrasing was decidedly Anglo-Saxon.

Mr Warner intoned plaintively: 'Gentlemen, let's keep the conversation on a higher plane.'

After that Jardine became more sphinx-like than ever. Australian reporters could extract nothing from him and complained that he was frequently discourteous and supercilious. A number of them approached him just before the third Test for details of the England team, which they needed to catch the editions. Jardine told them: 'The team has been selected and now reposes in my pocket. And it will remain there until I choose to issue it. We're here to win the Ashes – not to provide stories for newspapers.'

It was not the final clash, and on the eve of the fourth Test, Jardine refused to meet any Australian pressmen. The message came through Herbert Sutcliffe, who said Mr Jardine would talk only to English pressmen.

But that selectivity did not extend to one member of the British press party, Gilbert Mant, a London staff member off Reuters News Agency. Mant was an Australian, a fact which Jardine quickly learned on the voyage out. I was friendly with Mant, but he and Jardine had hardly any communication throughout the eight months of that tour.

Mant felt that Jardine considered him a cuckoo in the nest because he was Australian; he also believed that, although Jardine was capable of great charm at times, the English captain's usual attitude on social and official occasions during the tour was one of aloofness, disdain and sometimes outright rudeness.

Jardine's hostility towards Mant remained so unbending that when the reporter was married at the end of the tour, Jardine was the only member of the party who pointedly did not extend congratulations.

Hugh Buggy, who represented the Melbourne *Herald* on that tour, later wrote of his first encounter with Jardine at Adelaide in 1932 when he was among an army of reporters and former international cricketers assigned to cover the tour: 'I met him at the Hotel Richmond, a tall, lean, austere figure, who somehow recalled a portrait I had seen of the Florentine monk, Savonarola. His eyes had the same intensity, he meant business and quickly revealed it.'

There was no let-up in this attitude, and the Australians, understandably, resented being shut out, especially when they recalled their pleasant relations with Percy Chapman, Jardine's predecessor, who treated all pressmen as his good friends and led the Englishmen to a 4 to 1 victory.

After that first meeting, Buggy tried again. He said to Jardine: 'You have a big battery of fast bowlers in your side.'

'Yes,' replied Jardine.

'You must be the first English team to bring out four fast bowlers. Will you use them all in a non-stop fast attack?'

'That remains to be seen,' said Jardine, declining to answer any more questions about the team.

Jardine was still annoyed over the Sydney *Sun* report on the game in Western Australia. From being cautious in the beginning he went on to become frigid and when an Empire hurricane blew up over what he called leg theory he affected not to care a hoot about what the newspapers said of him or our bowling. I honestly believe he didn't care either. If anything it made him more determined than ever to win the Ashes by the greatest possible margin in the way he had planned.

To be strictly fair, it must be said that there was really nothing unusual about Jardine's silence with pressmen. Many Australian Test captains have been equally as reticent. Herbie Collins, Warwick Armstrong and Bill Woodfull were never ones to engage in merry chit-chat with pressmen. And in a later era Sir Donald Bradman was to give reporters the impression that they were trying to trick him into saying something indiscreet.

Jardine certainly took on a small army of critics when he crossed swords with the press. Most of them were camp followers of journalism. The few humble professional journalists were outnumbered about five to one in the press box by the 'experts'. As the tour progressed, more and more former international cricketers and interstate players were engaged by newspapers to write informed comment on the Tests. They comprised an Australian eleven of former Test players and half a state eleven.

The group of experts included two former Australian Test captains and an array of former batsmen and bowlers. Most of the experts were accompanied by their 'ghosts', ordinary reporters who (as one newspaperman put it) 'with due humility at the elbow of the great converted their profound opinions into readable English'.

One ghost had the most enviable job of all. He was Jack Ingham of the *Star*, who had come all the way from Fleet Street to write the daily comments of Jack Hobbs. The experts and their ghosts, as well as ordinary reporters, faced the daily drudgery of a ball-to-ball report which ran to thousands of words.

Fleet Street was totally unprepared for what was to become the year's biggest news story, one that in any history of the 1930s must take its place along with the depression, the rise of Hitler, the abdication of King Edward VIII and the outbreak of World War II.

So unprepared was the British press for the tour to be any different from those preceding it that only three journalists travelled out with the team from London: Jack Ingham, Gilbert Mant and Bruce Harris of the London *Evening Standard*, and he wasn't a cricket writer but a leading tennis writer.

Mant wasn't a cricket writer, either, but a general news reporter; his instructions were to write a factual account of the tour, providing detailed scores for the British press. The tour was considered so routine before it began that he was allotted a maximum of 25,000 words. But as bodyline swept all other news off the front pages, he cabled 100,000 words on the tour.

A fourth member representing the British press joined the touring team in Australia, an Exchange Telegraph agency man, whose job was to send only scores and the briefest description of play. The point must be made, therefore, that the touring press party did not contain one specialist cricket commentator. Hobbs was somewhat restrained on the subject of bodyline, being acutely embarrassed in the circumstances by his public attack on fast bumper bowling by some bowlers in England in the previous season.

Fifty years after bodyline, the touring English team to Australia was to have thirty-odd commentators following it around, supported by live television and radio descriptions of play.

With the limited international newspaper and newsreel coverage of the time, I think it's fair to say that the British public did not receive the fullest possible impact of the emotion and drama of bodyline as it was felt in Australia, where the coverage was much more detailed and full-bodied. It would be untrue to say that reports sent to England were deliberately played down; they simply didn't go far enough to capture the full fury of the upheaval. Reporters cabling back to England were more inclined to concentrate on the description of play instead of getting to the heart of the bodyline dispute. Not so in Australia. Gilbert Mant was to say in later years that he regretted not having departed from style and written more comment and personal opinion – a style of journalism taken for granted these days.

It must have been a difficult tour to cover. While dealing with what was for them a new form of attack, reporters had to try to keep a sense of balance amid a tremendous controversy, and not many succeeded.

As the whirlwind blew up, the situation grew more intense each day. Day after day the press box vibrated to a sharp clash of opinion. In addition to the expert scribes, a team of general news reporters were turned loose from early in the morning till late at night in hotels where the teams stayed, trying to pick up details of any wrangle that might be going on at high levels for dissemination to an Australian public eager for every word.

Despite the rumpus and the cabling overseas of a flood of verbiage every day, Jardine would make no public reply to the criticism of leg theory.

Only once did he break his silence, at a luncheon speech in Launceston. He said:

This leg stump attack appears to have originated in the Australian newspapers. We do not know very much about it and cannot understand how it has received the publicity it has.

We have placed a more difficult field than is ordinarily used with a fast bowler, and we have so far been successful in curbing the activity of the batsmen and brought disaster to some.

I can assure you there is nothing new in this form of attack and nothing dangerous in it, and we hope it will go on being successful.

Jardine was under a great strain. Apart from the enormous outcry against the tactical game he directed, he was constantly under fire personally. To add to his burden, newspapers carried many stories alleging dissension in our team. Some of these stories were true, some partly so, but most were exaggerated. The breach between England's captain and the press made facts hard to come by, and it was not surprising that rumour flourished.

Jardine never wavered and remained aloof and, in the presence of pressmen, hermetically sealed and immobile. He showed no signs of cracking, and I must say I admired his courage. I think his attitude towards criticism was one of sheer contempt. He regarded his tactics and my bowling as fair and within the rules of cricket and believed nothing else mattered.

When the controversy was in full spate, the old internationals writing for newspapers strutted the stage, sniffing and snorting at either my bowling or the way in which Australian batsmen played it. I liked the way one newspaperman, writing of his experiences on the tour, described their labours. He said: 'They handed down their judgments to the industrious ghosts with all the solemnity of a High Court judge delivering a pregnant pronouncement on a constitutional issue, and they provided the newspapers with a mixture of conflicting views calculated to baffle the most ardent cricket enthusiasts.'

Jardine, I know, was displeased because some of us were friendly with certain Australian cricket reporters. He disliked the fraternizing and no doubt saw it as an opportunity for those players who were disgruntled to air their complaints. Jardine was to do something about this situation at the time of the third Test.

Although I came to dislike one or two Australian correspondents for their rank unfairness, the tour was enhanced for several of us by the friendliness we found among others. I met many Australians who were in every way pleasant and sensible fellows. They understood the situation and accepted it. Whenever we met for a drink and a chat, we were never embarrassed by being asked awkward questions.

More pompous nonsense was talked and written about the tour than any other. Almost every former cricketer-cum-journalist who was present wrote a book about it. I had a crack myself, taking a tilt at the press but mainly trying to justify my bowling methods on academic grounds. Some writers, of course, blamed sensational press reporting for the whole confused drama, but I have not read one balanced or really adequate book on the tour simply because most writers had an axe to grind or could view it only in a very limited way. Everything was so controversial it was impossible to tell the full story, or anything approaching it.

How easy it is to accept a distorted view of the tour can be understood from a reported comment by Len Hutton, captain of the MCC visiting the West Indies in 1954. He is on record as saying that even 'the infamous 1932 tour of Australia' could not have been as bad as his present tour.

Infamous is hardly the word for that tour. Exciting and controversial, yes, but not infamous. The dictionary describes infamous as 'notoriously vile or abominable'. The tour was certainly not that.

I recall one piece of writing before we arrived in Perth. It was contributed by J.C. Davis, critic of the Sydney *Referee*, who expressed misgivings at the selection by England of four fast bowlers. Davis said: 'If the battery achieves success, it may be done by contravening the spirit of cricket.'

As far as the Australians were concerned this was, indeed, a prophetic judgment.

CHAPTER TEN

Man on the Run

WE SAVED IT UP for the fifth match of the tour because we wanted to get Don in strong company before giving him the full blast of our fast leg theory tactic. I was fresh from the match against South Australia in Adelaide where I scored 81 in 42 minutes, including two sixes, one of which was among the biggest hits ever seen in Adelaide. I scored my first 50 at the rate of 2 runs every minute and, while Jardine elegantly collected 16, I scored 70. I was caught out on the boundary while going to the well once too often. Clem Hill described it as 'one of the most magnificent innings ever played at Adelaide'. It was to be a different story on my next visit.

The Australian XI batsmen in that match got the full force of Bowes, Voce, Allen and myself. Even Allen made the ball get up, but one paper described him as medium-paced compared with me. I got Bradman in both innings and removed Woodfull for a duck in the second innings.

It was a refreshing sight to see Bradman clumsily waving his bat in the air. Bradman and Woodfull were out to strokes that were foreign to them. Woodfull chopped at a ball wide of the off stump, and Bradman made a wild swing and missed a ball which knocked down his off stump.

London newspapers reported that many old players considered I had bowled faster than Tom Richardson, and certainly faster than anyone seen in Melbourne for years. The batsmen didn't seem to be able to handle the bowling which consisted of about two bumpers and a number of short-pitched balls to the over bowled to a leg field of five or six players.

I remember a picture published in the Melbourne *Sun*, showing Leo O'Brien ducking to one of my deliveries and Duckworth standing about 18 yards back leaping in the air to stop the ball.

Jack Hobbs reported in London's *Star*:

Allen and Larwood bowled like demons and sent the ball down their fastest and best to shake Bradman's wonderful confidence. They did it. For the fourth time in the tour Bradman failed to make a big score . . .

Then Don faced Larwood again and the first ball did it. Bradman, drawing away to cut a shortish delivery, missed the ball, which hit the top of the off stump. In the circumstances Bradman's attempted shot was bad. He was drawing away, sure proof that he didn't like the bumpers.

I felt a lot safer in the press box, for the bowling looked very dangerous stuff. The newspapers will have very unpleasant things to say about these undoubted shock tactics and attacking methods England evidently intends to adopt.

The *Evening Standard* correspondent said: 'Provided that Larwood retains his present demon speed, the Bradman problem has been solved. Bradman dislikes supercharged fast bowling.'

The *Manchester Guardian*'s commentator, 'Cricketer', said: 'Jardine's plan of the shock bowlers attacking Bradman and Woodfull so far has succeeded and has demonstrated that Bradman is a mortal after all, which must be counted as hundreds of runs advantage to England. Bradman is not likely to feel naturally ordained to score a century. He must score by efforts like an ordinary man.'

That was an extraordinary match. We collapsed for 60 in the second innings, the giant Victorian bowler Lisle Nagel taking 8 for 32, with his flighted medium-paced off-spinners. The Australian XI were set 125 to win but, on a poor batsman's wicket, I doubt if they would have got 50 after I had removed Bradman and Woodfull for a score of 19. Rain washed out play and saved them.

When told that English critics were saying I had cast a shadow over him, Don said: 'Tell them to look at the score I made against Larwood at Leeds.' Asked how he was likely to fare against shock bowlers in the Tests, Bradman replied: 'Don't worry about that – I will be as right as pie.' Don went on to strike a blow for bowlers by saying that fast bowlers were being compelled to bowl at batsmen because batsmen were declining to play off-balls.

Arthur Mailey said in a Sydney newspaper: 'Should the English bowlers adopt the "leg field" in the first Test, we must not object on the grounds of sportsmanship. It is a legitimate theory encouraged by batsmen themselves. I have sufficient faith in the Australian batsmen to feel they can combat this menace in their own particular way.'

I knew I had Don on the run. I had upset his equilibrium and put him right off his game. Leg theory had succeeded far better than I expected. Don, caught in two minds by the leg trap, had jumped out of the way to avoid rising balls over the leg stump, at times using his bat with a clubbing action that would have done credit to a wood-chopper.

Although I knew I had Don rattled, I wasn't sure whether my success would last. I knew how brilliant Don was, and I noticed that several times in the game he had got his body out of the way of the line of flight as I was about to deliver, and square-cut the ball right off his stumps. Only a batsman with phenomenal sight and footwork could do that. Don's square-cut off the stumps was not a wallop – it was a crisp stroke perfectly timed. Even when he hit a defensive shot, anyone fielding the ball in the covers would wring his hands.

Some writers referred to the absence of Jardine from the match. He had gone trout fishing but hurried back to Melbourne, where the crowd demonstrated against our tactics. One of those who made some comment was Stork Hendry, the former international, who hooked me so well in England in 1926.

In the Melbourne *Truth* Hendry said:

Douglas Jardine, captain of all the bally old English cricketahs, went trout fishing while Larwood was trying to decapitate Don Bradman and Bill Woodfull at the Melbourne Cricket Ground last Saturday afternoon. It is unknown how many fish Doug caught, but it is a much discussed fact that he caught something to bring him back to Melbourne in a hurry when he got wind of the manner in which the English wickets were falling on Monday morning. Now, just why did Mr Jardine go off hunting for trout? Ah ha! Ah ha!

'Tis being unkindly said that Douglas, who hates to have his staunch old English demeanour ruffled, didn't care to remain in Melbourne and face the criticism which was inevitable following the devastating Mr Larwood's shock tactics.

That, of course, may be nothing more than the uncharitable raving of rumour. But it is still a fact that Jardo went fishing when he could have been watching a real exciting game of cricket.

It is still more undeniably fact that England's shock attack of last weekend was put on especially for the 'benefit' of the unfortunate Mr Bradman. It was the Englishmen's policy to break Don's morale at any price. They realized what a menace he constituted to their Test hopes – and likewise Woodfull too – and adopted the tactics of 'if you can't bowl 'em out, well, knock 'em out'!

Larwood placed his field in a manner that left no doubts about his intention to 'bowl at the man'. It's no use trying to evade that plain fact. Nobody wishes to cast any unsportsman-like epithets in the direction of England. If that's her idea of cricket, good luck to her.

But the tactics haven't succeeded in breaking Bradman and Woodfull. The future and the Tests will prove that. Australia's chances in the first Test match look much brighter at present than they did some time ago. The English batting weaknesses have been exposed; but the fact must not be overlooked that the match-winning attacker, Larwood, belongs to the enemy.

I do not believe that Jardine went trout fishing to dodge any leg-theory issue. It helps prove my point that leg theory was just something we intended to try and not something that we knew to be devastating in its newness or application.

We did not expect such an outcry from the Australians

whose fast bowlers had been bumping them down at English batsmen since last century. Nor did we expect it to succeed anywhere near like it did. Our success encouraged Jardine to use the same tactics in the next match against New South Wales. I didn't play, being held in reserve for the first Test. But Bill Voce kept up the attack, and Jack Fingleton took a battering, taking balls all over the body rather than taking the risk of cocking up a catch in hitting the ball to leg.

I found on this tour that I had reached top form. I had never bowled faster in my life, and I was able to get the ball up, even off a good length. I think this is what gave Don Bradman such a shock in Melbourne. It was not the extra-short one that worried him, but the ball rearing up off a good length and moving into the body. He would normally hook this one or move into his wicket to hit it round the leg side, but my extra speed this time had caught him off guard.

Most people who knew my bowling considered me to be about 2 yards faster than ever before. In an attempt to explain that, I can only say that at the age of twenty-eight I had reached the fullest point of maturity and, physically, I felt better than on my previous visit in 1928.

Without putting too fine a point on it, my stomach was in better shape this time than on the last tour. The strain of bowling fast for sustained periods can make you feel nauseated, and can even cause you to revolt against food. That's how I was affected in 1928. I tended to eat a great deal of fruit and to drink lemon squash in the breaks. The soft drink simply made me feel bloated and this, combined with the exertion, caused my stomach to be in disorder.

I solved that in 1932 – by drinking only beer. Even in the tea breaks, I used to have a glass of beer brought out on to the field for me instead of soft drink. If the crowds had known, how they would have bellowed!

Arthur Carr's advice to Jardine wasn't so bad after all when Jardine asked him how he could inspire his two Notts fast bowlers on the 1932 tour. Carr said, 'Feed them steaks and beer.'

Of course, the stimulation of playing for my country in the midst of an almighty row also brought out the best in me.

My bowling at this stage was directed right over the leg stump, and there was little variation in it. The batsman standing with a two-eyed stance was right in front. Australian batsmen were accustomed to walking in front of their wickets to defend against balls dead on the wicket or to push them around to the leg. Slow wickets enabled them to get away with this, but when they encountered my extra speed combined with the short leg fields, those who were not quick-footed took many blows on the ribs and thighs and legs, making the bowling look much more dangerous than it was.

When we went to Australia in 1932, cricket there was by no means in its healthiest state. It was pretty much a time of mechanical scoring and big scores, particularly by Bradman, Ponsford and Woodfull. Apart from Bradman, McCabe and Jackson, the batting was fairly slow.

Nevertheless, Australian cricket was coming into its own again after the trouncing it had had from Percy Chapman's team in 1928. The break-through began in England in 1930 when Bradman started his run of mammoth scores. The resurgence in Australia continued through 1931 but was not helped by very slow wickets. The bowling in some of the interstate sides could hardly be described as hostile.

Test matches were played to a finish in Australia, and most batsmen merely tried to tire out the bowlers before going for runs. It was the type of cricket that breaks a bowler's heart and bores a crowd stiff. In that respect, it was not unlike cricket today.

This could never be said of Bradman. He really went for the bowling and was probably the greatest magnet the game has ever known. When he was in batting, and the word got around, they would come from all directions – managing directors, clerks, office boys, typists, shop assistants, and they would all disappear and find their way to the Cricket Ground. Reporters covering games in which Bradman played could not afford to slip away for a quiet drink. They would find that by the time they had had a couple Bradman had put on another 40 or so runs.

I think Bradman, without leg theory, would have dominated the series. He would have scored his 200s and 250s, and the crowd would have gone to see him bat. But I doubt if they would have gone in great numbers to see what remained of the Tests. I may be wrong here, but I think they might have turned up if England had got a drubbing. Like any other followers, they wanted to see their own team win. But more than that there was a lot of feeling against Englishmen at that time. The world depression was felt very acutely in Australia, and in the view of the man in the street, Britain was responsible for much of the economic ills. It was felt, rightly or wrongly, that Britain should have looked after Australia better and protected her from what was happening elsewhere.

It was a time in Australia of dole queues, evictions, lines of jobless and a scramble for relief work. Spectators who went along to watch big cricket wanted to forget their troubles, but more than ever they longed to participate in a triumph of some sort. They needed a taste of honey. A man I came to know on the tour told me of what he had seen in a town called Captain's Flat in southern New South Wales. For every single job available there, sixty or seventy men waited. The foreman would throw a pick handle high into the air and the man who emerged with it out of the wild scramble got the job.

To cricket crowds, Bradman was a hero, a brilliant, dazzling figure who shone like a beacon in the grim atmosphere of economic hardship. A boy from the bush, he had triumphed to such a point that his deeds uplifted people's spirits; women flocked to see him play, bestowing on him a film star quality, a kind of idolatry; even in those days when people were far more conservative about exhibiting their feelings publicly, women struggled to get near him to touch and even kiss him. It was known as Bradmania.

Bradman, in the midst of the depression, was already quite wealthy through radio and newspaper contracts and various endorsements, including Bradman shirts. His success and prowess, although passionately admired by the Australian public, were such that some of his own team-mates were jealous. But to the public at large, Bradman was seen as the embodiment of success, and the hope for beating the traditional enemy.

Apart from the economic factor, which I think played a part in the attitude of the crowd then, there were other reasons why Australians regarded Englishmen differently from the way they do today. Australians in 1932 were a little insular. The country was much more isolated than it is today, and Australians were not the travellers they are now. Cricket and football were the only major sports played; there was not the great diversity of sports that exists today, and I think this helped to make barrackers then incorrigibly partisan.

Since World War II Australians have become more tolerant and understanding, and one hardly ever hears anybody in Australia these days being called a Pommie as a term of derision. Yet that term was on almost everybody's lips in 1932, and it was intended as a racist slur. So many thousands of British immigrants have been integrated in Australia that an Englishman is no longer considered an oddity.

In the 1964–65 Test series against Ted Dexter's men, you could notice Englishmen and Australians side by side drinking canned beer and even barracking together in a good-humoured way. In 1932 Englishmen were very few and far between among spectators. I can recall that at Sydney in a New South Wales–England match in 1928 one lone figure sat there constantly calling out: 'I'm a Pommie and I'm proud of it.' The crowd around him shouted back: 'Shut your bloody mouth and watch the cricket.'

Now in Melbourne or Sydney and, to a lesser extent, in Brisbane, Adelaide and Perth, you will find thousands of English people watching a Test match. And they are not all vehemently partisan, nor do they think of England as home any more. Frank Tyson is a case in point. He tore through the Australians in 1954–55 (taking 7 for 27 in Melbourne) and won the Ashes for England. He became a schoolteacher in Melbourne and has settled in Australia. Later, before one Australian team left for England, I heard him say in a broadcast: 'I am a bit afraid of our bowling weakness.' by *our* he meant Australian. He has become Australianized, and so have many others.

About the only people who didn't care were the kids. In Australia small boys have always imitated the methods of Test cricketers. In the early twenties they were copying the extraordinary antics of Cecil Parkin of Lancashire, one of cricket's comedians. He was billed by the press as a mystery bowler, and he used to send them down fast, slow, medium paced and then occasionally high in the air like a balloon. Everywhere you went in Australia, and even in paddocks in the bush, you'd see boys imitating his unusual run.

Early in 1933 a twelve-year-old boy named Ray Lindwall was imitating my run by measuring out twelve good strides to deliver off the fourteenth step in a public street in the Sydney suburb of Hurstville. Immediately after the New South Wales–England match, small boys began bowling short-pitched balls to packed leg fields in many cases on rough pitches and in parklands and paddocks. This was to perturb Australians, generally, because many boys were hit and free fights started. Schoolteachers in every part of the country were to threaten their pupils that they would flog them if they caught them bowling in the new style.

CHAPTER ELEVEN

A Word is Coined

I WAS READY for them this time. The mob on the Sydney Hill had upset me in 1928 with their barracking, but this time I knew better.

There is something different, something appealing about playing a Test match in Sydney in a setting that was first a swamp, then a market garden and for years has been acknowledged as one of the finest cricket grounds in the world. A long line of trustees going back to the seventies have never sought to destroy its charm with great monoliths of concrete. The ground has held more than 70,000 people at an international Rugby League game, but the policy of its founders in deciding that its prime purpose was cricket has never been altered.

I think the Sydney Hill mob still has the edge on anybody for humour and acid comment – at least I found it so in 1932. It was in the atmosphere of a packed Hill that I played against Australia in the first Test of that series. England and Australia were fairly evenly matched on paper, but Australia wasn't as strong in bowling. Bill O'Reilly, of course, was their trump card, and they also had Clarrie Grimmett to call upon.

This was to be one of my greatest Tests against Australia. I took 5 wickets for 96 runs off 31 overs in the first innings and 5 for 28 off 18 overs in the second. England won by 10 wickets; Australia scored 360 and 164 and England 524 and, on the last day of the match, one run to take the game. One solitary figure turned up on the Hill to see out the finish. He was, indeed, a real sport.

Our Test team was not revealed by Jardine until the coin

was tossed. That was the practice he was to follow right throughout the tour. Jardine did this for two reasons: first, deliberately to annoy the press and, secondly, to keep up the psychological pressure on the Australians so they would not know what tactics might be used or whether any surprises would be sprung.

What the public and the press did not know was that members of our own team were also kept in the dark. I didn't have much doubt that I would play as long as I remained fit, because Jardine always told me I was his spearhead. But it was different for some of the others. All were keen to play, and Jardine made the full seventeen members of the touring team sit in the dressing-room and don their flannels just as if they were expected to take the field. Naturally, some of the lads were very disappointed when they were not selected.

Maurice Tate, for instance, was still good enough to play for England but was too much of a gentleman ever to express his disappointment. There were others. George Duckworth, who played in every Test on the previous Australian tour, was discarded for Les Ames. Duckworth was the better keeper and Jardine knew that, but his attitude was that any Tom, Dick or Harry could stand 14 or 16 yards behind the sticks and take the balls and whistle for his batting. He needed Ames to stiffen the batting. There was always excitement in the dressing-room, and one could hear the chatter of the waiting crowd throughout that thrilling pre-match atmosphere, but none knew for certain he was going to play until Jardine pinned the team up on the wall without a word.

This was an example of the Skipper's remorseless approach and served notice that there were no favours to be handed out. To play for England ability and form alone counted.

I have never known anyone more dedicated than Douglas Jardine was to winning those Ashes. He was so keen that his feeling communicated itself, and I think everybody wanted to do their best for him.

Jardine came to me and told me I could help him to win.

'You are my main weapon, Harold, and I know you can help me,' he said. He asked me to bowl leg theory and I did. He was decent to me, and I wanted to help him. I wouldn't say I was told to bowl leg theory. I was asked to do it, and I complied. In any case, I was convinced that I wouldn't get many wickets any other way. I was up against good players and wickets that suited them. I have heard it suggested on many occasions since that I would have got just as many wickets on that tour if I had bowled to an orthodox field in a normal way. It is very debatable. If all the batsmen had been attacking players, I might have had a chance, but there were too many grim defenders in the team. Even on those wickets, which were faster than in England, I don't think I would have had a chance with Bradman in the mood he was usually in.

If I could have swung the ball, I probably wouldn't have worried about leg theory. The Australians were the same, just plain straight up and down. And yet, in Australia, today, I notice that many bowlers can swing the ball long after the sheen has gone. I think there is a possible explanation for this. In 1932–33 the balls were all hand made and the stitching was much neater than today's mass-produced leathers. In the mechanics of swing bowling, the smoother ball was then less effective than the poorer quality product of today. I am not putting this up as the sole reason. The summers of 1928 and 1932 were particularly dry, and thus the faster you bowled the less opportunity there was for swing. Even with a new ball I didn't swing much more than 6 inches, but at my pace it was enough if the ball was under control.

The absence of Bradman from this Test led to some speculation, and in our disappointment we wondered if he had had second thoughts about his confidence in playing shock bowling.

Since then, though, I have realized that Don was medically unfit at the time. He was, of course, among those chosen and told the selectors he was available and anxious to play but a little concerned about his health. The Australian Board of Control asked Don to submit himself to a medical examination, and the report which was sent to the board indicated he was not fit. The doctor who saw him advised him to take a month's rest, and the board told him he would not be required to play.

Instead of a month, Don took ten days and, after a further examination, was pronounced fit and selected for the second Test. It would appear that at the time he was trying to do too much. He was involved in writing and broadcasting, as well as cricket, and so much was expected of him at the wicket that his failure under the new leg stump attack must have weighed heavily upon him.

Bradman admitted later that he was a worried man at this stage. Immediately after the Melbourne match against the Australian XI he spoke to cricket officials about the high-velocity attack but apparently found little sympathy for his views. Later he approached a friend on the Australian Board of Control to see what could be done to alter the situation. After the third Test he even wrote a private letter to Lord's. He urged the MCC to extend the leg-before-wicket area to the off-side to give bowlers a better chance. At least Don acknowledged that bowlers weren't getting a fair deal, something he had chosen to ignore until they got on top.

Don's batting colleagues received a shock a week or so before the first Test when he asked to be dropped in the batting order. He invariably went in first wicket down, but this meant that a batsman of less calibre would be sent in with instructions to take the fire out of the attack. When Don didn't play, his place was taken by Jack Fingleton at first wicket. Don watched the game, getting a close look at Jardine's attack. It helped him devise a plan which he hoped would cross-trump the bowling.

Despite Bradman's absence from the crease, the Sydney Cricket Ground was jam-packed. They were queued up long before dawn to get in, and looking around you wouldn't have thought they could have squeezed another half-dozen in. Before the start I had a chiropodist come to the dressing-room to bandage each of my toes. I also put on two pairs of socks to try to cushion the shock of stamping down on the hard ground. I did this before every match.

The crowd on the Hill wasted no time getting on to me. Every time I dropped one short, they erupted like a human Krakatoa. They gave me hell over my chicken farm, calling out all sorts of nondescript terms with a poultry flavour. I remember things like: 'Eh Arrold, is that the way you chuck the chooks' eggs about?'

I was determined not to be put off this time and decided to play them at their own game. Whenever I appealed for a catch behind or an LBW decision a great howl went up from the Hill that could hardly fail to be heard miles away. Whenever this happened I would, mischievously, give them the old sign – the same as Churchill's victory gesture of later years but with a different meaning. This would set them howling again and, for a change, I got some fun out of it. I think they loved it, but you'd never guess from the hulla-baloo. As a variation I used to make a gesture with my right thumb at my nose. This also set them yelling and added to my enjoyment.

A lady wrote to me taking me to task for my antics. She said: 'Please try to control your shocking temper and above all, refrain from making vulgar signs.'

It wasn't long before the letters began to arrive. One threatened that I would be tarred and feathered, another that I was going to be murdered for my bowling tactics. I showed this letter to Jardine, who gave it to the police, but as it was unsigned nothing happened.

I received one letter from a Hill barracker at that time which pleased me. It was from a Mr A.E. Jay, a visitor from Melbourne. He said:

Dear Mr Larwood,

This is primarily to apologise for an incident which occurred on the opening day of the present Test match. While you were running to bowl the ball I called out hep right, hep right, etc., keeping time with your run, thinking it might put you off your length. It was most unsportsmanlike and I'm sorry. . . You seem to have come in for more than your fair share of barracking. But believe me, boy, we barrackers don't wish you any harm, but we're out to do everything possible to help Australia win and that is our method of doing it. We'll do exactly the same thing tomorrow but there is nothing personal in it. If you look at it in the right light you'll take it as a compliment that we are picking you out for special treatment. It is generally the most dangerous one we select. I want to see Australia win. So when we try to stampede you tomorrow remember it's not you we're up against, it's your ability. Take no notice because you give us what we want – you give us our money's worth.

From the time we went on the field in that match, and right through the Test series, the crowd used to roar from beginning to end. They would count me out until I delivered the ball, trying to put me off.

Cricket spectators today just don't realize what it was like then. I have never heard anything like it before or since. Spectators would remain fairly quiet for the first few overs when I bowled ordinary theory. I might put a bumper or two down in those few overs, but I kept the ball well up to the batsman, trying to use the shine. The wicket was so hard that every time you bowled you could see where the shine had been taken off.

So dead was the wicket and the conditions so dry that Bill Bowes, a good fast bowler in England, was useless in Australia. Voce and I were fast because we put everything into our deliveries and got response from the wicket. But Bowes was a pure arm bowler.

You could feel the tension of the crowd pressing in on you all the time out in the middle. From the time Jardine switched the field over to the leg side placing, they didn't stop yelling.

As always in that match I was flat out right from the first ball. It was never my custom to do any exercises before the game or warm up on the field as they do these days. Having changed in the dressing-room, I would sit and have a smoke, walk out on to the field, pick up the ball and pfft! I'd put the batsman on his mettle at once. Only once in the series did I fail to take a quick wicket. After Voce nailed Woodfull for 7, Ponsford and Fingleton defended stubbornly, preferring to take many balls on the body instead of hitting them to leg, but I got both of them and then Alan Kippax LBW for 8. Years later Australian players told me that Kippax said as he returned to the dressing-room: 'He's too bloody fast for me.'

Just how I bowled then and in the following games depended on the batsmen. I used to sense each one. I didn't bowl every ball short of a length. I couldn't afford to pitch them on the off or even the off-stump or to over-pitch. Most of my deliveries were just a little bit under-pitched on the leg stump. From where they normally pitched on a good length, they rose over the stumps. I know I was surprised to find that I got much more lift than Bill Bowes and Bill Voce, both much taller men. I put my short ones down but they went well over the batsmen's heads.

Stories that most of the balls flew at batsmen's heads have been highly coloured. Most of them rose around the hip, and were hittable to leg if the batsman could or would play a leg-side stroke.

I feel sure the leg-theory attack would have been dropped after this match if the Australian batsmen had attacked and battered it. They were a powerful side and every recognized bat, except Woodfull, was renowned as a hooker. We gave them every opportunity to play the hook. There were six men in a tight cordon close around the leg and another two near the fence but usually behind square leg. I used to bowl from wide out on the crease to right-handers to make the ball go at them from an angle.

That part of the leg-side field, from square leg right round to long-on, was usually left unguarded to encourage batsmen to hook. Jardine has been criticized by purists for leaving this gap unguarded when his fast bowlers were being hit. But that was why Jardine left the gap open – to encourage batsmen to hook and give them a chance to score runs if they could.

We were all surprised when the leg-stump attack suc-ceeded as it did in the first Test. I expected to be hit by several players but was surprised to find that most batsmen were more intent on ducking out of the way of rising balls than trying to score. There was no feeling of certainty among us yet because Bradman had still to face a real test. I had a feeling that his absence, whatever the fate of leg theory, was making it a lot easier for us.

Stan McCabe, who was twenty-two, wasn't worried by the bowling. He came in when 4 wickets were down for 82 and I had taken 3 for 15. McCabe, who was discovered by Chappie Dwyer, later an Australian selector, on a visit to the New South Wales town of Grenfell in 1926, came to Sydney later at the age of nineteen and went straight from a club side into the state XI. In 1930, though yet to score a century in a first-class game, he was picked in the side that toured England.

McCabe's mother and father, who came from solid pioneering stock, journeyed from Grenfell to Sydney for the match. As Stan left the enclosure to go to the wicket he said to his father: 'If I happen to get hit out there, keep Mum from jumping the fence.'

McCabe gave no sign that he was worried by the fast ones. He rattled my first ball to the fence just in front of square leg. Methodically, he set about pasting Bill Voce and me by stepping across the flight of bouncers and hooking them seemingly off his eyebrows for boundaries. McCabe's batting was so effective that Jardine had to scrap the leg-theory field and resort to an orthodox attack. McCabe retaliated with classic drives, cuts and glances and was 127 not out when stumps were drawn. Next day he continued to bat in carefree style collecting 60 in the 55 minutes Australia remained at the crease, carrying his bat for 187.

I remember when Bill O'Reilly, the last but one, came in. Stan walked across and said: 'Don't worry. He's not as fast as you might think. Just put your bat in front of them, and I'll handle him.'

I had two balls to bowl. The first one flew off Tiger's bat even before he began lifting it. Bill raised a big laugh among all of us when he called out to McCabe: 'Not so bloody fast, eh? – I'll say you can handle him.'

Stan's 187 in the overheated atmosphere of the match was probably his most popular innings ever. I think he would agree, however, that it was not the most classical innings he ever played. The crowd was ecstatic, and they saw the type of cricket they had paid to see.

Stan handled the bowling as it should have been played. He picked his shots and also had a bit of luck. He gave me every chance. When he was getting his big score, I really relished the cricket – I always believed that when anybody was hitting me I was going to get him out every ball. I don't think I thought of dropping leg theory because of McCabe's stand. He proved it could be played with courage and a bit of luck and, of course, first-class batsmanship.

The Sunday newspapers were full of stories about Stan's heroic batting, but he ignored them because he was modest enough to believe it might not do him any good to read a lot of praise. The innings helped Stan to become the most gallant Australian batsman since Trumper. He was not the perfect stylist that Alan Kippax was nor was he a ruthless swordsman like Bradman or C. G. McCartney. He was never brutal with bowlers even though at times we seemed to be at his mercy. McCabe always gave the bowler a chance and seldom refused a challenge to try a great stroke.

I don't think Stan ever bored a crowd. Critics have linked his Sydney innings with one in Johannesburg in 1935 when he scored an unconquered 189 and another at Trent Bridge in 1938 when he got 232 out of a total of 300, batting as nonchalantly as if he were at a net practice. I think Stan regarded the Trent Bridge knock as his greatest.

After the first day's play, at Her Majesty's Theatre in Sydney, Cyril Ritchard popped in an extra verse in the show, 'Our Miss Gibbs'. It went as follows:

Now this new kind of cricket takes courage to stick it,
There's bruises and fractures galore;
After kissing their wives and ensuring their lives,
Batsmen fearfully walk out to score.
With a prayer and a curse they prepare for the hearse,
Undertakers look on with broad grins;

> Oh! They'd be a lot calmer in Ned Kelly's armour,
> When Larwood the wrecker begins.

One of the misconceptions that have arisen over the 1932 tour is that I knocked Stan about so badly in that first game that he was demoralized and unable afterwards to make a good score. Nothing could be further from the truth. I don't remember how many times I hit Stan, but it was no more than if he had been batting to ordinary off-side bowling. He was hit a few times around the thighs and legs just the same as he would have been in any circumstances facing me. Stan would have been the first one to confirm that. Another story I've heard is that there wasn't a paling left on the Sydney Hill fence. Presumably they had all been pulled out so the barrackers could attack us. Quite a few palings were uprooted but for a different reason: spectators right up against the fence wanted to get a better view of the game, which is not a bad thing.

One or two other things happened in that match which were misconstrued later. Claude Corbett and some other correspondents were to report later on how I bowled myself to a standstill, continuing even when my side was so strained that I was compelled to hold my hand on it after every delivery. It was claimed I insisted on doing that because Jardine wanted Gubby Allen to reap the wickets of the 'rabbits' in the second innings. They said that before it became apparent that I was to be England's Ashes winner there was a strong feeling among North of England professionals that Allen was to be the 'first' fast bowler, and we decided to hold him back at all costs.

It was not so. I bowled because Jardine asked me to bowl. He had me on for 11 overs in one spell. Jardine was not worried about personalities. He would bowl anybody if he thought they could take a wicket. He would have put the wicketkeeper on and donned the gloves himself if he thought it would have done any good.

I think the correspondents got the wrong idea and did not learn till later that Jardine and Allen had a slight falling out. It was in the first Test that Allen told Jardine he would not bowl to a leg-side field. He could afford to do so – he was an amateur and not dependent on cricket for a living. An Australian by birth, Allen was born in Darling Point, Sydney. He came to England with his parents when he was a boy and was educated later at Eton and Cambridge. He was one of the doughtiest fighters in the England team.

Allen told Jardine on the field: 'You forget, Douglas, I am an Australian.' Although I was not then aware of it I heard later that Allen had invited Jardine to send him back to England on the next ship rather than insist that he bowl to a packed leg field. I know what would have happened had I raised a similar objection!

Correspondents also reported that there had been an unpleasant incident at the start of the Australian second innings between umpire George Hele and Sutcliffe. It was said that when Hele handed the ball to Sutcliffe the Englishman sarcastically remarked, 'Couldn't you find a smaller one?'

Hele was said to have boiled at the imputation and answered that the ball had gone through the customary gauge test.

The truth is that Sutcliffe was merely trying to be funny.

I hate to think what might have been written if some of the correspondents had known what I took on the field to give me a kick while bowling. Every now and again I would reach in my left trouser pocket and take out a pinch of snuff. A good sniff and my head would clear as if a black cloud had just passed overhead and disappeared. It reminded me of my days as a miner. Before going down I used to be searched like everybody else for tobacco and matches. We couldn't smoke down there because of the danger, and the only thing that gave us a boost was snuff. It helped ward off fatigue and kept us going. After taking a sniff on the field I usually gave the batsmen my 'snorter'.

I enjoyed another little secret against the Hill mob. When off the field, I used to stroll into one of the many bars around the edge of the Hill and have a beer in mufti. They hardly ever recognized me, expecting me I think to be about 6 foot 6 inches. I would stand there listening to them saying the most appalling things about me. Once or twice they recognized me when Bill Voce breasted the bar with me; Aussies who a few seconds before were probably declaring what they would like to do with me would then turn round and want to buy me a beer.

In that match, apart from Stan McCabe's big score, centuries were made by Sutcliffe (194), Wally Hammond (112) and the Nawab of Pataudi (102).

Pataudi's century was the slowest I have ever seen in my life. He was anxious to follow in the footsteps of two other members of his family line by scoring a century in his first Test against Australia. The others were Duleepsinhji and Ranjitsinhji. Pat upheld the family tradition, but it took him 5 hours 17 minutes.

The Nawab was by no means a man without humour. After watching him potter around for an hour and a half for about 25 runs and then, for a similar period, without any improvement Vic Richardson crossed the wicket between overs and said to him: 'Pat, what's wrong? Aren't you seeing them too well?'

'Oh,' said the Nawab, 'I'm waiting for the pace of the wicket to change a bit.'

'Good God!' Richardson said, 'It's changed three times while you've been in.'

C. G. McCartney wrote about that game in the *Daily Mirror*:

Larwood's bowling was magnificent, and he thoroughly deserved his success. He is faster and has better control of the ball this tour than on the last, and provided he can stand the strain of important matches he will be the big danger of Australia throughout.

His performance – 5 for 28 – was the finest sample of sustained fast bowling I have seen for years.

The wicket was showing signs of slight wear when Australia began their second innings but there was nothing to warrant the poor showing of our batsmen.

Australia made a disastrous start at her second visit to the wicket, Woodfull and Ponsford being dismissed for next to nothing. Ponsford was again clean bowled round his legs but this time by Voce, by a ball that was straight and of ordinary length. Ponsford again walked across too far – a movement which is becoming habitual to him. Woodfull was clean bowled by Larwood with a very fast good length ball.

McCabe's wonderful batting form in this match, together with that of Hammond, has put some colour into the game and has done something to offset the dull and drab displays of the others.

'Larwood bestrode our narrow world like Colossus', is how the Sydney *Sun*, in a leading article, paid tribute to my bowling in the first Test.

There was terror in his name – he was a killer. Our batting heroes could not face him.

To the general public it seemed that his new leg theory bowling was scaring the batsmen away from the wickets. He became a legend, a good deal of which was sheer imagination. Yet there was a psychological factor behind it.

Jack Hobbs said in the *News Chronicle*:

It was pathetic to see old Test stalwarts walking back with so meagre a reward. Naturally I wanted England to win but when Ponsford, Woodfull and Kippax left the wicket I felt really sorry. I have played so many Tests with these men and it now seems possible that their failure will mean that one or more will drop out.

I have only the highest praise for Larwood. His magnificent work was well backed up by others, both in bowling and fielding, while Jardine's amazing keenness forced itself upon all. Now we can say we are one up. It is indeed a big fillip to our chances. but we must not be too optimistic.

On the first day of the Sydney Test, members of the bulging press box worked overtime as they groped for a new name to describe the bowling of Bill Voce and me. How were they to put a name to the fast attack containing about two bumpers to the over and supported by a packed leg field?

Towards the end of play the literary capacity of the press

box had given birth to these terms: 'Shock attack', 'Hurricane attack', 'Leg stump attack', 'Fast leg theory', 'Fiery attack' and some others I can't remember. London newspapers played it straight with posters like: 'Larwood plays skittles.'

Warwick Armstrong said in the *Daily Telegraph* in Sydney:

There are no hookers in the game now.

In my heyday back in the 1920s and before the First War Larwood would have been taken off after being thoroughly thrashed by expert Australian hookers. They hooked the stuff all day.

(When a newspaperman drew Bradman's attention to this comment, Don pointed out that Armstrong was 6 foot 3 inches, and a ball coming at Armstrong's abdomen was coming at his head.)

The *Sun* declared that the leg-side bowling was deliberately intended to injure batsmen, and everybody was searching for a suitable phrase. On the second day, that malevolent coining, *bodyline*, was born. More than one journalist and cricketer-cum-journalist over the years has claimed the honour of being its originator. I felt then and I still do that it was a very doubtful honour to claim. I still prefer to use my own phrase, fast-leg theory, but bodyline belongs to history, and it would be useless to deny it.

Once bodyline emerged, it was used by everybody. It ran through the press box, and even members of the Australian Board of Cricket Control adopted the hateful word. And they were the very people who regarded all reporters as impostors, thrusting themselves into the glorious game. I always thought Claude Corbett was responsible for 'bodyline' but Jardine blamed Hugh Buggy and often looked at him with cold hostility when they met in the corridors or lounges of the hotels where we stayed. I was wrong, and Jardine only partly right.

Soon after the Australian XI match in Melbourne the *Australasian*, a Melbourne weekly paper and forerunner of the *Australasian Post*, contained an article by Jack Worrall. A Test cricketer of the 1885–99 period, he was described as 'Australia's wisest sports critic of the day'. Jack had the habit of telling all his friends, 'old cricketers go either in the head or in the legs'.

Tucked away in his article were the words, 'half-pitched slingers on the body line'. In writing that Worrall probably had in mind a phrase used earlier in the Melbourne *Argus* by the late R. W. E. Wilmott who wrote under the nom-de-plume of 'Old Boy'. He described our attack in that Melbourne match as 'being on the line of the body'.

Buggy read the phrase in the paper and remembered it. On the first day of the Sydney Test, he had instructions to send his reports to the Melbourne *Herald* urgently. In those days reporters sent their stories by telegraph, not by phone or teleprinter as they do today.

Just before lunch Buggy was asked for a quick lunchtime cover to catch the edition and used a variation of Worrall's phrase, 'bowling on the line of the body'. In his telegraphed message he said: 'Voce was hit for six, again bodyline bowling.' It was a paraphrase of the term he intended to use and was simply telegraphese meant to indicate that Voce had again bowled on the line of the body.

Back in the office of the Melbourne *Herald*, Australia's leading evening daily, Ray Robinson began to sub-edit Buggy's story. Robinson, a cricket authority from Sydney (he died in July 1982), picked the word 'bodyline' out. It seems that he too had read Worrall's phrase and decided to use bodyline as a headline. But the editor, the late Syd Deamer, would not allow it. He did not object, however, to the phrase 'bodyline bowling', going in the body of the report.

The word 'bodyline' caught on rapidly after that, appearing everywhere. Buggy was therefore not the originator of the phrase 'bodyline bowling' but with Robinson the co-originator.

As Robinson pointed out in his immensely readable book, *Between Wickets*, bodyline was a compromise and as such defeated much of its original purpose.

When Buggy was in London in 1936 as an MCC team toured Australia, the editor of the *Star* asked him to write an article on bodyline as its originator. Buggy claimed this was not so and declined the offer.

Years later Buggy told me: 'It wasn't my reason for not writing it. I didn't want to be lynched in the Strand.'

CHAPTER TWELVE
The Speed Gallery

'LARWOOD'S SUSTAINED ACCURACY and tremendous speed were admired on all sides – I think he bowled faster over a longer period than I can remember seeing from him or anybody else.'

Don Bradman wrote that in 1950. He was referring to the first Test in 1932, which he watched from one of the stands as a spectator. Coming from Don, I regard that as a compliment.

Just how fast was I?

I never knew my speed when bowling and was unable to judge it. The ball never seemed to be going fast enough, and when I let it go I always wished it would travel a little quicker.

I remember seeing Ted McDonald bowl about 1927 when Notts were playing Lancashire. I said to one of the lads: 'If I'm fast as this fellow I'm really fast.' The Notts player said: 'Don't be silly, you're yards faster.' When years later I was asked to compare my speed with that of Ray Lindwall I said, 'I wouldn't have a clue, I never saw myself bowl.'

The question of who was the fastest often crops up and provides more than one answer. There's no real yardstick to gauge it by. I can only quote some opinions of other people.

Young Joe Hardstaff, the Notts and England player who averaged almost 50 in his twenty-three Tests, said as recently as 1963:

I was weaned on fast bowling. When I learnt my cricket at Trent Bridge, men like Harold Larwood, Bill Voce and Harold

Butler jostled each other at the nets for the privilege of nailing the poor batsmen. And in 25 years in the first-class game I saw and played against them all . . . from the fast to the frightening. Larwood, Lindwall, Miller, Voce, Gubby Allen, Constantine, Martindale, Trueman, Statham, Tyson. I can reel off the names, a roll of honour of the greatest fast bowlers the game has seen.

So when people come to me and say, 'How do you rate Wes Hall with someone of the old school like Voce or Larwood?' I reckon I'm in a good position to judge. And I'll say this now for Wes. He's fast, real fast. I wouldn't have burst out laughing at the prospect of facing him and neither would anyone else I know.

But the fastest of all? No, sir. There's only one man who deserves to be known as the King of Speed.

The man who had it all – control, speed to turn a batsman pale and a big heart to go with it.

That was Harold Larwood, the man I call the Silent Killer.

They tell me Wes Hall has been timed at 90 MPH. Well, Loll Larwood was two or three yards quicker than him, so you can guess what kind of murder it was when he was letting them slip.

I'll tell you about that 'Silent Killer' nickname I gave him. I used to field at cover point to him. He never had a mid-off, but I still had the easiest job in cricket because nobody much tried driving Larwood in front of the wicket. As Loll came up on that smooth, carpet-slipper run of his and I moved in towards the batsman I used to pin my ears back and listen hard – to find out what kind of delivery he was going to bowl.

If I could hear his feet tap-tapping over the turf I knew he would be well within himself. He would still be quick, mind you.

But when I couldn't hear him running up I used to look at the batsman and think: 'You're a split second away from trouble, son, because I knew then that Loll was coming in on his toes. That meant only one thing – he was going to let slip the fastest he'd got.

Hardstaff rated the twelve greatest speed merchants of his

time in the following order: Larwood, Ray Lindwall, Wesley Hall, Bill Voce, Keith Miller, Freddie Trueman, Brian Stratham, Frank Tyson, Ken Farnes, Leary Constantine, Manny Martindale, Bill Bowes.

Frank Chester, who wore the white coat for thirty-three years and whose memory goes back to before World War I when he was a professional with Worcestershire, wrote in 1956 that I was 'positively the prince of all fast bowlers', but not the fastest. He nominated W. B. Burns as the fastest he had seen for a few overs, but said Burns was erratic and therefore could not make the top flight.

Chester said:

With such speed, Burns could not develop accuracy and usually batsmen had to pay more attention to protecting their skins than their wickets. A wild fast bowler is much more dangerous in a physical sense than one who bowls consistently down the line.

Next in speed and towering above all others in class was the amazing Larwood . . . There was nothing to fault. His speed almost outstripped the eye and his control over the twin essentials of length and direction was perfect. It was rather like releasing a thunderbolt to put him on to bowl and if his action had not been so beautifully balanced he would not have maintained so much accuracy at such speed.

About 1928 I was timed in England at 96 MPH. I think some mathematician got busy with a stopwatch, but I couldn't vouch for the accuracy. In Australia somebody, using the same method I think, timed me at 99 MPH. There again I wouldn't know how accurate the assessment was. If Wes Hall were electronically timed at 90 MPH I think 90 would be a bit slow for me, and if Joe Hardstaff's opinion that I bowled 2 or 3 yards faster than Wes is accurate, then I must have been up round 100 miles an hour.

America's fastest baseball pitcher of a few years back, Bobbie Feller, was electronically timed in several exhibition demonstrations to have thrown the ball at 99.5 MPH.

George Bayer, the American golf professional recognized as the hardest and longest hitter in the world, was once tested by electronic device. It was found that the speed of the club-head on impact with the ball was 109 MPH. The golf ball, which looks mis-shapen in slow motion film when hit, travelled at about 140 MPH for a short time. Other golf professionals like Jack Nicklaus, Arnold Palmer and Bruce Devlin would be about on the same mark. Pancho Gonzales was estimated to serve a tennis ball at about 120 MPH, the strings on the racquet imparting a catapult action in addition to the lever of the arm. A ball delivered at 90 MPH would mean that the batsman has less than half a second to sight it and make a stroke.

Years after that tour an article by Hugh Buggy revealed that two Australian batsmen who faced me in the bodyline Tests had told him they had failed completely to see some of my deliveries. When I was able to ask Buggy who the players were he told me it was not breaking a confidence to name the batsmen as Bill Ponsford and Leo O'Brien, the Victorian left-hander who had been brought into the second Test. They told Buggy some of my deliveries were so fast they could not see them until the balls hit their bat or struck them in the thigh or stomach. I always thought these players saw me pretty well.

I have been asked many times why it was that others with much greater physique could not attain the speed I was able to produce. Bill Voce, for instance, a very big man, could lift, one-handed, any ordinary-sized man merely by grasping his coat lapels. He used to amuse us by tearing in half a tin of tobacco, saying it was the easiest and quickest way of opening it.

I think the answer is in the co-ordination of every muscle which is brought into play. The arm, shoulder, wrist, body and legs all have their functions, and the man who is able to achieve perfect or near-perfect co-ordination will be the fastest. My speed was not the outcome of violent physical exertion as much as it was the conserving of energy until the exact moment of delivery. My run-up was rhythmical and disciplined, and I was perfectly balanced at the precise moment when my left foot came down and my arm came over.

My nervous system would come into play at this moment too. My whole body and almost every group of muscles would suddenly leap into action as I propelled the ball. Up to that moment I was completely relaxed and unwound myself like the sudden snapping of a clock spring as I let the ball go.

Only regular exercise to keep the muscles strong and supple enabled me to avoid any serious strains, torn muscles or injuries, apart from the left cartilage. But I don't think I could have bowled as fast without perfect co-ordination. Looking at some big men who bowled fast, I could never understand why they weren't faster than me. I guess they weren't relaxed and, in this way, wasted so much energy on the run to the wicket that when they reached the crease they had shed some of their strength and penetration. Added to all these things there must be a will to bowl fast. As far as I was concerned there was nothing better calculated to put a hot branding iron on me in 1932 than the barracking of the Australian crowds.

There were 64,000 fans at Melbourne Cricket Ground to see Don knock the cover off the bodyline ball. He went in second wicket down in the second Test to one of the greatest storms of cheering ever heard on a cricket field.

Don strolled to the wicket in his usual confident way, a slow walk to accustom himself to the change of light from the dressing-room to the field. He had to wait for the cheering to abate before he could take strike. Bill Bowes sent one down well outside the off-stump and a little on the short side. Bradman moved across slightly to pull the ball to the leg side, a stroke he had hit the fence with many a time. He clipped the ball into his stumps. Poor Don – the crowd was stunned, we were staggered and all was wrong with the world.

It was a shocking long-hop and deserved to be clouted to the fence. That's what Bradman tried to do, but I think he was a victim of one of the slowest wickets I have ever bowled on. The ball came off so leisurely that Don had almost completed his stroke when it came off his bat. The ball just stopped against the wicket. It was certainly a murderous wicket, and we all thought it had been doped to take the sting out of our battery of four fast bowlers. If the wicket, normally the liveliest in Australia, had not been deliberately watered down for the game, its preparation was certainly carried out very poorly. Anyway, Don didn't get a chance immediately to use the plan he had worked out to beat me and satisfy his countless fans. I didn't know of this until years after when Johnnie Moyes from the Sydney *Sun* filled in the details:

Bradman returned from this little beach cottage owned by Tom Langridge where he worked out his counter-plot like a general who seeks to halt the enemy's attack and then advance to the assault.

When Bradman returned to Sydney he looked better, not completely well perhaps, but ready for action. Next day he called at my office and expounded his plan.

My task was to think out all possible objections and raise them like Aunt Sallies for him to knock over.

The plan was simple and direct as he stated it, though one could see immediately that putting it into effect would be neither simple nor straightforward.

The first fact in his appreciation of the situation was that he had to make runs. He was so quick on his feet that he could get out of the way of anything Larwood might hurl down the wicket. He could dodge all day, provided he was content to do that. But, it was a but with a capital letter, the public would not be content with that. They would grow weary of an exhibition of gymnastics and demand that he make runs. The Hill would wax both facetious and querulous.

The old law of supply and demand would operate. The public would make the demands. How was he to arrange supplies? He would walk away from his wicket and try to hit the ball through the off-side field. If he succeeded it would put the bowler off his balance and force him to weaken the leg field and strengthen the off field.

Then he could revert to normal batsmanship. His plan was in effect to meet unorthodoxy with unorthodoxy. He must make runs.

I tried to counter it. If one ball came through quicker and

lower he'd be left straddle-legged with a cross-bat looking as though his style was fully impregnated with a scent of gum leaves, as some of his detractors still affirmed.

To this he replied that first of all a ball that pitched short would bound over the wicket. If it was even close to a good length he would not move away. Further, if its direction was towards him, it would pass outside the outside leg stump whether it was high or kept low. The hook shot was no good, he thought.

I pointed out that he played two hook shots, one, past mid-on like the drive off a high bounding ball in tennis and the second, a normal one. He had considered all that. In the first place he played the stroke with the ball coming towards the shoulder. It was easy enough against a normal bowler but Larwood came into the body and a miss would mean a broken head and hospital, which would help neither Australia nor Bradman.

As far as the normal hook was concerned he pointed out that he was not tall, that the ball was flying as high or higher than his head and that he could not possibly get on top of it and keep it down. He disposed of every argument. He considered them all and rejected them . . .

My view was one of apprehension. That his scheme cut across all the accepted canons of batsmanship was not entirely the cause of this. The champion writes his own textbook always. It appeared to me, however, that with one of Larwood's pace, even Bradman could not bring off the seemingly impossible. Still, he had made his plan and it was to be rounded off match by match according to the information gleaned.

Don made amends for that duck. In the second innings he reached 103 not out and this score, together with 10 wickets for the match secured by Bill O'Reilly, tipped the scales sufficiently to give Australia victory. How Bradman dominated that innings is shown by the fact that his runs were made out of a total of 191 in which seven of his fellow-players made only 10 runs among them, four failing to score.

Here was the Bradman whose cricketing career had been

ended for him by a commentator about three weeks previously. After the Board of Control ruled that Bradman could not write and play at the same time, and he had on medical advice missed the first Test, a cricket expert and amateur journalist provided a Sydney paper with a scoop. He reported in a three-column spread to a shocked nation that Bradman had pernicious anaemia and would never play again. But it was the kind of scoop that editors like to forget. The story was blown out for the simple reason that Don was not suffering from anything remotely like pernicious anaemia. He was to go on to score another 11,000-odd runs and forty-seven centuries in first-class cricket before his career ended.

The story was as wild as some of the reports on Don's dismissal for a duck. One Melbourne newspaper's account of the dismissal by a former Test player announced in its headline, 'Good length ball got Bradman.' On another page a description by another Test player was headed, 'Bradman out to shocking long hop.' Yet another cricketer-turned-reporter described it as 'clean bowled'.

That second innings of Don's must rank as one of the greatest of his life. He was under considerable strain but rose to the occasion. Although he was obviously put off his normal game, he played well enough to make me think he might yet tame bodyline; although I knew that wicket was so dead it didn't give me a chance, I had my doubts about how I'd go in the following Tests. Voce, Bowes, Allen and I were more or less innocuous on the wicket.

As soon as Don started darting to and fro across the wicket, I knew I had him worried. I used to say to myself as I bowled to Bradman: 'I've got you frightened. Wait till I give you this one.'

But I had to applaud some of the shots Don played. Bradman was a good one, all right.

Don upset the applecart a little when he got into position on the leg just before I bowled to square cut me or use his bat like a trench digger to hit me to the off. In bowling to his leg stump as I did I was trying to dictate what shot he should play – a hit to leg. But he wouldn't peck at it.

When he began moving to the leg to hit me to the off, I couldn't let him get away with it. The captain had my field set, and I had to bowl to it. When Don tried to counter me in this way, it became a matter of him or me.

So I used to watch him just before my arm came over. Mostly he would move to the leg, but sometimes he would step quickly to the off and hit the rising ball down into the ground on the leg side with a swipe resembling an old-fashioned cow shot.

I used to try to sense what Don was going to do. If I saw him trying to move back to the leg in that split second before delivery, I used to follow him a little bit. I did the same thing with the off. I suppose it amounted to bowling at the man. But he made it that way.

Don's antics in Melbourne in jumping about the crease made spectators think I was deliberately trying to knock his head off. Some other batsmen gave the same impression. All of them ducked to good-length balls. Woodfull, whether deliberately or not, gave the impression that I was trying to hit him. In the Melbourne Test, I hit him over the heart with one that was a plain straight ball just short of a length. It rose just over the stumps, and he should have played it. He was ducking at the time.

A similar incident occurred in the Sydney Test. Woodfull ducked, and the ball hit him on the thigh. I appealed for LBW. So did Ames, the wicketkeeper. Umpire George Hele ruled not out and turning to me said, 'Harold, if that ball had been 2 inches lower, I'd have had to give him out. I couldn't avoid it.'

'I thought it was out as it was, George,' I said.

'No, it was 2 inches too high.'

And yet I got barracked for appealing.

Bradman and Woodfull were the only ones who used to 'show' a little when they got out of the way of a rising ball. Their mannerisms made the crowd think I was trying to kill them. I hit Don only once in nine innings.

Woodfull, Ponsford and Fingleton were in trouble because they were slow-footed. Richardson was a powerful hooker and cut loose on me sometimes. I'm glad he didn't

do it all the time. He also gave the crowd the impression I
was trying to hit him. He was quoted in several newspapers
as saying he took block a yard outside the leg stump and yet
my delivery came straight at him. The inference was clear –
that I was out to brain him.

Richardson and McCabe almost killed bodyline in this
Melbourne Test. Richardson scored 34 and McCabe 32 in a
determined stand in which both players attacked our fast
bowling. They clouted the ball so heftily to leg that the
inner ring of leg-side fielders were forced to move back
because of the danger to them. The partnership was broken
not by the demoralizing effect of bodyline but because
McCabe fell to a freakish catch by Jardine off Voce. Our
bowling was being flogged at the time, and I've often felt
that if McCabe and Richardson had been together for about
another hour bodyline would have been finished.

Many people believe today that bodyline was a whirlwind non-stop attack of bumping balls. It wasn't. Bodyline
was a shock tactic, a sharp prong which depended on quick
penetration for success. Once the bowlers tired, and the
prong was blunted, bodyline bowling became mechanical,
even mediocre, and any batsman worth his salt should have
been able to hit it at will.

Bodyline wasn't bowled at Australia's batsmen as much
as most people seem to think. Jardine made frequent
bowling changes to keep his attack fresh. There were times
when bodyline became futile, and he was forced to resort to
an orthodox field. Bowes, who was later to become
something of a terror in England, where some batsmen also
developed a neurosis because of the bodyline spectre, was
so innocuous in Australia that he played in only one Test.
Voce appeared in four, and Allen, who wouldn't bowl
bodyline, played in every Test.

In all the Tests I bowled 220.2 overs, Voce bowled 133.3
and Allen 171. Hammond bowled 120.5 and Verity, the
slow left-hander, bowled 135 overs. It couldn't be claimed
that Hammond bowled bodyline because he wasn't fast
enough.

Even Bradman didn't get as much bodyline as most

people think. He half-succeeded at Melbourne with his shots to the off, and he was so brilliant and quick on his feet that if he'd been given balls pitched repeatedly in the same area he might have completely mastered bodyline. Also, bodyline was bowled at only the recognized batsmen.

Australia won the Melbourne game by 111 runs with good fighting cricket. She beat us fair and square, and we had no excuses, although we were a victim of our own tactics by being caught on a slow wicket with four fast bowlers. Jardine had something to say about the game in his book:

Had the Melbourne wicket played anything like it played the previous night (the second-last day) I feel confident we should have accomplished our task of getting 208 runs, and accomplished it easily.

This was the general opinion which no doubt accounted for the small attendance, smallest of any day of the match.

The wicket which played so well overnight appeared to be treacherous. Had I received only three balls these were quite sufficient to prove to my satisfaction at least that those correspondents who gave as their considered opinion that there was nothing wrong with the wicket, must either have had their attention directed to some direction other than where the game was taking place or must have temporarily lost their powers of observation and judgment.

After that match Australian newspaper posters proclaimed:'Bodyline beaten', 'Bodyline squashed'. They even stopped accusing me of being unsportsmanlike for a time. There was now great confidence in Australia's chances in the following games. It made Jardine more determined than ever, and it also made me anxious for another encounter – on a better wicket.

I remember the second Test for two other reasons. One of them produced the most humiliating experience in which I have ever been involved. It so happened that I had bowled about two overs in my second spell on the first day when I noticed the ball was out of shape. I showed it to the umpire and Jardine, and a new ball was brought from the pavilion. Woodfull then said to Jardine, 'No, we're not going to use that the way it is.' So between them they played pat-a-ball alongside the Test wicket. Jardine underhanded the ball to Woodfull who patted it back. About 50,000 people looked on. We just had to stand there like naughty boys while they engaged in this nonsense for about three overs. Every now and then Jardine and Woodfull would take a studious look at the ball as if the fate of a nation hung in the balance. The crowd was incensed and called out angrily. I was so embarrassed I blushed.

It wasn't long after that I had trouble with my boots. It was really my left one. It had ripped right along the instep, and the uppers were coming away from the sole. At home, on the softer grounds, my left foot used to slide along a little, and the tension on it was not quite as great. On the hard Australian ground, the spikes used to hold me solid, and that was one of the reasons why I was so much faster in Australia.

At that time I had only one other pair of boots with me in the dressing-room, and they were brand new; I had not even worn them at net practice. When I went off, the Melbourne crowd was furious. They booed me off, probably thinking I was putting something over them. In the dressing-room George Duckworth said to me, 'Look, Harold, put mine on. I'll go and get this one repaired for you.'

We both wore size 7, and I was glad of George's offer. I put George's boots on, and when I went out on the field to sarcastic cheers Jardine immediately put me on again.

The same thing happened with the second ball – the left boot ripped along the instep. When I went off once more, sections of the crowd shouted abuse, and I was hooted right off the field. Probably they thought I was taking a shower or having a drink. It wouldn't have been the first time an English bowler had hoodwinked an Australian crowd – S. F. Barnes did it in a Test match in Sydney in 1911. He left the field ostensibly for reasons of nature, but used the 'rest' period to smoke a cigar and have a rub-down before continuing to bowl.

As I walked off I tried to indicate to the crowd that there was something wrong with my boot, but it only made them angrier. George had gone off to get my boot mended, and there was nothing else to do but put on my new ones.

After one over I found them so tight and painful that I was limping. Jardine came across. 'What's wrong with you, Harold?' he asked.

'I think the skin's off my toes, Skipper,' I said.

'Oh, heavens. Go off again and change those boots.'

The crowd was yelling madly by now, thinking I was going off again.

'No, Skipper, I daren't,' I said. 'I think the crowd would lynch me.'

'To hell with them – you go off.' I didn't go, though, and told Jardine I'd stick it out.

'I'll have to ask you to have another over or two, Harold,' Jardine said.

I was wild at the crowd's attitude. I bowled as hard as I could. The harder I bowled the more it hurt, and the more it hurt the harder I bowled. The barrackers certainly bluffed me that time. But the batsmen had a torrid taste of bodyline. I bowled bumpers with maximum venom, and Jardine moved the full placement of fielders on to the leg side, capitalizing on my aggression.

That afternoon, when I hobbled into the dressing-room, there was hardly any skin left on my toes. I was able to wring blood out of both pairs of socks.

About this time, while most commentators were still blaming me for introducing bodyline, it occurred to me that it would be a pleasant change if letter writers and other antagonists turned their attacks to the man who first introduced the idea of *real* bodyline bowling. It wasn't an Englishman. Nor was it an Australian. It was Brigadier Gerard, a Frenchman!

The first reference to bodyline bowling in English literature as far as I could make out was in Conan Doyle's historical sketch, *The Adventures of Gerard*. Conan Doyle apparently was a lover of sport, and Gerard was one of the great Napoleon's cavalry leaders. For a time he was a prisoner-of-war in England and a guest of a wealthy English sporting peer, Lord Rufton.

In later years Gerard spoke of the passion of the English for sport and boasted of his triumphs over them at their own sport of fox-hunting, pheasant shooting, boxing and cricket. Conan Doyle quoted Brigadier Gerard in this way:

The English have a game which they play in summer called cricket. I learned to play that on the lawn before Milord's mansion. Ah, that is a game for soldiers and brave men but not for children.

It is played thus: one man tries to hit the other with a ball, against which he has only a stick to defend himself. Three pegs are driven in the ground, beyond which he must not retreat. Rudd, the head gardener, was a great player of cricket and so was Milord himself.

It was for me to defend first, and for Rudd to attack. He missed me, but in spite of my nine campaigns under the great Napoleon, I must confess that I turned pale when the ball whizzed past me, before I had time to raise my stick, and knocked down the three boundary pegs.

It was then for Rudd to defend himself, and for me to attack. As a boy in Gascony, I had learned to throw hard and straight, and I felt sure that I could hit that Englishman.

With a shout, I ran forward and hurled my ball. But with surprising quickness, he raised his stick and the ball flew to an amazing distance. It was again for me to attack, and for him to turn pale.

But he was a brave man, that gardener, for he stood up a second time. I felt certain that my hour of victory had arrived. He wore a red waistcoat, and I made that my target.

You would have thought that I was an artilleryman and not a hussar, so swift did my ball fly to its mark. He fell, and knocked down the three pegs. He was a cruel man, that Milord Rufton. He stood and laughed, and did not go to the help of his servant.

It was for me, the victor, to rush forward, and lift him to his feet (for he could not stand), to embrace him and cheer him with words of praise and encouragement.

He was a fair-minded man, that Englishman. He acknowledged that it was skill and not chance which had given me the victory.

'He did it a purpose, he did it a purpose!' He said it again and again.

CHAPTER THIRTEEN

'Murder', They Said

No game was ever yet worth a rap for rational man to
   play
Into which no accident or mishap could possibly find
   its way.

ADAM LINDSAY GORDON, Australian poet

JARDINE WAS VERY HARD ON ME. He bowled me in more
matches than anybody else on that tour. Often he told me I
wouldn't be put on to bowl. 'I only want to keep you fit and
in the match atmosphere,' he would say.

But when bowlers like Maurice Tate couldn't get the
batsmen out Jardine would come to me and say, 'Harold,
I'm afraid I must have you on for two or three overs.'
They were only country matches, and I didn't think it was
fair.

I remember one game against a Victorian country team
at Bendigo. The second Test had ended only two days
before, and I had bowled thirty-five overs on the heart-
breaking Melbourne pitch. And my feet were still sore.
We were staying at the Shamrock Hotel. Jardine, the
managers and the amateurs, taking with them Sutcliffe,
were the guests of Major Alan Currie at his station
home, Ercildoune. The rest of us professionals were not
invited.

Before leaving for the station Jardine put the names of
the team to play against Bendigo in a slip in the letter-rack
of the hotel. I looked at it and saw that I was to be twelfth

man. I was wild. 'I won't be there,' I said to a few of my drinking mates standing around in the Commercial Room, and taking out a pencil I struck my name off. A local man walked up to me as I stood near the fire and said, 'I hope you never get another wicket in Australia!' I turned on him and told him a thing or two. He apologized, saying he had only meant to convey that I had already got enough wickets and was actually paying me a compliment, not insulting me. I accepted his explanation, we finished friends and had a drink together.

The word got out, and my outburst was widely publicized. The impression was given that I thought it was beneath me to be twelfth man. That wasn't quite correct. I had arranged to go out the following day for a drive in the Victorian countryside. I wanted to get away from cricket for a little while.

I went to my bedroom and stayed there. Jardine, Warner and Palairet came to the bedroom later and tried to coax me to play. I didn't argue with them. I just showed suppressed anger and told them I wouldn't play.

But Jardine beat me. He approached the Bendigo officials and arranged for Bendigo to bat thirteen men and England twelve.

Jardine told me that would save me the embarrassment of feeling that I was only twelfth man. He knew that wasn't the reason for my objection just as well as I did, but there was nothing I could do except play.

I wasn't supposed to bowl in the match, but Jardine put me on. I took 4 fairly quick wickets (for 29). Newspapers reported that I did not exert myself and bowled at only quarter-pace, implying that I did so because I was peeved. I didn't have to bowl fast against country batsmen. Most of them were beaten before they left the dressing-room, anyway. I never got any pleasure out of bowling fast at batsmen who were not first-class. I enjoyed the challenge of bowling to real batsmen, and it was never my idea of fun to knock tail-enders about or batsmen who had not had much experience against really fast bowling.

The match produced some bodyline feeling. Some

members of the crowd showed hostility towards us, and there were shouts of 'How do you like it?' when Sutcliffe was hit on the hand by a fast ball from Storker, a local express. A section of the crowd urged the other fast bowler in the team, Harry (Bull) Alexander to 'rock them in'. Alexander, a big bounding fellow who played for the district team at Essendon, a Melbourne suburb, had been given his nickname as a result of his habit of charging at the wicket and bellowing whenever he made an appeal. He was very fast but erratic, spraying them all over the pitch. In the Bendigo game, we used a normal offside field as we did in all minor games on the tour.

I remember the match, too, because of what was said by the acting Mayor of Ballarat, Councillor J. Harrison, in a speech at the official luncheon. Councillor Harrison surprised everybody with his direct, hard-hitting comments. Ignoring any customary words of welcome, he said:

Woodfull has not adopted leg theory bowling by fast bowlers, and I am gratified that Australia has not done so. That is your method. I hope that Australia will never retaliate with leg theory bowling. We in Australia are admirers of skill. It will be a bad thing for cricket if this leg theory is not suppressed. Cricket is a gentleman's game, and I hope we can bring about the good feeling that has always existed up to now. We should not like to see brute force brought in to suppress skill.

Jardine replied thus:

You have debated one side of this subject. It is not my place to debate it. I believe that it has been said that a cricketer is 'easy money' and that you cannot libel a cricketer. I only ask you to consider this question: See how many times Larwood has hit the wicket. It is a fairly familiar cry of the Australian barracker, 'Bowl on the wicket.' You might consider Larwood's record in this respect.

(In first-class matches in Australia on that tour I had taken 29 wickets, 13 of them clean bowled, including 6 tailenders. Twelve had been caught off my bowling and 4 given out LBW.)

I was a little distant to Jardine for a day or two after the twelfth man affair. It had been my fifth consecutive match. When I cooled down, he told me he had wanted to keep me fit by running me about the field. His intention was good, but I thought at the time it was a bit hard on me. Later I realized that there was purpose in everything he did. I had to admire him for his determination.

During the match the secretary of the Board of Control, Mr W. H. Jeanes, wired to Bendigo demanding to know who had authorized the arrangement to bat extra men. He was told, 'Bendigo's people wanted to see Larwood bowl.'

There was another minor Bendigo incident, one that didn't involve me, but I remember it. At the hotel, Pataudi had been given the Royal Room, one in which the Prince of Wales had slept. Palairet apparently didn't like the arrangement and deposited his own luggage in the room. Despite Pataudi's mild remonstrance, he had to bow to the manager's wishes.

We all practised hard in Adelaide preparing for the third Test. Some members of the team who hadn't yet played in a Test worked hard at the nets in the hope that they would be selected. Adelaide was packed with visitors.

Long before dawn on the first day, Friday, 13 January, crowds queued up waiting for admission. Police had trouble keeping them orderly, particularly at the southern gate, where fights broke out because of the slow progress through the gate.

Early that morning a group of reporters covering the tour tried to get the names of the English team. But, as was his custom, Jardine refused to divulge the list. He was annoyed because of stories that were being written about Gubby Allen refusing to bowl bodyline. Newspapers quoted Allen as having told Jardine: 'You forget, Douglas, I am an Australian. I will not bowl bodyline. If you insist I will go back to England on the next boat.' Jardine had scoffed at the stories and denied them, but they were right.

Before the game began, all seventeen members of our

team had to don their flannels in the dressing-room. Nobody except a few of us could be certain of playing until just
before Woodfull tossed the coin and Jardine released the
names. Paynter was to play in his first Test, replacing
Pataudi, and Verity, who had been omitted from the
second Test side, was to return to the XI in place of Bowes.
Freddie Brown was twelfth man.

A few of our lads went on to the ground just before 11.30.
The huge crowd (it was a record 39,301) gave Woodfull a
warm reception when he walked on. His greeting was
rivalled by the one given to Jardine who, capless and
smiling, went across to Woodfull and shook him warmly by
the hand.

Before a battery of cameras Woodfull tossed and Jardine
called. The crowd was tickled when one of the photographers rushed up, intercepted Woodfull as he was on the
point of picking up the coin, and photographed the shiny
two-shilling piece as it lay on the grass. The crowd guessed
the result of the toss long before it was announced over the
amplifiers because Jardine, alone, walked across to the
centre of the oval and examined the wicket. When he
rejoined Woodfull the two captains, followed by the
players, left the ground. It was a quiet introduction to the
match; the calm before the storm.

We batted first, and it was typical Test match play, a little
slow if anything, but hard fought. On the second day we
had reached a total of 341, Leyland having got 83, Wyatt 78
and Paynter 77. Verity made 45. Tim Wall bowled
tenaciously to take 5 for 72 off 34 overs.

The trouble started soon after Australia began its first
innings at 3.25 PM. It was another poor start with Fingleton
back in the pavilion and only one run on the board. He was
out to Allen. Then in the last ball of my second over I hit
Woodfull over the heart with one that was just short of a
length. He doubled up in pain, and the crowd hooted me
wildly.

I was still swinging the ball and bowling to an off-field
with four slips.

When I was on my way in to bowl the first ball of my

third over to Woodfull, Jardine stopped me in mid stride by clapping his hands, and motioned the field over to the leg side. That was the signal for a tremendous burst of hooting and abuse, but Jardine persisted with his field placing. Jardine and Sutcliffe fielded on the leg, with Allen posted close in at silly short-leg and Voce at deep backward point. The crowd counted me out as I began each delivery and hooted all the time.

When Jardine had walked across to me a few minutes earlier, after I hit Woodfull, handed me the ball and said, 'Well bowled, Harold,' Bradman was standing only a few feet away at the bowler's end. I knew what Jardine meant. He was trying to put Bradman off, trying to unsettle him by letting him think the ball was being bowled deliberately to hit the man and that he might get the same. Jardine was a master of the finer points of psychology.

In the same manner, Jardine used to try to bolster the spirits of some of our players, whom he knew to be squeamish about bodyline. As an incoming Australian came out to bat, he would say to those around him: 'Here comes another yellow bastard,' meaning that the player was lacking in courage. He usually referred to Bradman as 'that little bastard'.

Jardine wrote about the injury to Woodfull in his book, *In Quest of the Ashes*. He said:

With the last ball of his second over Larwood again brought the ball back and Woodfull, stepping outside his off stump, failed to connect with his bat and received a nasty crack on his left side. Pandemonium instantaneously broke out. After sympathizing with Woodfull and bidding him take his time, I walked down the pitch to Larwood where I found Hammond encouraging Larwood to take no notice of the sights, signs and sounds of trouble that were brewing at the ring side.

I added my own words of encouragement and asked him if he was able to run the ball away at all, to which he replied that far from making it go away he was turning the ball back. I was accordingly not surprised when at the start of the next over Larwood made a sign to me that he wanted a leg side field.

Had either he or I realized the misrepresentation to which we were to be subjected, neither of us would have set that par· ticular field for that particular over.

Woodfull is an old hand and had he been grey and groggy as most of the Australian press suggested, he knew perfectly well that he had only to ask me for leave to discontinue his innings, for his request to be instantly and readily granted. I do not imagine that Woodfull himself would claim that he was either grey or groggy.

Jardine's recollection of how the field for Woodfull was changed over to the leg side was incorrect. He motioned the field over, not me.

The Skipper always changed the field over. I probably did tell him that I was getting the ball back. That was my break·back, and I could bowl that at any time. But after two overs I would certainly have still been swinging the ball. Several newspapers at the time reported that I was on my way in to bowl when the field was switched over. Players in that match whom I have spoken to since support that view.

Jardine's own statement on the incident demonstrates his approach to the game in that series. He played the game hard. He asked for no quarter and gave none. As Woodfull did not ask for a respite to recover from his injury Jardine could see no reason why he shouldn't use any tactics within the rules. Woodfull was prepared to bat on, therefore he must be prepared to accept whatever form of attack was used.

In making 22 before Allen bowled him, Woodfull was hit several times by good balls just short of a length. Ponsford suffered more than anybody in the match, I think. He proved he could take a hiding in getting 85 runs. You could really only regard his bruises as minor, because anybody who scored 50 runs against me must expect to get hit a few times, no matter what kind of a field I had placed. Although both these players were superb defenders their footwork was poor against speed. They were magnificent batsmen against all classes of bowling, Ponsford being beautiful to watch, but the extra fast stuff put them off balance. I was always glad to see their backs, and I was always glad to see Fingleton walking back to the dressing-room, too.

They might have been slow, and they might have taken balls on the body when I thought they should have hooked. But they had guts.

Soon after Woodfull was out, he was lying on the massage table in the dressing-room receiving treatment for a bruise to his chest when Plum Warner walked in and Woodfull made his protest that one team was playing cricket, the other wasn't.

As soon as Woodfull's words reached Jardine's ears, he hurried into the English dressing-room, locking the door behind him. 'I want you all to be quiet,' he told us. 'I've got something very serious to say. This remark has been made. No one must talk about it outside this room. I shall deal with it. It is the most disgraceful remark I have ever heard.'

The remark was leaked from the Australian dressing-room. Some pressmen averred that Jack Fingleton was the culprit, but he denied it. Others thought it was Bradman. Fingleton blamed some unauthorized person in the dressing-room for letting the cat out of the bag. Jack was earning his living as a newspaperman at the time, and it must have been a terrible burden to keep such a story to himself. Jack denied it, however, and we must accept his word. It is true that pressmen sometimes went into the dressing-room, and it may well be that Jack's theory is right. The culprit remains a mystery. But it certainly made a powerful impact. I am certain of one thing – it was not Woodfull because newsmen at the time told me he was very disturbed that the information had got out.

A sequel to the incident was that Plum Warner claimed Woodfull had apologized, but this Woodfull publicly denied. Nearly every newspaper published the alleged apology and the denial.

A story in the Adelaide *News* read:

The joint managers of the English team in a statement to the press today said that Woodfull had expressed regret to him and Mr Palairet, the other joint manager, about Saturday's incident when Woodful criticized them for not playing cricket. The incident is now closed, all are now the best of friends,' said Mr Warner. But Woodfull denies this statement. Late this afternoon he said he had made no apology to Mr Warner. Obviously, Warner was deeply wounded by the slur.

The ball that hit Bertie Oldfield started everything off. It was most unfortunate. I had stopped bowling bodyline, and the field was set mainly on the off. I wouldn't have pitched one short at Bertie only he could bat, and he had settled in. The last thing I would have wanted to do was hit him. I pitched it short on the off stump. Bert swung at it going for a hook, but it came off the wicket slower than he expected.

He had spun almost right round, having just about completed the stroke when it hit him on the right side of the temple. I think the result would have been even worse if the peak of his cap had not broken the force of the ball. An X-ray revealed more than a black eye – he had suffered a linear fracture of the right frontal bone.

I was the first one up to Bert. I might have broken even with Gubby Allen, who was fielding at short leg. I was very upset. It was Bert's fault, and he was gentleman and sportsman enough to admit it at once. I am certain the ball came off the edge of his bat and that he walked into it. I was frightened at how serious Bert's injury might be; I was also frightened at the abuse and barracking of the crowd. I thought they were going to come at us. It was so bad that Maurice Tate, who was sitting in the enclosure, got up and went into the dressing-room saying, 'I'm getting out of here – somebody will get killed.'

I felt that one false move would bring the crowd down on me. I was glad when we finished off the last three batsmen and were able to go in to the comparative safety of the dressing-room.

The Melbourne *Herald* reported at the time:

Then developed one of the most amazing demonstrations made in a Test Match in Adelaide. The crowd on the mounds wildly hooted Larwood as he ran to the crease to bowl each ball. They howled at the fast bowler and counted him out with vigour.

The atmosphere was electrical. Every time Larwood took up the ball a rumble of hooting began. It rose in a steady crescendo when he started his run ... The demonstration spread from the outer mounds to the stands and storms of hooting rent the air right through Larwood's over. The crowd, especially those in the outer ground, were absolutely enraged ...

Former Australian captain, M. A. Noble, wrote:

In all my experience of cricket I have never known such an atmosphere of such disgust and anger as prevailed this afternoon. A batsman had to be struck in the head sooner or later. That batsman happened to be Oldfield. He was struck on the forehead and the doctor who was called in to see him said that if the blow had been an inch lower the consequences would have been serious. Oldfield's injury was unfortunate for Australia and not the design of the bowler. . .

The match continued in a tense atmosphere. Jardine didn't improve the crowd's mood when he strolled out wearing his most colourful Harlequin cap. I shall never forget Jardine in that moment. There are two kinds of courage, hot and cold. Hot courage is when a man rushes into a dangerous situation on the spur of the moment without a thought for the dangers confronting him. Cold courage is when a man knows the dangers before him but presses on without regard to the consequences in a calm and calculating way; Jardine had cold courage.

That resolute attitude of Jardine's was to be shown later on after the outbreak of war when, instead of accepting a safe job with the coal industry in Sheffield, he went to France before Dunkirk with the British Expeditionary Force. Sent by Dunkirk headquarters into Belgium to discover why troops there had not made contact, Jardine found them all dead, commandeered a troop carrier and drove himself back through German lines.

I don't think any captain of any cricket team anywhere

has ever had to bat in an atmosphere of such hostility and abuse. When he broke the shoulder of his bat and sent to the dressing-room for another one, he was advised from the mounds over and over again: 'You won't need it, you bastard!'

While the tumult was still at its height that afternoon – the third day of the Test – members of the Australian Board of Cricket Control met at the ground to frame a protest to the MCC against our bowling tactics. They had asked the English team managers if bodyline could be stopped, and Warner replied that he had no control over tactics – a statement which was clearly incorrect. Warner was either unwilling or unable to get the better of Jardine on the issue. Reporters were summoned to a conference room where the secretary of the Board, Mr Bill Jeanes, handed them a copy of a cablegram and told them they could copy and publish it.

The message said:

Bodyline bowling assuming such proportions as menace best interests of the game making protection of body by batsmen the main consideration and causing intensely bitter feelings amongst players as well as injuries. In our opinion it is unsportsmanlike and unless stopped at once it is likely to upset friendly relations existing between Australia and England.

Hugh Buggy, whose service for the tour was also being taken by the Adelaide *News*, asked Mr Jeanes: 'Is the board going to leave that last sentence in the cable about friendly relations between Australia and England? Isn't it a bit hysterical?'

Mr Jeanes replied: 'The cable has been sent.'

The cable incident was clumsily handled. The board sent the cable at ordinary rates, not realizing that it would be next day before the words reached London.

After the press conference announcement, the news reached London in three minutes flat by Gilbert Mant's Reuter cable at urgent rates. Journalists there immediately woke Lord Hailsham, the MCC president, at 2 AM. One can imagine Lord Hailsham's reaction on being summoned from his bed in the middle of a chilly night to be told Australia had officially denounced the English team as unsporting!

It later emerged that the decision to send the cable – at 3.12 PM on 18 January – certainly wasn't unanimous. Eight board members voted for it, five against. The members who framed the protest cable were Billy Kelly of Victoria and H. W. Hodgetts, R. F. Middleton and B. V. Scrymgeour, of South Australia (the four to whom Woodfull had complained about Jardine's tactics four days earlier).

News of the protest caused a sensation throughout the cricket world. Thousands of words on it were cabled back and forth across the world for days after. Johnnie Moyes, one of Australia's leading cricket commentators and an outstanding historian of the game, wrote later about the match:

. . . when Australia batted there was early evidence of suppressed resentment that would sooner or later find an outlet. Woodfull was hit over the heart. In all fairness it must be said this was a legitimate hazard. There was no leg field. The ball was such as any fast bowler might have delivered and it was not pitched on the batsman's body. Larwood was therefore entirely guiltless.

What followed was not legitimate in the opinion of the crowd for the leg field took up its position and the bodyline started. This seemed to the onlookers to be entirely divorced from British standards of fair play. They did not like to see a man bruised and battered and suffering from a severe body blow over the heart subjected to further risks which he was not in the best shape to avoid. It seemed like kicking a man in the ribs when he was down, and the crowd expressed its resentment not always in words free from offence.

Later Oldfield was hit on the head when batting gallantly, a hit that narrowly missed being most serious. The atmosphere degenerated into a foulness that seemed likely at any moment to culminate in a bitter upsurge of violence and end in a riot. Again, bodyline was not the cause except perhaps indirectly for all the batsmen had tasted the bitterness of it and their teeth had been set on edge.

Woodfull, who always played cricket according to the spirit as well as the letter of the law, was bitter and disillusioned. No wonder he was moved to wrath when Sir Pelham Warner ventured into the dressing-room with words of comfort. It was no time for platitudes, it was no time to express regret to a captain who had been battered and who had seen his wicketkeeper taken from the field with a split head, as though from the field of battle. But after all, Warner was powerless to interfere with Jardine's field tactics. While this was going on the Board of Control delegates were framing a cable to the MCC. Conceived in a conviction of unfairness, it was to impute a lack of sportsmanship to the opposition, a charge which above all others would anger the rulers at Lord's. For a time there was a chance that Test cricket might go into the discard . . .

Johnnie clearly disliked bodyline, but he never allowed his feelings to intrude in his dealings with me; I always found him a gentleman to deal with, and I saw a lot of him on the tour.

The events in Australia excited debate in newspapers which was repeated in many other journals throughout the Empire. Nevill Cardus in the *Observer*:

Jardine has at last found the right side. He ought to leave it unaltered, except by putting Duckworth in in place of Ames.

The Australian batsmen lost a gorgeous opportunity on a wicket which was a batsman's heaven. Shock bowling conquered again. I am no lover of the modern leg theory violence, but cannot withhold admiration at Larwood's ability to give batsmen a startled, brief life on a magnificent wicket.

My chief reason for thinking England will win the rubber is the decline of cricket everywhere. Not two members of the present English side would have been placed in the 1902 or 1905 team, while there are not two Australians who would not look small and ineffectual compared with Clem Hill, Noble and Victor Trumper. But the game is itself greater than the players. As there are no masters in the present series we are enjoying rare fun.

The *Star:*

The real offence of the leg theory is that it keeps cricket at a pitch of excitement rare even for Tests. Every accident including some not connected with it is being attributed to leg theory. Many English cricketers prefer to see us without the leg theory, because it gives the other side a chance to protest. We believe England's job is to win within the rules. We hope she is going to do it.

The *Daily Telegraph:*

It is high time that lovers of cricket in England and Australia should declare their impatience of the sulphurous atmosphere in which the Tests have become involved. It is impossible to estimate the exact meaning of the Australian complaints against the English bowling. The printed opinions of old Australian Test players are not in agreement about the descriptions of play and suggest that unskilful batting rather than dangerous bowling caused the loss of wickets and injuries. Of the absolute legality of leg-theory bowling there can be no question; but England will heartily agree that such a defence of this sort of play is not sufficient. On the other hand, Australia cannot forget that fast bowlers have been dangerous before. The strain of Test play must always tend to produce unfortunate incidents; but players, spectators and critics should minimize them or they may become a noxious element in cricket.

The *News Chronicle:*

We don't know what reply if any the MCC will make to the Australian protest. The whole controversy is rather mystifying. Why is leg theory not cricket? Why if applied unfairly, have umpires said nothing? All fast bowling is dangerous. McDonald and Gregory were famous exponents of the shock attack.

Sir Julien Cahn, leader of many English teams on tour, speaking at a London dinner said: 'I do not believe in much of this Test controversy. I have entertained all Australian teams. All are good fellows, and I'm not going to have anything said against Larwood, because he belongs to my club.'

Arthur Mailey was quoted as saying that he would like to see a committee of prominent international and ex-international cricketers discuss the whys and wherefores of bodyline quietly. He suggested men like Warner, Woodfull, Jardine, Hobbs, Noble and Ryder, all of whom had captained England or Australia.

'The whole thing is a problem which is most difficult to solve in an equitable manner,' said Mailey. 'If it is allowed to continue, batsmen will be compelled to wear baseball masks and heavy padding; then the fast bowlers could fire away until they were worn out.'

Jack Ryder, the Australian captain before Woodfull, said:

Before I came to Adelaide I often had things to say in favour of a leg theory type of attack. I believed that aggressive front of the wicket play would do much to conquer it and that it could continue without harming the game. But the incidents in which Woodfull and Oldfield have been concerned here have made me think otherwise.

It seemed on Saturday that when Woodfull was hit and Larwood immediately changed to leg theory that if it were not an attempt at intimidation it was rubbing it in rather hard . . .

In many respects I admire Larwood. He is one of the fastest and best bowlers I have played against. He is too good a cricketer to be made notorious by the tactics he is adopting. The position is in the hands of the captain. He must talk matters over with the bowler. Jardine is conversant with all there is to know about the game. There is nothing in the laws of cricket to stop leg theory. And Jardine seems to take advantage of every opportunity the law gives him.

By applying the methods they have the Englishmen have done the game much harm. The danger to players is not so obvious on the slow and easy wicket here as it is in Melbourne and Sydney. I think, however, that Adelaide people have seen enough to convince them that leg theory is all wrong. I have.

It seems that the fast bowling battery was chosen by England primarily to check Bradman's run of high scores. The plan succeeded until Bradman made a brilliant century in Melbourne, and it proved such a success with the other batsmen that Jardine is loath to discard it.

No cricketer or supporter of the game is opposed to good-length bowling on the leg side, no matter how fast. It is the ball short of good length bowled to lift high which cannot be tolerated.

Feeling continued to run so high that I was not surprised during the Test when I went to an Adelaide theatre one night and overheard a small child, after coming up and looking at me, saying to her mother: 'Mummy. He doesn't *look* like a murderer!'

The Australian Board of Control appointed a committee to investigate and report on what action was needed to eliminate bodyline bowling from cricket. The committee was made up of Woodfull, Victor Richardson, Roger Hartigan and M. A. Noble.

Bodyline had ceased to be a mere controversy. It was now a crisis. And, privately, Jardine was worried that Lord's would not support him. In the tension-filled hours while everyone waited to see what the reaction would be from Lord's, Jardine said to Gubby Allen, 'Those bastards will not back me up.'

He was particularly worried about the use of the word 'unsportsmanlike' in the board's cable and remained difficult to mollify when some team members, among them Allen, told him this assertion would be the one thing Lord's would not be able to accept.

On 23 January after the Test ended (which England won by 338 runs) the Board of Control received the devastating Lord's reply to its cable of protest. The MCC cable read:

We Marylebone Cricket Club deplore your cable. We deprecate your opinion that there has been unsportsmanlike play. We have fullest confidence in captain, team and managers and are convinced that they would do nothing to infringe either the laws of cricket or the spirit of the game.

We have no evidence that our confidence has been misplaced. Much as we regret accidents to Woodfull and Oldfield we understand that in neither case was the bowler to blame. If the Australian Board of Control wish to propose a new law or rule it shall receive our careful consideration in due course. We hope the situation is not now as serious as your cable would seem to indicate but if it is such as to jeopardise the good relations between England and Australian cricketers and you consider it desirable to cancel remainder of programme we would consent but with great reluctance.

Australian cricket authorities, of course, didn't want to cancel the rest of the tour. They were making splendid profits. Adelaide had attracted record crowds. The Sydney and Melbourne grounds had been packed to capacity, and vast crowds flocked even to the minor games. Bodyline gave cricket in Australia a much needed fillip. Without it I feel sure that having regard to the Depression the tour would have been a financial loss.

On the last day but one of the Test, while I was being given the full treatment from the crowd, I received a telegram from Archie Jackson as he lay dying in a Brisbane private hospital. It read: 'Congratulations magnificent bowling. Good luck all matches. Archie Jackson.' This was the same Archie Jackson whom I caught on a bowler's wicket at the Oval for half an hour or so in 1930; the man who stood up to me and took a bruising while Don Bradman drew away.

A fortnight before sending the telegram he had written in a newspaper article reproduced throughout the Empire:

If legislation were introduced to eradicate leg theory cricket would became an invalid, and comparable with a one-legged man, about to satisfy up to a point but unable to obtain supreme heights of action.

Larwood is one of the most likeable and docile fellows one could wish to meet. He would not hurt a fly, and his success is the reward not of intimidation tactics, but of sheer skill combined with pluck and resource.

Leg theory bowling is as much a part of bowling as the off theory. As such it should be dealt with by cricketers in the field and not by legislators who have never taken part in big cricket and who are unaware of the trials and tribulations which beset bowlers on shirt-front wickets under blazing southern skies.

CHAPTER FOURTEEN

Supposing Somebody Died?

'ENGLAND EXPECTS her men to bowl 'em out or lay 'em out. Next – cricket under arms?' This headline appeared in *Truth*, the Melbourne weekly, immediately after the Adelaide Test. It was fairly typical of the comments in some Australian newspapers. The rest of the article is quoted to show the feeling that existed in some quarters:

The third Test match at Adelaide between Australia and England, if it has done nothing else, has attained pronounced success in driving several further extremely lengthy nails into the coffin of cricket. The great game is being obliterated in an obnoxious warfare of lowly scheming and intrigue.

England has descended to the backlane tactics of 'If you can't bowl 'em out knock 'em out,' and the indignant protests this has drawn from Australia caused the match to develop into something in the nature of a first-class gang squabble.

Collectively, if not individually, the English side bids fair to become the most unpopular sporting combination ever to visit this country. Its tactics are at last arousing general hostility, and while this may be due mostly to the feelings against one man, or even a few members of the side, the team as a whole must suffer as a consequence.

It is unfortunate, for among the Englishmen are some of the best and most good-natured athletes who ever entered an arena; but they, too, are forced to share the burden of unpopularity that has been garnered by individual mannerisms and tactics.

Candidly, Australia is fed right up to the neck with the hypocritical humbug of Captain Jardine and sees little to enthuse over in the seemingly guileless evasions of manager

Australia's Bert Oldfield collapses after a Larwood thunderbolt caught him on the temple. Adelaide Test 1933

In the same match Aussie captain Bill Woodfull, hit over the heart, drops his bat in agony

Bodyline in action – Larwood about to deliver the sizzling ball . . .

. . . the rocket is delivered. Both pictures at the Melbourne Test

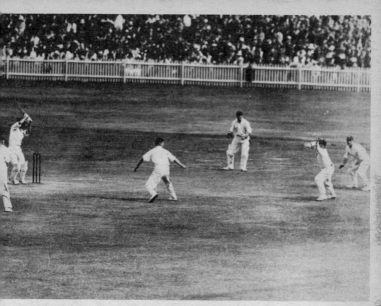

Jack Fingleton slips one past Larwood's inner leg cordon in the Test match on 7 December 1932 (Photo Sydney Morning Herald)

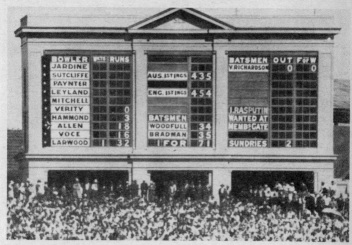

BOWLER	WKTS	RUNS
JARDINE		
SUTCLIFFE		
PAYNTER		
LEYLAND		
MITCHELL		
VERITY		0
HAMMOND		3
ALLEN		18
VOCE		16
LARWOOD	1	32

AUS. 1st INGS	435
ENG. 1st INGS	454

BATSMEN	
WOODFULL	34
BRADMAN	35
1 FOR	71

BATSMEN	OUT	F or W
V. RICHARDSON	0	0

J. RASPUTIN
WANTED AT
MEMB:GATE

SUNDRIES	2

The bodyline rumpus packed them in at Sydney in the fifth Test, 1933, although the Ashes were already in the bag. Larwood broke down in the second innings

The bodyline partners – Larwood and Voce – who were in the middle of the controversy

Clarrie Grimmett and Stan McCabe (187 not out) go out in the Sydney Test to make a 'death or glory' stand against Larwood's rockets

Bill Voce, Larwood's partner in the bodyline speed battery, about to let fly.

(Photo Sydney Sun)

No. Copies of Origin No. of Words Date Time Official Instructions

K2301.   LONDON   9   3RD   930AM.

LCO LARWOOD AUSTRALIA HOTEL SYDNEY

WELL BOWLED NOTTS

                    MARYLEBONE

In any enquiry respecting this message please quote Reference No.

The first line of this telegram contains the following particulars in order named

No.	Office of Origin	No. of Words	Date	Time	Official Instructions

K2292 LONDON 7   25   931AM...

LCO LARWOOD AUSTRALIA HOTEL SYDNEY

BRAVO..

     MARYLEBONE.

S.h. etc. no.   The first line of this Telegram contains the following particulars in the order named

Station from.	Words.	Time Lodged.	No.
BRAM 19	LONDON 9	11th 12 4pm	

  LCO LARWOOD

  BELLEVUE HOTEL BRISBANE

WELL BOWLED CONGRATULATIONS

  MARYLEBONE.

Three cables sent to Larwood during the 'bodyline' tour of Australia. They had a hollow ring afterwards!

Although England needed only one run (with all wickets intact) to win the first Test at Sydney in 1932, this lone Aussie spectator turned up to see Sutcliffe hit the winning shot

The England team in the famous third Test at Adelaide 1933. Larwood is in the top row, third from right

1.

2.

1. A youthful Don Bradman, the
freakish champion from whom
bodyline was hatched.
(Photo Sydney Morning Herald)

2. The stern visage of Douglas
Jardine, the patrician, aloof English
captain of the bodyline tour

3. Close-up of a hero: Stan
McCabe, whose 187 not out against
Larwood's bodyline rockets on the
Sydney Ground in the first Test in
1932 was one of the most blood-
stirring and courageous Test
innings of all time.
(Photo Sydney Morning Herald)

3.

Bodyline batsman Jack Fingleton in action. Larwood described him as one of Australia's most courageous players.

(Photo **Sydney Morning Herald***)*

The hatchet is buried. Larwood and Bradman shake hands when they meet in London again after many years

· TO ·
HAROLD
FOR THE ASHES
— 1932 - 33 —
FROM A GRATEFUL
"SKIPPER"

A memorable and personal tribute from Jardine to Larwood. The ashtray (very appropriate!) was presented before a crowd of 20,000 in England

Larwood meets King George V in the match against the West Indies 1928. Arthur Carr (captain) makes the presentation

Hero and worshipper – a sad ending. Jack Gregory, the legendary fast bowler whom Larwood idolized, ended his Test career in attempting this catch off Larwood in the first innings of the first Test in Brisbane in 1928. Gregory, whom Larwood had worshipped as a boy in England, injured a cartilage in the incident

The well-known partnership of Sutcliffe (left) and Hobbs who made so many splendid openings for England

Australia's famous opening pair – Bill Woodfull and Bill Ponsford

When he retired after the bodyline fracas, Larwood went home to Nottingham to grow flowers

His cricketing days over for good, 'Lol' kept himself busy among the 'Lollies'

Bringing with him a family of five and memories of the bodyline controversy, Harold Larwood arrives in Australia at Fremantle on the Orontes *in May 1950 – as a migrant.* (Photo Daily News, Perth)

When Larwood arrived in Sydney in 1950, first person to meet him was an old antagonist, Jack Fingleton.

(Photo Sydney Sun)

Fifty years after bodyline – Larwood at his Sydney home in October 1982, at the age of seventy-seven

On the fiftieth anniversary of bodyline, Larwood poses in the living-room of his Sydney home alongside a picture of the 1932–33 bodyline tourists

'Plum' Warner. Mr Jardine doesn't appear to like us very much, and there is a marked reciprocity of feeling on Australia's part in this direction.

If there were a most popular man competition promoted in Australia at the moment and Douglas Robert Jardine constituted all three starters in it, it would be safe enough to wager that he wouldn't fill a place!

Judging by incidents in the Test game at Adelaide we would seem to be passing through a changing period of cricket. Oldfield was seriously hurt and the English Skipper promptly despatched a consoling message of sympathy to the wicketkeeper's wife in New South Wales. Woodfull, too, was well in the firing line.

The Australian leader was hit over the heart by fast bowler Larwood. The real ethics of sport demanded that Woodfull be given a breather for a few overs but, instead, Messrs Jardine and Larwood conspired to bring about his complete downfall by packing the field around him, and putting up a terrific leg barrage. It was evidently a nice way of expressing their regret that Woodfull was not rendered useless for further play, as Oldfield was to be later in the battle.

It certainly seems as though the old order is changing. Soon we may expect to read reports of matches something like the following:

'The Fourth Test between Australia and England turned out to be a great fight. Australia won with the loss of only six men, three of whom were killed outright. The others succumbed to injuries received early in the battle.

'England emerged from the fracas minus eight killed and three reported missing. It has not yet been discovered how they were missed as it was considered impossible for Australia's offensive of tear gas, poison shells, and jam tin bombs to miss anything. However, the Board of Control, in conjunction with Defence Department officials are inquiring.

'When asked what was likely to come from the inquiry, Sir George Pearce, in characteristic fashion, replied, "Nothing," as he considered the contest had been conducted in the friendliest of spirits.'

LATER

'It has now been definitely established that the missing Englishmen are located at Darwin. They are in hiding there, and expect to leave for home by the next plane, attempting the Australia–England record. They will be disguised as spare drums of petrol.

'Perhaps, when cricket is played in such a hearty spirit, we shall see some of the thrills that for so long have been absent from it.

'Woodfull and Fingleton will open for Australia from the inside of armoured cars. Larwood will commence sending them down from an 18 pounder placed in a strategic position behind the main grandstand and Jardine, armed with two fountain pens and a couple of dozen telegram forms, will prepare to despatch messages of condolence at cut rates arranged by Mr Archdale Parkhill.'

Newspaper readers will be thrilled with reports from the front like this:

'Larwood's first delivery was a bonzer. It dropped fair on top of Woodfull's tank and made it look as flat as a pancake in which mother had forgotten to put the baking powder. In the excitement of this early blood drawn by England, Jardine almost neglected his duties as captain. Finally, however, he despatched a message of sympathy reading: "Woodfull has been left with a hand and will probably retain the sight of one eye. This is to be regretted and Larwood and myself are both sorry."

'Plum Warner, acting as message boy for Jardine, wanted to know whether the Skipper and Larwood were expressing their regret at not having seriously hurt Woodfull. Jardine declined to answer on the ground that his contract forbade him to make any comments.

'While this was going on Bradman had come in first tank down. After having a look at the field, he went off and re-turned, flying low in a Puss Moth, and easily kept out of Larwood's range. After remaining for a couple of hours he met disaster when attempting to sweep low over Fingleton's armoured car. It was decided to have a bob-in subscription to raise funds to buy Don a rubber-wheeled chair.

'Jardine wired a message of condolence to Mrs Bradman and asked whether there was anything he could do. Mrs Bradman wired back, "Yes, put in your bob."

'Fingleton was next to go. He poked out his head to see why Gubby Allen was not putting them on the tank and was well taken by Ames, who sneaked up on him with a butterfly net. Jardine telegraphed to Associated Newspapers: "Poor Fingleton, you've lost him."

'Sir Hugh Denison replied: "That's nothing – we've lost more than that in the last few years."

'The game continued. Larwood, after a consultation with the captain, changed his range when McCabe and Richardson were together. He flew them high, and one burst among the spectators in the outer.

'Mr Archdale Parkhill sent a message of congratulations to Jardine and asked him if he would like special telegraph lines reserved and extra telegraphists employed. "Certainly", replied Jardine, who later requested the services of three stenographers and two shorthand writers.

'The game was held up for half an hour while the English managers argued that as there were so many dead-heads on the outer they should be removed and more room made for paying patrons. The latter, they said, preferably should be recruited from the deaf and dumb asylum in order that Jardine would not be disturbed at his work.

'Australia's innings closed for three killed, five seriously wounded and two badly maimed. Ironmonger didn't take the field as he had forgotten where he had left his Roman shield and poison spear.

'The start of England's first innings was delayed owing to Sutcliffe's offer to fight anybody who said he should open up. Larwood was finally selected to take the field first, but another hitch occurred when he reported that his boot was hurting him.

'Mr James ("£1000") Whitelaw cabled an offer to provide a pension for life for England's two openers. England's two openers replied with a request that Mr Whitelaw provide a couple of suitably inscribed coffins instead. Mr Whitelaw answered, "Certainly! I'll also undertake to supply your wives with a two-year supply of free washing soap."

'Mailey telegraphs that an umpire has walked on to the field to inform the crowd which is entrenched behind sandbag parapets, that no decision can be reached as to when England will start. Noble wires that the umpire's body will be removed from the field after dark.

'An Australian bowler operating a patent trench mortar had mistaken the umpire for an Englishman. "I can remember a similar incident when I captained an Australin team against Warner's men in 1901," Noble states.

'"Don't believe it. He can't remember anything," says Mailey from the ground. "Anyway, it was a good length ball that bowled Bradman."

'Jardine was asked to open for England. "I can't," he replied. "I've got to send a telegram." It transpired that the captain was engaged in a long-distance chess game with an opponent in England. The game was expected to last three months. It was stressed that scoring a little faster than usual he might make six runs in that time. He was not to be tempted, however, but sent a telegram instead.

'The battle ended in Australia's favour, England forfeiting after seeing Wall practising with two revolvers concealed in shoulder holsters and three machine guns.

'The selectors then called a meeting and announced that the Australian team for the fifth Test would include Ambrose Palmer, Jack Carroll, Tom Lurich, Hughie Martin (if available). They had thought of sending Strangler Lewis but after discussion it was decided that he might be tempted to drop his headlock for leg theory.

'Barracking arrangements by special request of Mr Jardine will be left to Killarney Kate.

'The Board of Control also had a meeting. It agreed to the urgent representations of the Marylebone Cricket Club that the Roman shields used by the batsmen should be reduced by three inches in diameter owing to the number of men given out shield before wicket.

'It was also decided that Test matches in future should be private fights. The public will be kept out. No one will hoot Larwood or barrack Mr Jardine and the whole of the English side will pay its own expenses while in Australia. Thus keeping the beastly public out, and ensuring that Tests will be played in a silence broken only by the crunching of shattered bones.

'O YEAH!'

At least a million people must have read this heavy-handed satire, and in the same issue a story appeared obviously inspired by the remarks expressed by a Sydney judge, Mr Justice Sheriden, in which he had stated that my leg-theory bowling was covered by the criminal law.

The article said:

Is Larwood, with his present type of bowling, unwittingly placing himself within the displeasure of the law? Would the police be justified in intervening to stop him? Supposing somebody died as a result of injury from one of his fast balls, could a coroner commit him for trial for manslaughter?

All these highly interesting possibilities were discussed with *Truth* the other day by a well-known legal authority, who has particularly interested himself in what the law might have to say about injuries or deaths resulting from an orgy of fast leg-theory bowling.

'It has already been held in British Courts,' says this authority, 'that if while engaged in a friendly game such as football or cricket one of the players commits an unlawful act, whereby death is caused to another player, he is guilty of manslaughter. The act, although it be in accordance with the rules of the game, would be unlawful if the person committing it intended to produce a serious injury to another.

'A man might also be adjudged guilty of manslaughter if he committed an act which he knew might produce serious injury and if he were shown to be indifferent and reckless as to the consequences.'

'In other words, a bowler might say to himself, I know that something like this laid so and so out the other day, but that's their lookout, and keep on doing the thing which he knows by then might cause serious injury. If, then, somebody happened to get killed, the bowler would be most certainly liable to be called to account by the law.

In most Australian states the Police Offences Code includes

a provision that a man might be called to account for 'an assault with intent to do grievous bodily harm'. Assuming that any of the foregoing qualifications could be applied to the state of mind of a bowler then, in the opinion of the legal authority, the matter might well become one for the attention of the police.

According to the legal luminary, there is a case in English law which tends to strongly support these contentions. In that case a footballer died as a result of a charge by another footballer. The charging player was indicted for manslaughter . . .

Truth puts forward these views for what they are worth, in view of the agitation everywhere for the adoption of similar tactics by such bowlers as Alexander or Gilbert. Deliberate bowling at the body will undoubtedly carry some very unpleasant implications for the bowlers if anything really serious happens.

Judge Sheriden, in New South Wales, has already referred to the dangers of the legal position and it is well that they should be recognized. That the police should have to interfere with the playing of an international game of cricket would be intolerable. Yet that may easily happen if the present position is made worse by retaliatory methods.

English newspapers did not regard the legal possibilities quite as seriously as some Australian newspapers, and one London newspaper produced the following story:

Described on the charge sheet as an itinerant player, Harold Larboard, aged 28, of Nottingham, was charged at Adelaide Quarter Sessions with recklessly and wantonly attempting to do grievous and bodily harm to certain citizens of the Australian Commonwealth, to wit, the Australian XI, by means of a lethal weapon known as the leg trap.

Detective Kaunstauk stated that when Larboard was arrested he had in his possession an infernal machine made of a hard round substance, suspiciously like a hand grenade.

When taken in charge he was about to hurl this weapon at the person of Bradman.

Justice Sherrydown created much laughter in Court by

inquiring, 'Who is this Bradman?'

When charged, Larboard replied, 'Ah knoaws nowt about it; thee go an' see Mester Wa-arner.'

The next witness, Mr Alan Kopecks, described as a radio announcer, explained that leg trap was a contrivance for getting the Australian team out without allowing them to score any runs by bowling in the direction of the wicket instead of at the pavilion . . . In summing up, Justice Sherry-down described the leg theory as a very serious offence. He added: 'To be compelled to bat in chain armour is detrimental to free action, and arnica is but small consolation.'

He thereupon pronounced Larboard guilty, the sentence being that while in Australia he be ordered to bowl underhand with tennis balls.

Our troubles would have been very few indeed if this had been the only material published. But stories of serious dissension in our team spread quickly and were widely published before the Adelaide Test ended.

Not every Australian newspaper, of course, set out to make us appear a villainous bunch, but some seized quickly on any snippet and played it up in a way which gave the impression that the English side was on the verge of internal revolt because so many members disagreed with the 'unsportsmanlike' tactics.

Here is one example showing how rumour was largely misconstrued as fact:

Incidents without parallel in the history of any previous touring team are making the present visit of England's Test combination one that must culminate in a mild scandal either in this country or when the team returns to England. These incidents are exclusive of anything that happened on the field and have taken place on the social side of the tour.

The undercurrent of unpleasantness that has so long been in evidence has bubbled over into a boiling torrent. There have been amazing scenes in which some of the more promi-nent men have fared and it looks guineas to gooseberries on a first-class showdown startling the sporting world before the fourth Test match is played in Brisbane.

There are numerous reasons for the unhappy state of affairs that exist among the men of England who are anything but merry. One of the chief causes of discontent has been the treatment meted out to Maurice Tate, who is probably the most popular member of any touring side in recent years.

Tate is liked and respected by the majority of his team-mates and his appearance on any arena in Australia is vociferously and enthusiastically noted by the crowd.

Slow smouldering resentment occasioned by Tate's treatment blazoned up when the bowler was once discarded for the Adelaide Test. What is regarded as the deliberate humiliation of the Sussex man so affected a batsman who is England's most dependable run-getter that he gave expression to his thoughts in open declaration that it was immaterial to him whether he made runs or not.

Whether this prominent player's feelings underwent a change by the time he reached the wicket is not known; but it is significant that he did not make runs in either innings, and showed no disappointment because of that fact when he returned to the dressing-room.

Tate himself is feeling the position very keenly. The constant insulting of his ability by using him solely in picnic games and matches of minor importance has caused a remarkable drooping of the spirits of this unusually exuberant and cheerful player.

The decidedly unfriendly atmosphere between Tate and Jardine, his captain, became supercharged following an incident at Glenelg last Friday night. The pair faced each other while strolling along the pier, and Tate did not bother to hide his amusement when a bunch of kiddies, remembering the incident of Bowes clean bowling Jardine at practice, commented on the incident in a way that children sometimes have.

On their return to the hotel at Glenelg at which they were staying, Jardine spoke to Tate about the incident. Sharp words were exchanged, and according to eye-witnesses, the discussion resulted in something of a scene.

Quite a few people who have been close to Jardine during the week state that there is more than a suspicion of signs of a conflict on his countenance. Anyway, Jardine has given a hint of seeking another environment.

Whatever the reason, the captain who was living at the Pier Hotel, where the remainder of the team is, made inquiries regarding quarters at the Richmond, which is also the place of accommodation of the Australians, and it can be definitely taken that Tate and Jardine do not exchange very many words with each other. Such a position between the captain of an international cricket team and one of his star bowlers must be intolerable; but – well, there it is.

It is known that unless injuries to other bowlers so impair England's attack to make his inclusion necessary, Tate will not figure among those selected for either of the remaining two Test matches. He will, in fact, be extremely lucky to play in any game of importance as things stand at present.

Glenelg police guardedly deny that their services were required at any time, either in connection with a row between the players or on another occasion when a party was in progress in honour of certain English players.

Four or five of the party – not Englishmen – are said to have spent a couple of hours in the company of the police but there is no official verification of this.

On another occasion, it is rumoured, some of the English players returned to the hotel late at night after a round of the Glenelg side-shows. One member of the party ordered drinks all round just as Jardine is believed to have walked in and informed the 'shouter' that he couldn't do such a thing.

'Can't I?' the other is alleged to have replied. 'It's my money and I can dashed-well spend it as I like.' One word led to many others, all of a heated nature, and finally a glass of beer was thrown.

Adelaide has been simmering with excitement ever since the Englishmen have arrived. Interest in bodyline bowling, and the resulting injuries to Woodfull and Oldfield, have been quickly superseded by an intense anticipation of what the outcome of the evident signs of discontent in England's ranks will be. These things are the topic of every bar and cafe in the city.

Jardine's disciplinary measures and his methods of handling his men both on and off the field have not endeared him to them. It is certain that the English MCC will have many pertinent matters with which to deal when the team returns.

A touring side from that country has never before been so much at war with itself, and Jardine's culpable lack of popularity as a leader must be the subject of some inquiry.

It is tragically unfortunate for cricket that these things should be, and it is certain that the English authorities will take steps to ensure that there is no repetition when future tours are being arranged.

Incidents like the alleged beer-throwing were played up and given considerable publicity. Stories of dissension reached such a pitch that the night before the Adelaide Test finished we were asked to attend a meeting at our hotel. Next day the managers issued a statement saying there was no dissension and that team members were behind Jardine as captain.

One report of that meeting said:

With something of an atmosphere of the 'Star Chamber' hovering about the meeting, every member of the English team was gathered secretly in a private room at the Glenelg Hotel late on Wednesday night. Words weren't minced in the discussion that followed.

While the meeting was not called expressly for the purpose of reviewing the Jardine–Tate position, it is understood that this was mentioned. Finally, a motion was passed that players did not desire to enter into any public controversy and that they deplored the introduction of personal feeling into the game.

On Thursday morning a carefully worded communiqué from 'Plum' Warner was handed to the press at Adelaide Oval.

In effect this stated that the team wished to deny that there had been any dissension or disloyalty in their ranks, and that they desired to assure the public of England and Australia that they were, and always had been, loyal to Jardine under whose leadership they wished to achieve success in an honourable manner.

It can be stated definitely that some members of the visiting team are in conflict with the official managerial notification.

Tate and Duckworth, both of whom have been stood down for three Tests, much to public surprise, Mitchell, who has been an onlooker at big games – and expects to continue as such – and Pataudi, who has been acting as 'Lemons' lately, have strong views on certain matters.

The meeting that was called on the Wednesday night, the night before the Test finished, was not a special meeting – at least it didn't begin that way. The entire team always had one meeting a week, usually on a Saturday night. We used to have a drink to our wives, sweethearts and children at home. Some of the players, of course, were teetotal. It was the sort of thing to keep the old flag flying. Jardine and the managers were always there.

That was how that meeting came to be held that night. But once we were there the question of alleged dissension in the team was raised. I am a little bit hazy on the exact details, but I think Warner did most of the talking. I feel certain that Jardine offered to stand down as captain if it was felt that his handling of the team in the bodyline crisis was causing team members embarrassment. I think he sent off a cable to the MCC to this effect, too.

Jardine was so concerned at developments in that Adelaide Test that he sought a vote of confidence in his captaincy, and this came up at the meeting.

I'm sure my memory is correct in recalling that Jardine wanted to leave the room while the vote was taken but was persuaded to stay by the managers and the players.

Sutcliffe had drafted a statement, which was read to the team. It really avoided the essence of the bodyline issue and was more to do with rebutting newspaper stories of dissension in the team. The statement denied rumours of dissension and disloyalty and wanted to 'assure the public of England and Australia that they are and always have been utterly loyal to their captain'.

When it came to a vote for Jardine everybody expressed their confidence in him because it was a vote for England. Jardine might have been unpopular with a few of the players, but everybody respected and admired him, and many of us liked him; and when it came to winning back the Ashes, every man in the team knew he was the one person who could lead us to victory. We all had one thing in common: we wanted to win the Ashes, and that was the thing that united us and ironed out any differences.

At that meeting there was some talk about fraternizing in the Australian dressing-room. Several of our players, mainly those who could not get in a Test, spent a lot of their time in this way. Jardine knew these players were disgruntled and no doubt could see that this was one way in which grievances might be aired through the press.

There were grievances in the team, but they were not nearly as serious as was made out. They were not caused by bodyline but were only due indirectly to it. There was some dissatisfaction from those who could not get in a Test, players like Duckworth, Tommy Mitchell, Tate, Bowes, Brown and Pataudi. Pataudi scored a century in his first Test but didn't do so well in either innings of the second and was dropped after that. Jardine considered his batting too slow. As far as the amateurs and professionals went, there was the usual distinction between us. We seemed to split up into twos and threes, the professionals and the amateurs mainly staying among their own groups.

I knew Allen didn't like bodyline and wouldn't bowl it, but that had nothing to do with me, and I never discussed the subject with him. As far as I was concerned he was an amateur, and a very reserved one. We were friendly enough on the field but didn't have much to say to each other off the field. We weren't drinking mates. It was the same with Bobby Wyatt and the other amateurs.

The only other person in the team who was against bodyline was Wyatt. I knew he didn't like it but, there again, it was a subject I did not on any occasion discuss with him. Nor did I ever hear him speaking out openly against it. 'Plum' Warner gave the impression to some Australians that he was against bodyline in a minor way, but he seemed more interested in the gate receipts than in the effect of bodyline.

If, as was suggested later, Warner had to walk warily, he certainly did it very skilfully. He never gave me the impression that he was opposed to my bowling methods and, in fact, encouraged me because he was as keen as anybody to beat Australia. Before the second innings in the Adelaide Test he came up to me and said: 'I'll give you a pound, Larwood, if you can bowl Fingleton out quickly.'

'I'll be trying whether you offer me a pound or not, Mr Warner,' I said. He didn't seem to mind what method I used; after all, he was one of the men who selected me and the other three fast bowlers. I bowled Fingleton for a duck, giving him a pair for the match and he was dropped from the Tests after that.

Many years later when I told Fingleton about that he said, 'Gee, Harold, he must have wanted to see me out pretty badly.'

I think he wanted to see Jack Fingleton disposed of because he blamed him for leaking the story about Woodfull's snub in the Adelaide dressing-room which caused him grave embarrassment at Lord's and elsewhere.

No matter what anybody then said, or what they have said since, only Allen and Wyatt expressed any disapproval of bodyline on that tour. Wyatt didn't mix with the professionals off the field, and usually was to be found in his bedroom playing classical records. He was a very studious type of person.

As far as I understood it, everybody, with these exceptions, favoured bodyline because they could see it gave us a good chance of winning the Ashes. But, when some of them couldn't get in the Tests, they began to moan about bodyline, not necessarily because they regarded it as unsportsmanlike but perhaps as an excuse for being passed over.

I think a lot of Pataudi's statements at public functions were misunderstood. He was a very witty fellow but often engaged in mild sarcasm. Whenever he met anybody at a party or a public function he would say things like, 'It's a dangerous thing to score a century in our team – you'll get yourself dropped quickly if you do that.' This often gave the impression of bitterness and rivalry among the players, but Pataudi didn't mean to be taken too seriously.

The boys who couldn't get into the Tests used to wear a tie with a rabbit motif on it, to indicate their status. It was more or less a joke, and I suppose it was their own little way of showing that they were taking their disappointment on the chin. I think Pataudi inspired the idea. Duckworth was probably as keenly disappointed as anybody because he was a splendid wicketkeeper, and better than Ames, but didn't play in a single Test, because of his batting. And yet in Melbourne he took off his boots and gave them to me. Any member of the team would, virtually, have done anything when it came to pulling together for England. Personal differences were sunk for a cause that was common to all of us.

It was said that Tommy Mitchell declared at Perth that he was ready to return home by the next ship because he felt he was not wanted. I think Tommy may well have said so. But the reason was not because he was fed up with the team. He was very homesick, and no doubt thought the concentrated fast attack would squeeze him out.

Some correspondents claimed that when Maurice Tate joined the team in Melbourne he was not welcome as there were already too many players. All of us were pleased by his arrival because he gave us a rest in the less important matches.

I think it was unfortunate that he couldn't get a game in a Test. He was still good enough to bowl for England but didn't fit in with Jardine's plans to use fast bowlers. Maurice still had so much nip off the wicket, even at that stage, that I think today he would be classed as a fast bowler. I remember being asked in 1950 how I thought Alec Bedser would have fared as a foil for me in 1932. I said Alec would have done the same thing as Maurice – he'd have been sitting in the dressing-room looking on. I don't think Alec was as good a bowler as Tate.

Maurice Tate probably grumbled over his failure to make the Test side, but he would never have said anything openly to embarrass Jardine. Maurice was too much of a gentleman. I doubt very much whether he had much to say to Jardine about his disappointment and, certainly, there was no beer-throwing incident.

As for the suggestion that I regarded myself as a sheet-anchor and tried to 'lord' it over Jardine: I wish I could have felt that way. I would have had a much easier time on the tour. Jardine wasn't the kind of man you could dominate, especially if you were a professional. Although I was annoyed with him on several occasions, and thought he was too tough on me, I never had any serious open clash with him, and he remained very much my superior throughout. Freddie Brown was another of the unhappy men on the tour. He didn't play in a Test because he failed to come up to expectations. But I thought he was a better player then than when he led the MCC team in Australia in 1950.

There was probably some truth in the story about Jardine wanting to change his hotel at one stage. I know that one night a group of us professionals were having a pretty good party and Jardine, whom we thought had already left for the weekend, rang our room to speak to Fergie, the scorer. We thought we'd have a bit of fun with the Skipper and began to whistle, shout and horse around as if it was a pretty lively time all round. The Skipper didn't think much of our behaviour and was a little frosty during the next few days.

After the evening meeting during the Adelaide Test, members of our team stopped going to the Australian dressing-room. I think Jardine might have insisted on this when the question of his captaincy was discussed.

As far as I was concerned, the meeting made no difference to my friendship with the Australian players and pressmen. Bill Voce, Tommy Mitchell and I usually got about together, and I spent a lot of time with Stan McCabe, Bill O'Reilly and several of the other Australian players. Jack Fingleton often had a drink with me. We didn't talk much about the politics of the game over a glass of beer but, on the subject of bodyline, I used to tell them that I hoped nobody would get hit. I think a player like Stan McCabe realized I had a job to do.

None of them showed any feeling against me off the field. I had very little to say to Don Bradman or Bill Woodfull even on the field. The players on both sides were perhaps not quite as friendly as some of us would have liked, but there was no kind of feeling to spoil the game on the field. Australians might not have liked bodyline, but on the field they made no complaints, except when some played to the gallery.

I am sure that Gubby Allen did not make his feelings about bodyline known to any pressman. He didn't mix very much with the press boys. Gubby kept his attitude and feelings very much between himself and Jardine. I know that in the Sydney Test when Stan McCabe was cracking him all over the field the Skipper came across and said, 'I think you'd better change your field over to the leg side and bounce them, Gubby.'

Allen replied, 'No, if you want me to do that you'll have to take me off.' There was no unpleasantness in the brief exchange.

It is my belief that Pataudi was the one who told pressmen about dissension in the team, in revenge for Jardine dropping him from the Test team. Pataudi didn't like Jardine and made no secret of it. But that was not the reason for his failure to win a Test place after the Melbourne game. I know that Pataudi told newspapermen one story about Jardine. In a bar one day he said he had been told at Oxford about Douglas's qualities. The Nawab said, 'Before I left England several people told me that there were many qualities I'd like in Douglas. Well, I've been with him now for nearly three months and I haven't found one yet that I care for.'

Plum Warner was cultivated by several correspondents when Jardine refused to speak to them after the Adelaide Test. On a train bound for Brisbane one night before the fourth Test, he told a correspondent I know well that he thought bodyline would eventually do harm to cricket. He emphasized that he had no control over the captain. This comment was reported and picked up by every newspaper and gave the public the impression that there was a cleavage of opinion between him and Jardine. I feel sure the astute Warner said what he did in his own interests. If he did indeed hold this view – and I doubt it – he withheld it until after the tour. Reporters used to tell me, jokingly, that covering the tour was like being a war correspondent.

Jardine admitted later in his book that perhaps his policy of remaining tight-lipped had been an ill-advised one.

But despite the argument and hostility of the crowd, the tour was a marvellous success off the field. We were feted wherever we went. Bodyline increased our popularity, and hosts and hostesses in every city and town bombarded us with invitations to dinners and parties.

Englishmen living in Australia felt obliged to offer us hospitality because of the situation, but if we had accepted most of the invitations we wouldn't have had a second to ourselves. We had to turn down many offers.

Many people have claimed over the years that Douglas Jardine didn't have a friend in Australia. It was not so. He was very much in demand, especially by socially prominent families, and spent a good deal of his leisure time in their company.

At least one correspondent has pointed out that when Jardine went off to Tasmania for a quiet period at least one attractive woman there was fascinated by his charm, culture and strength of character. But I am sure Jardine went on the trip in search of trout, his second love to cricket. When the bodyline storm was at its peak, he placidly collected his fishing rods and took a break.

They can say what they like about the tour, but I wouldn't mind another one as enjoyable.

CHAPTER FIFTEEN

High Politics and Paynter's 'Blinder'

> Victories that are cheap are cheap. Those only are
> worth having which come as the result of hard
> fighting.
>
> BEECHER

'WHAT'S LIKELY to be the order for the Test, Skipper?'

We were in Toowoomba, Queensland, a few days before the fourth Test was scheduled to begin in Brisbane, and I was chatting to Jardine. I felt close enough to him to be able to ask who might be in England's team without being rebuffed.

'There won't be any Test unless I get a suitable reply to my cable.'

'Why is that, Skipper? What cable?'

Jardine told me he had sent a message to the MCC telling them he would not lead England's team unless the Board of Control's claim of unsportsmanlike play was withdrawn. He had asked the MCC to use its influence to see this was done.

The Board of Control had just sent its second cable to the MCC on 31 January. Although phrased more carefully than the first cable, it did not retract the objectionable word. The cable read:

We appreciate your difficulty in dealing with this matter without having seen the actual play. We unanimously regard bodyline bowling as adopted in some games in the present tour as opposed to the spirit of cricket and unnecessarily

dangerous to players. We are deeply concerned that the ideals
of the game shall be preserved and we have therefore appointed a committee to report on the means necessary to
eliminate such bowling from Australian cricket beginning with
the 1933–34 season. We will forward its recommendations for
your consideration and hope for your co-operation in their
application to all cricket. We do not consider it necessary to
cancel the remainder of the programme.

The word quickly got about that Jardine would not captain
us unless the term was withdrawn, and the team unanimously supported him. I don't think anybody disagreed. I
remember Jardine stayed up all night waiting for a reply
from the MCC. He was irate. He received a reply about two
o'clock in the morning but did not tell me what it said
except to indicate that it was favourable.

The MCC committee held an emergency meeting after
which they sent off another cable which contained an
interrogative sentence on the imputation of 'unsportsmanlike'. The MCC cable said:

We, the committee of the Marylebone Cricket Club, note with
pleasure that you do not consider it necessary to cancel the
remainder of the programme and that you are postponing the
whole issue until after the present tour is completed. May we
accept this as a clear indication that the good sportsmanship of
our team is not in question? We are sure you will appreciate
how impossible it would be to play any Test match in the spirit
we all desire unless both sides were satisfied there was no
reflection upon their sportsmanship.

When your recommendation reaches us it shall receive our
most careful consideration and will be submitted to the
Imperial Cricket Conference. (Signed) Findlay, Secretary.

On receipt of this message, members of the Board of Control were believed to have held an immediate conference by
telephone. The Queensland representatives on the board,
Messrs J. S. Hutcheon and R. J. Hartigan, opened nego-
tiations with Plum Warner. Warner left Toowoomba hurriedly to have a long talk with them.

But already other frantic moves were going on, all

behind the scenes, that would lift bodyline into the realm of high politics and international diplomatic drama.

Warner, who had desperately tried to contain bodyline, now felt he must bring some pressure to bear on the Board of Control to persuade it to back down. He decided to approach the British government's representative in Australia, Mr Ernest T. Crutchley, and invoke him as an intermediary in the dispute.

On 1 February, which became a day of decisive action, Warner sent a telegram to Mr Crutchley, saying: 'Have under consideration cancellation of remaining matches of tour including Test owing to failure of board to withdraw stigma of word 'unsportsmanlike' in their first cable. Beg you use your influence to get word withdrawn. Matter very urgent.'

Later that day Warner and Palairet carried our protest more directly to Mr Crutchley when they spoke to him on the telephone. They told him we felt we were in a false position in having to take the field with the stigma of the board's term still on us. The next development was the publication of the MCC's second cable. We looked upon this in two ways: some thought it amounted to an acknowledgement by the MCC that the board in its second cable message had withdrawn the term 'unsportsmanlike', and others regarded it as a direct question on the point to the board, providing an excellent way out of the impasse.

What happened next was not revealed at the time. Indeed, it did not become full public knowledge until fifty years after the bodyline eruption, although there were rumours at the time, all denied. The *Sydney Morning Herald*, through its writer Philip Derriman, disclosed in a bodyline series in December 1982 that the Australian Prime Minister, Joseph Lyons, had personally intervened in the bodyline dispute because he feared it would jeopardize the nation's depression-hit economy if it continued.

Mr Lyons not only tried to pressure the Board of Control to drop the hateful word 'unsportsmanlike' but also telephoned the then Australian Minister resident in London, Mr Stanley Bruce; there is every reason to believe he also telephoned the British Prime Minister, Mr Ramsay Mac-Donald on the issue.

These revelations mirror the extraordinary diplomatic and political tensions created by bodyline.

Rumours circulated at the time about the Prime Minister's intervention but, when he was asked about it by reporters on 23 February, 1933, he simply laughed it off.

The threat posed by bodyline to British loans to Australia could not be easily dismissed, nor that the sale of British goods in Adelaide and Australian wine in Britain fell sharply – ill feeling over bodyline being blamed.

Warner's appeal to Mr Crutchley had an immediate effect. From Canberra, Mr Crutchley telephoned the Prime Minister in Melbourne, warning him that the tour could be cancelled. Mr Lyons agreed it would be a grave thing if this were to happen, and he promised to contact the chairman of the Board of Control, Dr Robertson.

Action was swift, although the negotiators and inter-mediaries kept their actions secret at the time. On 1 February, the board chairman sent a telegram to the secretary of the board, Mr Jeanes. The telegram read:

Prime Minister interviewed me today. Stated that British representative had seen him and asked him to get us to withdraw word objected to. If not likelihood of England pulling right out. If we do withdraw has no doubt attack will be modified. Government afraid successful conversions endangered.

The Australian Prime Minister had already been at work trying to solve the problem before Mr Crutchley approached him. And there seems little doubt that the major reason for his concern was the conversion loans. These were old loans from Britain, renegotiated or converted to allow easier repayment, all vitally important to keeping Australia afloat in the depression. Many British politicians and bankers looked upon Australia as having the status of a colony in financial matters, and it was difficult for Australia's leaders to have anything but a conciliatory attitude over the loans. In a letter to Warner on 2 February, Mr Crutchley said that Mr Lyons had tried his hand at peace-making after the first MCC cable of 24 January, realizing the enormous harm which cancellation of the tour would have caused.

According to that letter, Mr Crutchley said the Prime Minister had persuaded Dr Robertson to induce the board to withdraw the word 'unsportsmanlike' but, in return, Mr Lyons had wanted an undertaking that Jardine would modify his bodyline field placements. It later emerged that Warner would not, or could not, give such an undertaking.

Bodyline had now reached absurd heights: an Australian Prime Minister and a British diplomat were bartering like common horse traders over where an English cricket captain could position his fieldsmen! Other diplomatic and political activity went on over the bodyline furore. After the Adelaide Test hiatus, the Governor of South Australia, Sir Alexander Hore-Ruthven (later Lord Gowrie), sent a cable to Number 10 Downing Street.

In London, the Secretary of State for the Dominions, Jimmy Thomas, was most concerned about bodyline's effect on Anglo-Australian relations.

A British Cabinet Minister, he consulted with Prime Minister Ramsay MacDonald and conferred with senior officials of the MCC.

Mr Thomas, made fully aware of Australian anxieties by Sir Alexander Hore-Ruthven, spoke out strongly against bodyline; but his fellow Cabinet Minister, Lord Hamilton, the new MCC President and perhaps appropriately the National Government's Secretary for War, backed Jardine.

Most of the political patchwork that went on was kept away from the public view; in Australia, for example, Keith Officer, an adviser to the newly formed Department for External Affairs, met some of the senior members of the English team with a view to finding a settlement.

A Brisbane afternoon paper announced that a settlement of the whole dispute had been reached, but other papers reported that neither Warner nor Palairet nor the Queensland Board of Representatives would say a word on the result of the conference or indicate what had been discussed. At the official welcome to us by the Queensland Cricket Association, however, Warner made a speech which indicated that the trouble was by no means settled.

I pray for peace, as much as any statesman ever prayed for peace at a time when his country was in danger of war.

A certain liveliness has been about in cricket, and I say this seriously, that it has meant a tremendous lot to me because I adore cricket and cricketers. All I can say is that I hope and pray that the sky is clearing and the stars are once again appearing in the cricket firmament.

With some emotion, he continued:

If you stretch out your hand to us we shall grasp it eagerly. And every cricketer in the world will grasp it just as eagerly. England and Australia are two great cricketing powers. We are the masters of cricket. We stand for everything in cricket. Anything that ruffles the calm surface of English and Australian cricket affects cricket all over the world.

I say from the bottom of my heart that England and Australia in cricket must never drift away from each other. I ask most earnestly that every man of good temper and good-will will do everything he can to make things right at the present moment, and personal influence radiates like wireless.

I ask you to join with me and hope that there will be a happy issue out of all this liveliness.

Jardine, who followed Warner, said simply, 'In the present trials and tribulations in the cricket world I hold very strongly that the least said the soonest mended. Believe me, it is not always very easy to remain silent.'

The issue remained clouded until 8 February, two days before the fourth Test. Most of the anger and recriminations were solved by the Board of Control's final cable to the MCC, but tension lingered on. The cable said:

We do not regard the sportsmanship of your team as being in question.

Our position was fully considered at the recent Sydney meeting and is as indicated in our cable of 30 January. It is the particular type of bowling referred to therein which we consider not in the best interests of cricket and in this view we understand we are supported by many eminent English cricketers. We join heartily with you in hoping the remaining Tests will be played with the traditional good feeling.

If the term 'unsportsmanlike' had not been withdrawn – and it was interpreted to have been withdrawn by the Board of Control's final cable – I feel certain that Jardine would have stuck to his guns. The situation was serious enough as it was but, if the tour had been called off, I hesitate to think what a major issue bodyline would have become.

Jardine always claimed that a conference would settle the trouble. But nobody seemed to be very keen to sit down at a table in this way. He said at the time that conferences settled few things, but he believed the leg theory could be discussed sensibly round a table. His point was that it was as legitimate as slow leg theory, and that you might as well ban left-hand bowling or bowling around the wicket, as bodyline.

Several unusual things happened in Brisbane. In the match against Queensland what became known as the Oxenham incident occurred. I was bowling to Ron Oxenham, a fairly good cricketer, an all-rounder, whom we all thought was a little bit conceited. I was bowling to an ordinary off field when he popped an easy catch to short leg. It was so obviously out that I didn't appeal and turned to go back to my bowling mark. When I turned around, I was amazed to find that Oxenham was still at the wicket. I appealed to the umpire. He said he couldn't see, that I had obscured his vision. I knew that was nonsense because I always ran well off the wicket to the left as I followed through. I appealed to the square-leg umpire. He said he hadn't been looking.

I was wild. I said to myself, 'I'll make you wish you'd left the wicket when you were out.' I dropped him several short ones at my fastest. They reared past his face. He went white. I was barracked and received a great deal of adverse publicity for poor sportsmanship. Nobody that I can recall seemed to think it important to mention Oxenham's poor sportsmanship in staying at the wicket when he knew he was out. I think ninety-nine out of every hundred people on that ground knew he was out. Oxenham was not the first batsman to stay at the wicket in this way, nor will he be the last. It is rare for a batsman who is out but receives the benefit of the umpire's decision to leave the wicket of his own free will. I have seen it happen only three or four times.

A non-cricket incident occurred in the Bellevue Hotel, Brisbane, where we were staying. The licensee of the hotel was Mick Maguire, a former Australian boxing champion. I remember he had four beautiful daughters. One night, while Mick was serving behind the bar, I was standing there having a quiet drink with Tommy Mitchell, Les Ames and Bill Voce.

An Australian bush worker came in. He was a big fellow, roughly dressed, and sporting whiskers. He started needling us at the bar. Tommy, only a little fellow, had a very quick temper. He took it for a while, and then decided he's had enough. Whipping off his glasses, he turned on the big bushman to have it out with him. The big bloke calmly produced a revolver. I vamoosed. It wasn't until the next day that I learned that Mick Maguire had jumped the bar and bundled the fellow out.

It was in Brisbane that I was hit for six for only the third time in my first-class career. A bowler named Gamble, who came in about No. 11 did it. A left-hander, he shut his eyes to a good-length ball, swung mightily, and the ball soared out of the ground. It was a stirring hit.

Jack Ryder hit me for a six in Adelaide in 1928 with a ball that went right over the keeper, the slips and into the stand.

Les Ames was the other one. Les and I were good friends and, when our counties played, we used to stay with each other. At Trent Bridge one day, he was batting when I had one ball to bowl before lunch, and I decided to give him a bouncer. And I think he decided it was going to be a bouncer because he hooked me straight out of the ground.

When a coppery glow beats down on Woolloongabba oval from the sun peeping through a veil of storm clouds and the humidity rises to the nineties, Test cricket in Brisbane is like playing a match near the Red Sea.

Humidity during the fourth Test was the worst I ever experienced, even more unpleasant than in India. When the weather is like this in Brisbane, a violent thunderstorm can swamp the ground. On one occasion in a Test there, the wicket covers were washed away. After such a storm has done its worst, and the sun peeps down again, the stifling heat frays the nerves of both players and spectators. When we played there in 1933 you could add to this discomfort a setting that was primitive and barren of amenities.

I couldn't imagine a cricket ground of the 1880s or 1890s being less agreeable. It is only fair to say that vast improvements have been carried out at Woolloongabba since. But, in 1933, apart from the lack of facilities, players and spectators were hamstrung by extraordinary rules and regulations, which could only be put down to a despotic administration. It would be no exaggeration to say the restrictions could hardly be equalled outside a military camp. Barbed wire sparkled on top of wooden fences, which separated the ground into various sections. The dressing-rooms for the players were isolated and guarded like the Berlin wall. I believe the barbed wire remained at Woolloongabba oval until 1946.

There was an occasion when Bill Brown, the Queensland state skipper, was out of the Australian team after the war with a thumb injury. He was not allowed to visit his team-mates in the dressing-room. And in 1952 the Australian vice-captain, Arthur Morris, was barred from entering the South African dressing-room even though he had been invited there by the visitors' captain, John Goddard. Exceptional hostility was shown towards pressmen, and any reporter who wanted to see either of the Test captains had about as much chance of getting through to the dressing-room as one had of gatecrashing a Buckingham Palace function.

In 1933 an Australian pressbox wag, Arthur Mailey, registered his disapproval by sending a query by telegram to Bill Woodfull to the dressing-room less than 100 yards away. Pressmen of the British Empire were perched up under a superheated galvanized-iron roof, where they sweltered more than on any other part of the ground.

Cricket administrators even imposed taboos on dress in the members' enclosure. Dungarees might have been appropriate dress, what with the dust and flying paper, but women who had the temerity to arrive at the gates wearing off-the-shoulder sun frocks were refused admittance.

The MCC protested to the Australian Board of Control in 1954 about conditions there. The board was loath to deprive Queensland of its Test match and, by some finesse, was able to soothe the ruffled feelings of MCC members. The board must have reminded the Queensland Cricket Association that public goodwill deserved more attention because correspondents found a remarkable change for the better had come over the administration.

One cricket writer observed: 'Some of the former *verbotens* had gone, there was more freedom of movement and wonder of wonders, a Queensland Cricket Association committeeman asked me to join him in a drink at a little bar that might have come from a film set of a saloon in Abilene or Tombstone.'

The remarkable thing about these irritating rules is that they should have been imposed in a city populated by the most friendly and hospitable Australians one could meet anywhere.

We didn't get any storms in Brisbane for what was only

the second Test played there, but they remained a threat most of the time. Brisbane in February becomes Australia's 'oven' and, with the thermometer registering over a hundred degrees, the awful heat took a lot of the sting out of my deliveries bowled to a packed leg field. Voce didn't play as he was unfit and Tommy Mitchell, the slow leg-breaker, came in. Allen and I did the fast bowling.

It was one of the toughest bowling jobs I ever did. I was so affected by the heat that even in my first spell I lost track on my run-up – an extraordinary thing for me – and trod so hard against the leg stump that it snapped off at the base, and I fell heavily.

The Australians batted well in their first innings. It was the only day in this Test series when I didn't get a wicket. At the end of the first day Australia had 3 down for 251 with Bradman 71 not out. Australia's openers for the first time in the series had taken the score beyond a century. I can recall that Vic Richardson was hooking me soundly, much to the delight of the crowd, and Woodfull, moving down the wicket, told him that in no circumstances was he to throw his wicket away and give me any incentive. Two of my team-mates close enough to overhear told me that Richardson replied: 'I'll show the bastard he can't bowl!'

Vic did that day. He got 83 before Hammond had him stumped, Mitchell bowled Woodfull for 67, and McCabe was out for 20 off Allen, when stumps were drawn for the day. I think I was too dry even to foam at the mouth; Australia seemed set for a big score.

That night Brisbane continued to swelter, and two city hotels were filled with disgruntled cricketers and correspondents. About eleven o'clock Jardine fired a quiet broadside into a group of pressmen gathered in the Bellevue Hotel. He accused them of deliberately plying me with drink to reduce my performance. But that was not so, and they rightly denied it. I was not present at the time.

I was elsewhere discovering that the hospitality of the Brisbane people could be overwhelming. About three o'clock, feeling very rosy, I returned from a private party to the Bellevue Hotel, where I found a group of exhausted pressmen in the lounge still talking cricket. Hugh Buggy was one of them. I bet them ten shillings apiece that I would bowl the 'Boy Wonder' inside three overs that day. It was the name Don Bradman was known by in the English side. He was then not quite twenty-five. The pressmen just laughed and assured me that the Boy Wonder was headed for another score of 200.

But that day not only did I bowl Bradman inside three overs, but I also clean bowled Ponsford. And I collected my bets.

One paper reported:

The answer to the question, Will Australia make a big first innings score? was provided by Larwood, almost immediately the second day of the fourth Test was started at Brisbane today. Working on a 'dead' wicket, he flicked off Bradman's bails and sent Ponsford's near-stump hurtling with a couple of incomparable 'specials' at the trifling cost of 16 runs to England (6 to himself), and the feat altered the game's prospects. Five of the batsmen fell for 73 runs so that the seven outstanding produced only 89, and Australia were all out for 340 half an hour after lunch.

But the Australians, always 'last-ditchers', fought back and due mainly to O'Reilly and Ironmonger we were 6 down for 216. We looked certain to bat one short as Eddie Paynter had been taken to hospital on the first day suffering badly from tonsillitis.

It was at this stage of the game word was received that Paynter was 'on his way'. I think Jardine might have had ideas about the Lancashire batsman, but this was not the reason Paynter left his hospital bed and went to the oval.

Bill Voce was mainly responsible for getting Paynter to the ground. He had been sitting at Eddie's bedside and went out to learn the score. It was a shock to hear what had happened, and he hurried back to the hospital where Paynter lay in a fever. Eddie was amazed, too, and insisted on getting up. They got him dressed, and Voce rushed him to the ground in a car.

I'll never forget Paynter's face as he came in to bat. He looked white and ill. At no time a great talker, he had even less to say that day than usual. He had the shakes.

I remember batting with Eddie. He remained pale throughout but never wavered. I also recall how considerate Woodfull was to him every moment of his innings. Paynter went back to hospital that night but returned to the crease next day and went on to make 83. I feel certain that without Paynter's score England would have lost the match.

We scored 356 in the first innings, Australia collapsed in its second innings for 175, and we went on to win by 6 wickets.

Paynter's effort was the pluckiest achievement I have ever seen on a cricket field. The courageous little Lancastrian was a better bat than generally given credit for but had always to struggle for recognition throughout his career.

I remember one or two other things about that match. Jardine, described by one London paper as a master of monumental patience, made his determination so plain that it raised the crowd's anger. At one stage he played 82 balls without scoring and didn't score a run for 83 minutes.

The London *Star* described one of my overs to McCabe as farcical. Stan ducked six times in succession without attempting to hit the ball. England's victory in the Ashes was hailed in England without any harsh words against bodyline.

One London newspaper reported:

The most human note in the winning of the Ashes at Brisbane yesterday was provided by Plum Warner, joint manager of the England cricketers, when overwrought with nervousness and excitement he could not bear to watch the final stages of the drama.

Only 53 runs were needed but teams have been out for less. Warner stuck it until Leyland was beaten but this shock and the fine bowling of O'Reilly was too much. He left the ground and put his ear to a loudspeaker.

When the announcer said, '144 for 4' he dashed back just in time to see Paynter clinch the series for England with a six. There surely could not have been a more fitting end to the match. Paynter's in-and-out-of-hospital knock did so much to win the game for England that we wanted him to make the winning hit.

The Australians evidently did, too, for with three runs needed McCabe deliberately sent down a full toss to the little Lancashire batsman which he smacked over the boundary. This was a nice gesture that still further strengthened the friendly spirit which characterized the game. And so to the champagne glasses, the pavilion handshakes and the congratulatory speeches.

Another London paper said in an editorial:

Although there is another Test match to come the struggle for the Ashes is over and the moment for congratulations has arrived. Most of the team have earned their share but the part that Jardine as captain, and Larwood as a decisive moral force have played under very trying conditions in securing the victory stand out above everything else. No captain and no player have ever been more harshly treated not by playing opponents but by the onlooking public, or more violently abused than they.

Both men, like the first-class sportsmen they are, have shown themselves quite imperturbable. The management of his men on the field by Jardine has been beyond all praise, while the stamina, skill and undeviating purpose displayed by Larwood have played a part in the victory which it is impossible to estimate and difficult to exaggerate.

Even the *Catholic Herald* came up with a crack on England's behalf against her detractors. It said:

A lot of Australians must be feeling foolish these days. The Australian Broadcasting Commission, after saying that it was impossible to play against the 'unsportsmanlike' leg theory, must have been mad when their champions made 250 runs for 3 wickets against it. Batsmen can score against leg theory if they concentrate upon playing cricket and do not play to the gallery.

Woodfull, possibly to impress the crowd with the terrible dangers he was facing, ducked to a ball that hit his crouching figure in the stomach! Then Ponsford and the redoubtable Bradman, after impressively and repeatedly demonstrating the dangerous 'bodyline' by walking away from it, heard the rattle in the timberyard and were bowled behind their leg! Perhaps the Board of Control were wise not to withdraw that word 'unsportsmanlike'; there is too obvious a place to attach it if it be allowed to run around loose.

While the match was still in progress, Neville Cardus said in the *Observer*:

There are several ancient monuments in London which are not presentable to the public gaze: I suggest that one of them be taken down forthwith and a statue of Larwood erected in its place. He is today one of the nation's heroes obviously. He has changed the face of Test cricket in Australia. Only a year or two ago Australian Test matches were becoming a blight and a bane: batsmen were swollen with runs. They gorged on centuries until they were fat. And they gave themselves to lazy rest on sleepy cushioned turf. Meanwhile, the game languished for want of action and energy. Larwood has put an end to this fatty degeneracy: by his strong arms he has transformed the slothful lawns of Australia into violent battlefields.

After many years we are again discussing Australian Test cricket in terms of a bowler's prowess: no longer is the tale of it a mechanical repetition of the names of conquering batsmen – Bradman, Ponsford, Hobbs, Sutcliffe; Sutcliffe, Hobbs, Bradman, Ponsford. The sturdy little man from Nottingham has got rid of stalemate, and also got rid of the batsmen's drowsy bed of luxury. And in this game in Brisbane in heat of Ethiopic scorchings, he has performed his deeds mainly by pure and classical fast bowling aimed at the stumps. He clean bowled Bradman and Ponsford at a moment of acute crisis for England: if Bradman and Ponsford had been able to stay in for another quarter of an hour they might easily have stayed in all day.

Larwood, by strength and superb determination, lifted himself above heartbreaking circumstances. For, consider his situation yesterday morning: the wicket was a comfortable hearthrug; the sun was pitiless (at breakfast time the temperature reached 87 in the shade). On Friday Larwood had been mastered, and now Australia's two record-breaking batsmen were somehow to be got out, and Australia's total was proudly poised at 251 for 3.

In three overs Larwood broke the back of Australia's innings: in three overs he saved his side from a purgatorial day in the sun, snatched the game's prize out of Woodfull's grasp and turned Australian confidence into mortification. And, as I say, the deed was done by fast bowling of the kind that Tom Richardson would have recognized and loved. What are we to think of the way Bradman and Ponsford allowed gorgeous opportunities to slip, by committing elementary, technical errors?

The accounts of the match from those on the spot assure us that both of these batsmen lost their wickets by forgetting the old simple first principle – always play straight down the line of a well-pitched ball on the wicket. Neither Bradman nor Ponsford could blame the bumping ball this time. Indeed I am beginning to think that leg theory is wasted on some of these Australian celebrities, and I am already certain that those of us who, in Christian charity, have been trying to sympathize with, and see, the Australian point of view – I am certain we have, out of our concern for cricket as a whole, been throwing our compassion on undeserving objects.

A Test match cricketer ought not to leave his defences uncovered and exploit a crossbat to a fast, straight ball. I suspect that if Larwood had concentrated his aim on the wicket over after over his successes this tour would have been greater still. Why send the ball flying around the head of a batsman who has not proved his capacity to stop great speed hurled at his leg, or off stumps?

It is rather pitiable the way the Australians have made no creative effort to deal with the fast bowling of Larwood and his leg theory. In all periods of cricket history batsmen have found themselves confronted with strange problems. Usually the solution has come from quick and concerted action. Not many years ago V. Trumper and C. Hill exploded the South African's googly bowling in a single day. These contemporary Australian batsmen seem to have failed to think out a really organized method of countering Larwood: some of them have ducked at the bumpers; some of them have held up their bats as shields; some of them have tried hitting the ball through, or over, the encircling leg field. But all these expedients have apparently been merely improvised at the last fraction of the last second.

I can gather no evidence from the reports of men on the spot, or from private correspondence, that the Australians have thought out, and agree upon, a method of tackling Larwood, and have given the method a unified, deliberate trial. I am afraid they have allowed Larwood to upset their powers of constructive thinking. Their attitude to his attack rather reminds me of a conversation which took place between Mr Winkle and Sam Weller: 'These are awkward skates, Sam,' said Mr Winkle. 'I'm afraid it's an orkard genlman as is using them,' answered Sam . . .

The Ashes were ours. Despite all the hullabaloo, that little night out at the Piccadilly Hotel had been well worth while. But it was also a time of sadness. Archie Jackson had died of a chest complaint in a Brisbane hospital while the Australians battled to stave off defeat. The Australians were perhaps the most dejected cricket team in history as they sat in a coach of the Brisbane–Sydney Express as it raced south the day after the Test ended. The body of Archie, acknowledged in Australia as 'the greatest master batsman since Trumper', lay in the rear of the coach.

Superlatives have been heaped on Archie, but I would say he was one of the most graceful batsmen I ever bowled to. Apart from having complete command of every stroke, he had the courage and perfect temperament necessary to a great Test player.

Old-timers thought of him as a reincarnation of the legendary Victor Trumper. He did not seem to hit the ball, he caressed it, using his blade like a foil to alter the angle of a direct thrust. Australians used to say Archie did not have the wrist power of the master, but the grace was there and also there was an amazing physical resemblance.

I remember when Archie scored his first Test century in the Adelaide Test of 1928. Three were down for 19 when he came in. He was on 98 when I gave him the best and fastest ball I could muster. The nineteen-year-old boy's feet moved slightly, his bat swung in a perfect arc, and the crowd went wild as the ball clipped the fence. Archie was the youngest batsman in history to score a century in his first Test innings.

CHAPTER SIXTEEN

The Sydney Hill Mob

JARDINE LOOKED AT ME. 'Why don't you want to play?' he asked.

'Well, Skipper,' I said, 'I've bowled my inside out, and we've won the Ashes. The pressure's off now, and I could do with a rest. Besides, I've never watched a Test match in my life, and I'd love to see one for a change.'

We were in Newcastle in New South Wales playing a match before the last Test in Sydney. I had just asked Jardine if he would rest me from the Test. I didn't want to play.

Jardine asked me a few more questions, and I thought he would agree to leave me out. 'I'd love to watch a Test match, Skipper,' I repeated.

Jardine suddenly decided, 'I'm sorry, Harold. I can't grant you the favour.' Then, pressing down on a near-by table with his right thumb and screwing it hard to the right, he said: 'We've got the bastards down there, and we'll keep them there.'

One of the funniest incidents in my life occurred in the Newcastle game against Northern Districts of New South Wales. A young batsman was facing me. I wasn't bowling very vigorously at him. I was certain I had him dead in front with one, and I appealed for LBW. 'Not out,' said the umpire. Next ball I had him caught behind, and I appealed again. No dice!

So, at the end of the over I said to this young fellow, 'Is this umpire your father?'

'No,' he said, 'he's my uncle.'

Sydney Cricket Ground was crowded to capacity for the

Test. I had thought that with the Ashes decided some of the interest might have waned. But bodyline was just as lively an issue. You couldn't move on the Hill. The game of cricket was really alive.

Australia went in first, with Richardson and Woodfull opening. Remembering Richardson's remark in Brisbane, I bowled at him with plenty of relish, and he was soon out for a duck, caught by Jardine. I bowled Woodfull for 14 and then Bradman for 48.

After a few overs, Jardine moved the field over to the leg side for the bodyline attack, just as if the Ashes were still to be decided. But Australia's down-the-list batsmen shaped better on this occasion. Leo O'Brien, the Victorian left-hander, got going with Stan McCabe and scored 61. McCabe got 73. Len Darling, another left-hander like O'Brien, who had been brought in to the Brisbane Test in the belief that he would counter our rising deliveries, also batted solidly in making 85. And Bert Oldfield, who had missed out on the Brisbane game through his head injury, did well before he was run out for 52. I remember that when Bert came in to face me in that game, his face was white. Which is only natural.

P. K. Lee, the South Australian all-rounder, was not overawed by the bodyline bogey and scored 42. Even Bill O'Reilly, who wasn't noted for his batting, got 19 because he wasn't afraid to hit the ball, and Harry (Bull) Alexander, the fastest bowler in Australia, lashed out to make 17 not out.

I remember when O'Reilly came in to bat. Before I ran in to bowl, he pointed to his stumps and called out, 'Here they are, Harold. You can have them.' But he needn't have worried. I never bowled any short ones at Bill.

Every time I dropped one short, the Hill roared. I couldn't even hear the famous Yabba barracking that day but no doubt he was there.

When we finally got Australia out after about one and three-quarter days, I headed straight for the showers, having bowled 32.2 overs to take 4 for 98. I was still in the showers when Jardine came in. He had just got out for 18, and we were one wicket down. 'Put the pads on, Harold,' said Jardine.

I usually went in No. 10. 'Put the pads on, Skipper? What for?'

'I may want you to go in.'

'Surely not me . . .?' But Jardine had already left. When I came out of the showers, I was fuming. One or two of the boys advised me that I had better do as Jardine had asked.

'This isn't fair,' I said angrily. 'I've just bowled my guts out, and now I have to go in as nightwatchman.'

I eventually calmed down a bit and sat with Les Ames and Maurice Leyland, who were also ready. It was about 5.45. Soon after a roar went up. We weren't watching the match, but we knew somebody was out.

Jardine arrived, looked at the three of us and said, 'Right, Harold. You can go in.'

I said to Ames, 'Get your bat ready, Les, because I'm going to get myself out.'

And I intended to. Sutcliffe had just been dismissed by O'Reilly for 56, and Wally Hammond was still in. The first ball I got from O'Reilly I slammed hard to Bradman at cover point. I started to run, but Wally Hammond called out, 'No, Harold, go back.'

'Come on,' I yelled. Bradman was a splendid field at cover, perhaps having the quickest and most deadly throw in the game, but it didn't matter because I was in no mood for using a bat. I expected Bradman to gather the ball in plenty of time to throw it to O'Reilly for a run-out. Hammond and I were passing each other in the middle when Bradman got the ball. I knew he would try to get me instead of Hammond. But instead of throwing to O'Reilly waiting at the stumps he tried to knock down the wicket. He missed and the ball went to the boundary, giving me four byes. Stumps were drawn and that was the end of play for the day.

Next day I was still batting on spleen. I attacked the bowling at every opportunity. I remember Bull Alexander bumping them down at me in every over, doing his best to hit me. I knew he was trying. The Hill enjoyed it immensely. They roared as each bumper reared past me. Bull was pretty fast, up near Bill Voce's pace, but not very accurate. The mob on the Hill kept egging him on. 'Knock his bloody head off, Bull,' they yelled.

I kept square cutting and hooking Bull, but I missed one, and it just grazed my nose. The Hill loved it. Bertie Oldfield, who used to stand close to the stumps even to fast bowlers, said, 'By gee, Harold, that was a close one.'

'Oh, I don't know, Bert,' I lied casually. 'I had time to count the stitches on it.'

The crowd kept on yelling. 'Give it to him.' 'Knock the bastard's head off.' As Bull rushed at the crease to let each ball go, the crowd cheered. But I played him pretty well, and luckily he didn't hit me. Fast bowlers never worried me; it was the slow ones who gave me trouble.

I remember that when I was around the 60s I thought of old Jimmy Iremonger and told myself he'd be proud if he could see me knocking Australia's class bowlers about like this. They were taken off at last and the slow spinner, Lee, put on. I hit him for three fours in one over and didn't realize I was approaching a century when Maurice Leyland came down the pitch to me and said, 'Hey, Harold, ease up a bit. Look at the scoreboard. You're 98.'

'That's 98 too many,' I said. I was still annoyed with Jardine for sending me in after I had bowled so hard.

I intended hitting Lee to the fence again but, as I went to play the next shot, an on drive, I thought of the century, was caught in two minds and hit the ball uppishly. Bert ('Dainty') Ironmonger, of whom it was said he could not stop a tram, took the catch, a rare feat for him.

That was the nearest I got to a Test century – 98 in 2 hours and 20 minutes including one straight drive for 6, one 5 and nine fours.

Every man on the Sydney Cricket Ground stood and cheered me. The applause and the cheers from the mob on the Hill were thunderous. I never realized the approach of Australian crowds until that moment. It proved to me Australians like a trier, they go for the underdog, and they appreciate good cricket no matter who provides it. They are tough: they barrack to unsettle a player, but they like anyone who attacks. I never expected the Hill mob to get up and cheer me after the abuse they had hurled. If I had that time over again, I would get those two extra runs.

Wilfred Rhodes wrote after my innings:

Larwood is a batsman of greater power – a batsman of whom a deal more would have been heard had he not been required to save himself for bowling. He is essentially a front of the wicket player – that, alone, guaranteed him success in Australia as soon as he was given a chance – and he plays straight down the line of the ball. Driving is his strong point.

He has been a remarkable cricketer on this tour. We still wonder, and we always shall wonder, where he gets his tremendous pace from when he is bowling. It is a mystery I have never been able to solve, and when I have seen him hit out with the bat I have wondered where he has found his rugged power. Without Larwood's 98 and Hammond's century we would be badly placed . . .

I realized later, of course, that I had made a mistake over Jardine's decision to send me in early. His explanation was that he had done so to ensure I got a good rest before bowling in the second innings. If my wicket had fallen quickly, it would not have have mattered so much, but had I got runs at the end of the innings, when I was normally sent in, it would have tired me and affected my bowling. Also, going in early was intended to remove the tension of waiting to bat. 'You're my main weapon, Harold, and I was doing it to keep you at your peak for bowling,' he said. Jardine was right, he meant well and I felt rather foolish for having been so annoyed. But if Jardine had only communicated with me a little more, I would have accepted the situation without demur.

You realize a lot of things later on. I thought the Australian crowds were very rough on me. Later I recognized that, being the spearhead, they were only trying to put me off. But it had the opposite effect.

We went on to score 454 in the first innings, only 19 ahead of Australia. In that second innings I had my tail up, going all out to beat Maurice Tate's record of 38 wickets, the greatest any bowler had taken in a Test rubber. Maurice got his record bag in Australia in 1924. I nailed Richardson early to give him a pair for the match. Woodfull and Bradman were in, both were well set, and I was desperately trying to break the partnership. Richardson's wicket gave me 33 in the Tests, and I needed another five.

My left foot began to feel sore, and I slowed down a little. Jardine was looking anxiously in my direction. Then I felt a sudden pain. I couldn't walk. Jardine came across to me.

'What's wrong, Harold?'

'I've done something to my foot, Skipper. I can't walk. I think I've broken a bone.'

'You'll *have* to walk. You'll have to finish the over.'

I began to get angry. 'I can't.'

'You'll have to.'

I had 5 balls to go to finish the over. Nobody thought to ask the umpire if it was in the laws for me to have to finish the over. In my anger and frustration I didn't think to ask him. All I could do was stand against the crease and swing my arm over. 'Here's five fours,' I murmured to myself.

Bill Woodfull just patted the balls back to me. He knew I was hurt. It was the kind of sportsman he was. In that instant Woodfull went up 100 per cent in my estimation.

Bradman was at the bowler's end. We didn't pass any remarks. At the end of the over I said to Jardine, 'Can I go now, Skipper?'

'No,' he said.

'Look,' I said, 'I can't run. I'm useless. I'll have to go off.'

'Field at cover-point,' Jardine directed. 'There's a man covering you there. You can't go off while this little bastard's in.'

Although Bradman must surely have known something was wrong with me, Jardine was too psychologically astute to allow me to go off while the Boy Wonder was still at the wicket. Don must have been glad to see me out of the firing line because he immediately began to hit out at the bowling. Hedley Verity was on, and Don began dancing down the wicket to him. About two overs later Bradman was clean bowled by the Yorkshireman for 71.

Clapping his hands to attract my attention Jardine came over to me and said, 'Right, Harold, you can go now.'

I half-limped alongside Bradman. Neither of us spoke a word. Probably the two greatest antagonists ever to meet on a cricket field walked off together. But I didn't realize it was to be my last Test appearance. I had died with my boots on.

I took no further part in the match. I knew my foot was bad but didn't think it was as serious as it really was. A Sydney masseur, Tom Langridge, who had a gymnasium and often gave me a rub-down, examined my foot, which was black from heel to toe. It was the result of stamping down as I delivered the ball. Langridge told me I would never bowl again without an operation.

Australia was out in the second innings for the surprisingly low total of 182, Verity causing most of the damage by taking 5 wickets for 33 off 19 overs.

In England's second innings a dispute arose over Bull Alexander's run-through on the wicket. Jardine pointed out to Woodfull that Bull was damaging the wicket. They had a discussion about it, while the crowd jeered, and eventually Jardine suggested to Woodfull, 'What about getting Harry to bowl in rubber shoes?'

'That is absurd – he has been bowling in spikes all his life.'

Enraged by this time, Alexander said: 'I'll bowl round the bloody wicket.'

'I don't mean you to bowl round the wicket, Harry,' said Jardine.

'I said I'm going to bowl round the bloody wicket.'

Alexander did so but quickly changed to over again. He began bumping the ball down at Jardine and, urged on by the crowd, struck Jardine a painful blow on the hip-bone.

Jardine was only a thin man, and the blow almost knocked him over.

As the Hill mob cheered, fieldsmen began to move in to offer their sympathy and see if Jardine needed assistance. But Jardine was not the kind of man who looked for sympathy. He waved them away and said, 'Let's get on with the game.'

Alexander continued to bump them down, but Jardine didn't flinch. He defied Alexander and the taunts of rowdy Hill patrons.

When Jardine came into the dressing-room after being out to Ironmonger for 24, several of us went over to him to see if he was badly hurt. The ball had hit him on top of the hip-bone and inflicted a wound which had bled profusely. Although obviously in great pain, Jardine said nothing.

It occurred to me then what I had done to some of the Australian batsmen. I had not realized how much they must have been knocked about or, for that matter, how it had ended for some good batsmen. I had forced Alan Kippax out after the first Test. He couldn't play bodyline. Ponsford was dropped after the Brisbane Test and Fingleton after Adelaide. I had bruised and battered a lot of players.

I was interested enough later to ask mathematicians at Sydney University to work out for me the force of impact of a cricket ball weighing 5.5 ounces making contact at 90 miles an hour. They told me that assuming that a batsman's ribs had moved in half an inch to absorb some of the blow the ball would strike a batsman with a force of about 2 tons. No wonder the batsmen were bruised, and no wonder they wore padding!

England went on to win the last Test by 8 wickets.

Jardine had something to say about the barracking of Australian crowds in his book. In the incident where Alexander damaged the wicket he quoted from an Australian newspaper:

There was a demonstration by a section of the big crowd which witnessed the play in the fifth Test match at the Sydney

Cricket Ground yesterday when the English captain D. R. Jardine complained to umpire Borwick about the fast bowler running on the wicket. The crowd jeered and counted out Jardine and barracking broke out afresh when he patted the spots on the wicket.

There was a regrettable scene in Alexander's fourth over. The fast bowler was still bowling over the wicket and one ball rose sharply and struck Jardine a sickening blow on the left side. Immediately there was a roar from the crowd. While some of the fieldsmen approached Jardine many spectators joined in sustained applause. That conduct was unpardonable.

To support his protests Jardine said that a former Australian captain had agreed with him that the wearing of the wicket against which he protested should never have been permitted.

On the question of the conduct of Australian crowds generally Jardine had this to say:

It is no use blinding oneself to the fact that a total absence of any attempt on the part of the authorities to control their crowds and demonstrations must give rise to a feeling that these performances, even if they have not the active support of the authorities, at least have their tacit approval . . .

The Australian, whether he be the man in the street or mayor of a town way back, is constantly at pains to emphasize the goodnaturedness and fairness of the Australian barracker. Towards the end of our tour there was a noticeable weakening of this conviction. But there was no doubt that a constant repetition of the wish to believe in this truth is responsible for its general acceptance.

The childlike faith in this belief, and its twin, that barracking is so amusing and the remarks so clever and entertaining, is an excellent way of auto-suggestion or Couéism . . . I have seen nearly every member of the visiting side treated to a strong dose of the crowd's disapproval. Ask any cricketer who has played cricket for England in Australia in the past 20 years and he'll tell you that boasts concerning the impartiality of an

Australian crowd are so vain as to be almost pathetic.

I am not suggesting that an Australian crowd should always be expected to be impartial. I am only pointing out how utterly unfounded is the claim to impartiality.

The parrot-like phrases such as 'Get a bag', and ''Ave a go', coming from the Sydney Hill certainly tended to become monotonous. But a great many comic remarks come from the crowd. I believe, too, that they have a good knowledge of cricket, second to none in Australia.

Jardine thought the only funny remark he heard in Australia came from the Hill. When about to take a drink from the twelfth man Jardine was tickled to hear a raucous character call out: 'Don't give the —— a drink. Let him die of thirst!'

Immediately after the series C. G. McCartney wrote in the Sydney *Truth:*

I say without fear of hesitation that the biggest factor in the Test series was our players' ignorance of the game of cricket. Some of our men lacked common knowledge of the game, which the visitors possessed in plenty. Our batsmen allowed themselves to be tricked by Verity, but the English batsmen could not be enticed into error by our similar spin bowlers . . .

In the same issue A. E. Liddicutt said:

Heartaches and headaches have followed the English crick-eters throughout their tour of Australia. To our batsmen Lar-wood, the demon fast bowler, has been the biggest headache and has given the most heartache. Larwood has also given our selectors more than enough to worry about and will have them mentally facing his demoralizing bumpers when they choose Australia's side to tour England in 1934.

Jack Hobbs cabled to the *News Chronicle*:

Larwood was the dominating factor in our win because apart from the wickets he took he made Bradman change his game.

He dominated Don. When I left England I thought, I shall be satisfied if we get rid of Bradman for a century each time. It is the 200 or more that I fear.

Don's average today is 56 and Larwood was the cause of its comparative small size. Bradman was brought down to the level of an ordinary batsman; the rest, virtually, were made tailenders. It was evident that Bradman had said to himself, If I am hit my career may be finished; and that isn't going to happen. So he played a gambler's innings, took no risk of injury – and in view of his slight physique I do not blame him, although sometimes he might not have given up so whole-heartedly.

Reduced to essentials the story is that we won the Ashes and were successful in four Tests, though we lost the toss four times, because of Larwood's wonderful bowling, Jardine's magnificent fighting captaincy, will to win and splendid team work from top to bottom. In short we were a great side, probably with the exception of the 1911–12 team the greatest England has ever sent to Australia in my time.

Jardine wanted me to go with the team to New Zealand. 'You've won the Ashes for me, Harold,' he said, 'and you've earned a rest. Just come along for a holiday.'

I told him I would think about it, and did, but decided against it. I was homesick for my wife and baby daughter June, and I wanted, too, to get an operation on my foot over and done with as quickly as possible.

I remember an amusing touch introduced at the final game of the tour against South Australia at Adelaide. Every MCC player except its captain wore a Harlequin cap from Jardine's little bag. He himself appeared in an ordinary England cap. It was a final snook at Australia.

I said goodbye to the team in Adelaide and boarded the transcontinental train for Perth to take a ship from Fremantle. Pataudi, who had also elected not to go to New Zealand, accompanied me and Palairet, too, was returning to England.

On the journey we were playing bridge with a member of the Australian Parliament when the train pulled up at night at a little place called Quorn. The whole townspeople, about 200 or 300, seemed to be waiting for us at the station. They kept shouting out, 'We want Larwood, we want Larwood.' I refused to go out. Some of them threw fruit through the window at us, and a bunch of louts came into the carriage and bombarded us with pomegranate seeds, which they blew at us using their mouths as pea-shooters. They had plenty of abuse to offer, but we ignored them and took it on the chin. I realized later that probably they only just wanted to see us and that had I gone out in the first place the scene might have been avoided.

It was a great feeling of relief and satisfaction to board the *Otranto* bound for London. Before sailing I received a telegram from Jardine: 'Bon voyage. Take care of yourself. Good luck always. Skipper.'

CHAPTER SEVENTEEN

'To Harold, for the Ashes'

THEY CAME ABOARD in droves at Port Said as soon as the *Otranto* berthed. I was surrounded by newspapermen from everywhere wanting to know everything that had happened in Australia. Representatives of the great national dailies in Britain, together with agency men, correspondents of magazines, and important provincial papers, had been sent to meet me at Suez, many of them with instructions to obtain the exclusive rights of my story.

But I was still under contract and had no intention of saying anything. Besides, the Orient company's officers on the *Otranto* had handed me a copy of a coded message which had been received from the MCC secretary. It said: 'Confidential communicate the following from Findlay to Larwood: Am sure you will regard matter connected with tour strictly private and not give any information to friends including Mr Carr or press who may meet you Port Said or elsewhere stop telegraph us Lord's saying you will be on your guard.'

I also received three cabled messages from my skipper, Arthur Carr, which mystified me a little. The first said: 'Important meet alone Suez please come ashore and rejoin boat Port Said letter wife. Carr.'

I cabled Carr, wondering what was in my wife's letter and almost immediately received a second message: 'Meeting you Suez don't talk to anybody until I see you. A. W. Carr.'

After receiving my cable Carr replied: 'Travelling with you from Suez no mystery wife's letter crowd journalists boarding *Otranto* see me first. Carr.'

I was imprisoned in my cabin being questioned by about a score of reporters when Carr came aboard. He came into the cabin and handed me a note. This was the alleged mystery letter about which so many sensational stories were written. There was nothing more to it than that Carr simply advised me not to give any information to the newspapermen until he had spoken to me.

Carr had travelled to Suez as guest of the *Daily Sketch*. The editor had felt that Carr could use his influence as county skipper to secure the story for them. Carr assured me he had made it clear that I was bound by the MCC contract to remain silent until the tour ended, but they insisted on sending him, together with their sporting editor, L. V. Manning, who was to act as 'ghost'.

Carr accepted their invitation but deliberately let them down. He came as a friend, because he wanted to keep the newspapermen away from me and shield me from further controversy. He knew newspapermen have a way of getting their stories. It was a team of disconsolate newspapermen who arrived back in London because none of them had got the story he wanted.

I received an avalanche of telegrams offering me terms to talk. The *Evening Standard* offered me £100 for 300 words. Another London paper indicated a willingness to pay £1 a word and invited me to write as much as I liked. The *Daily Sketch* got more than anybody, but it amounted to very little. Carr fed them some hastily conceived ideas on the future of leg theory but practically nothing on the tour itself. The issue of Friday, 7 April 1933, featured a story, part of which read:

All doubt as to whether Larwood's much discussed leg-theory bowling will be tried during the coming county cricket season in England is set at rest today by a radio message from L. V. Manning. He is on board the liner *Otranto* in which the famous Test bowler is returning from Australia.

Mr A. W. Carr (the Notts captain) and Larwood have been putting their heads together, says L. V. Manning, the *Daily Sketch* sporting editor, and nothing but legislative action by the MCC will stop the leg-theory tactics from being employed.

Asked if this would ruin county cricket, Carr replied, 'Rubbish! It will make it more exciting.' He also said he was not afraid of retaliation by other counties because no one but Larwood could bowl the real stuff. . .

When I arrived at Dover after travelling overland from Toulon, hundreds had gathered to greet me. My wife met me in London at Victoria and after pushing my way through what seemed like a crowd of several thousands, and hundreds of interviewers, I reached St Pancras Station to catch a train for Nottingham. Mr Findlay was awaiting me and reminded me that my contract prohibited me from discussing any of the scenes, incidents and controversies of the Australian tour.

I had hoped for a quiet arrival at Nottingham, but when I reached there just before midnight I was mobbed by thousands who struggled in and around the station. Arthur Carr did most of the talking, telling everybody that if ever I told the full story it would be amazing. I did say that the Australian papers had grossly magnified trivial incidents.

Next day there were more newspapermen and cameramen than fowls on my chicken farm, but I kept quiet and didn't venture outside. I said nothing publicly until the English team returned home on 6 May. The following day I dropped a bombshell in the *Sunday Express*, saying that Bradman was frightened, Woodfull was too slow and Australian crowds unfair. My interview, given to the sporting editor Charles Eade, appeared together with a letter from me approving the article after some revisions had been made and expressing thanks for the cheque I received.

I said:

Now I can speak. For months I have been muzzled because my agreement with the Marylebone Club made it impossible for me to write or talk about what happened to me and the rest of the English team in Australia – particularly to me, because most of the temper and venom of the cricket crowds there was directed at my unfortunate head. Yesterday the MCC tour ended and I was released from the obligation not to let the English public know just what we had to put up with.

Until now I had to suffer in silence the taunts and abuse of the crowds in Australia; not only the crowds either. The news-papers joined in the campaign to wreck us: but let me start at the beginning. On the way out we talked over the plans we should adopt to win back the Ashes. We knew we were up against a stiff task; that only by a definite scheme could we hope for victory. We decided to adopt leg theory, that is, to concentrate our bowling on the leg stump. It was Jardine who originally had the idea of building for victory with this plan of attack, though all the members of the side took part in the discussions, which finally led to its adoption. Voce and I were chosen as the two bowlers likely to bring it success; so in bowling as I did I was merely carrying out the pre-arranged plan. In other words, I was playing for my side, which every cricketer is supposed to do.

For doing that I had to endure four months anger of the crowds and the barrackers, who knew nothing about the finer points of cricket. Leg-theory bowling probably requires more accuracy than any other form. We were able to exploit it with complete success. That is where the trouble started. The people who went to the famous Hill in Sydney and the cheaper parts of most other grounds, particularly Adelaide, were not there to see cricket. They were there to see Australia win. That was all they wanted. Above all, they were there to see Brad-man score runs.

All the excitement there had been about Bradman's writ-ings, which had stirred the Australian crowds into believing Bradman to be a super-batsman. We showed that he was not, and the mob did not like their idol treated that way. Then there was Woodfull. He was expected to stay at the wicket all day while the others got the runs. He was a failure too. You ask why Woodfull and Bradman could not stand up to my fast leg-theory bowling. These are the true reasons. Woodfull was too slow, and Bradman was too frightened. Yes, frightened is the word. Bradman just would not have it. He was scared by my bowling. I knew it, as everybody did. Time after time he drew away from the ball.

If I was not bowling when Bradman came in, Jardine put me on at once. It might have been supposed that Woodfull would have tried to quieten the crowd, or indicate in some way he was not in sympathy with those noisy demonstrators, but he did not do so.

He, too, was slow and did not like to face me either. Time after time he would duck when the ball did not get up at all. Sometimes the ball struck his pads. Ames and I appealed for leg-before. These antics were silly and undignified but, coming from a captain, a man of Woodfull's long record, only encouraged the crowd to shout all the more loudly at me. Woodfull and Bradman were failures against fast leg-theory bowling. They were upset, and the crowds were upset to see their idols fall. Richardson and McCabe played me all right. Woodfull and Bradman could not.

Australia was being beaten so the crowd, not knowing what sportsmanship means, shouted abuse at the men who were winning. Can you imagine my feelings when 50,000 people booed my every step as I ran at the wicket? Do you know what a bowler thinks about when he realizes he is not only playing the batsmen, but the crowd as well?

On the previous tour I was treated the same way. I was only 24 then, and I must say that barracking and the angry shouts upset me. I was so distressed, in fact, I could not do justice to myself. My side could not bowl properly. It was not the conditions or the ground or the batsmen that beat me four years ago; it was the crowds. They tried to put me off and wanted to see me fail. They tried to upset me, and succeeded. The barrackers beat me in 1928–29. This time I was four years older, more experienced and tougher. The crowd could not upset me by their unfairness and hostility. When they jeered and booed they merely made me grit my teeth and bowl harder than ever. Of course, I said a few things about them under my breath, but I took care not to let them see I was affected. On the first tour I was upset. This time I was inspired. The next time I shall probably enjoy it. If I am selected I shall be ready and willing to go again. I know I have been reported as having said I would never make another tour. It is a lie. I never said it.

Many newspapers tried to put words into my mouth, but I have been loyal to my agreement with the MCC and not spoken out till now. A group of journalists came to interview me at Suez and offered to pay for news. I could have had £1,000 that day but would not tell them anything. You are the first newspapermen I have given an interview to. I am telling you my own story, just as I tell it to friends. The newspapers in Australia were up against me just as much as the barrackers. They spread stories of quarrels in the English team before we arrived. These were all lies. There was no trouble at all in the team. This campaign only caused the English players to stick together all the more. I take off my hat to Jardine for the way he stuck abuse hurled at him by the crowd – and what abuse and what a crowd!

People who only watched cricket in England cannot imagine the bitterness of the disappointed mob of cricket fans in Australia, yet they were allowed to dominate the game in Australia to such an extent that the Board of Control protested against our methods. Board of Control! What a title! It cannot even control its own crowds, and half of its members could not tell you the weight of a cricket ball.

When the Australians come here they are treated as gentlemen. When we go to Australia we have to suffer cheap wit and abuse from an unsportsmanlike gang which would not be tolerated for a moment here. The Australian people seem to be out to throw us off our game. When they failed they shouted insults, and hoped to win in that way. They made a lot of hot air about bodyline bowling. That is rubbish if you like. If I had bowled at the body how was it I kept hitting the wickets and getting the men leg-before?

The fact is, the Australians were fairly and squarely beaten. Their players failed and the crowds were not interested in the play with the result that they tried to get back at me because my bowling – to the captain's orders – had had a lot to do with our success. The Australians may not like my bowling. Well, I do not like their howling. It is not cricket.

This caused a new flare-up in the bodyline row. Cables flashed around the Empire once again, and I was rebuked on all sides. Things became so hot that Mr A. W. Shelton, president of Notts County Cricket Club, issued a statement on my behalf to explain the *Sunday Express* interview.

Mr Shelton said the interview had been written by another person from statements I made, and that I believed I was at liberty to publish a statement the day after the MCC team returned. I had signed the proof of the article without sufficient thought. Upon certain facts being brought to my notice after I signed the proof I had decided to withdraw it in order not to cause trouble between the MCC and me. Accordingly I had sent two telegrams to the editor of the *Sunday Express* on Thursday and Friday, the first of which was acknowledged in writing, withdrawing the interview, as well as the permission to publish it. At the same time I had returned the cheque I had received in payment. Mr Shelton said I wished to express regret for the article, the publication of which I did all in my power to stop.

The editor of the *Sunday Express* made this prompt reply in the *Daily Express*:

I have never heard such nonsense as the statements issued on behalf of Larwood. As late as Saturday he gave an interview to the *Daily Mail* reiterating the assertion he had made to us that he had been released from his pledge of silence to the Marylebone Club. We bought and paid for the interview at Larwood's suggestion. When late in the week he asked to be released from his contract he made it clear that he sought the release chiefly because he proposed to publish an account of his experiences in book form. I preferred to publish it in the *Sunday Express*.

The editor was quite right in some of the things he said. But the *Sunday Express* approached me, I didn't approach it. I have never approached any newspaper in my life with a proposition; they have always come to me. I thought of withdrawing the article only after the editor of the *Sunday Dispatch* had put pressure on me not to give any interviews. The *Dispatch* intended publishing in serial form a book on leg theory which was being ghosted for me. I was to receive about £500 for the serial rights. I received only about £50 for the *Sunday Express* article. I know it was less than £100, and I'm pretty sure it was only £50.

When I mentioned the article to Mr Shelton, he thought it would be unwise from the point of view of controversy and advised me to withdraw it. I tried to, but no doubt the editor was perfectly within his rights to publish it as I had already signed the proofs. I make no apology for the article. It is exactly how I felt at the time. I was still smarting from the Australian criticisms, and I was so involved in the controversy that I didn't think a few extra comments would make any difference. I was wrong because it provoked a strong reaction from Australia.

Mr E. E. Bean, a former chairman of the Australian Board of Control, said through his walrus moustache that my comment was offensive and seemed an act of insubordination. Mr Bean said:

Larwood seems to have created a difficult and delicate position for the Marylebone Club as the arbiter on international cricket in England.

That a professional cricketer should have the audacity to offer comment of such an offensive character, and so surcharged with personal spleen, seems an act of insubordination which no self-respecting authority should tolerate. The ungenerous spirit which the statement reveals towards those persons and organizations in Australia which sought consistently to extend the highest courtesy and kindness to all the English players suggests Larwood is entirely lacking in the sense of appreciation which Australians have the right to expect from any representative Englishman.

The deplorable incident, if allowed to pass unchallenged, will furnish an additional argument for those people in Australia who hold that the interest of the game is best served by the complete cessation of international visits for an extended period.

Arthur Mailey said in the Melbourne *Herald* he had never accused me of bowling bodyline, but I had certainly sent down a few bodylines in the interview. He admitted there was a strong flavour of truth about some of my statements but said other parts of my tirade were apparently spiced up.

Mailey said it was unfair of me to say Woodfull and Bradman could not stand up to my bowling.

'All members of the English team did not agree with the
Larwood–Jardine attack, but the difference of opinion did
not cause any serious breach,' said Mailey. 'There were no
beer-throwing episodes that we heard so much about nor
were there any stand-up fights. The English team was,
within itself, a happy combination. There were differences
of opinion naturally but the players did not allow their
personal views to affect the success of the tour.'

Alan Kippax, the New South Wales captain, said plain
facts showed that Woodfull was not too slow and Bradman
too frightened to handle my bowling as it was known
before the bodyline attack began. 'Allowing that Larwood's
statement that Woodfull was too slow and Bradman
frightened – with which I personally do not agree – were
correct, the fact remains that if Bradman were frightened
even Larwood knows that he was not frightened of his
bowling as we previously knew it,' said Kippax.

Mr W. J. Johnson, an Australian Test selector, said:

Australia does not care to use diplomacy where honesty will
serve the purpose. We must believe what we saw. Australia has
been beaten before, but has never been accused of squealing.
Larwood's reference to the fear of him by Woodfull and Bradman is significant. They were in fact attacked and intimidated
in the effort to secure their wickets. In the light of the magnificent records of both men it is hysterical to infer that they
are cowards.

Bradman said in interviews that he naturally greatly
resented the accusations of being afraid and emphatically
denied it. According to my ideas, Bradman said, it would
seem that to adopt orthodox methods and get hit was dis-
playing courage. Any other methods by which my theory
might be defeated envinced fear. 'Larwood's statements
were apparently a financial success, even if they had been a
failure otherwise,' said Bradman.

His outburst is unexpected and he has tried to justify his
bodyline method at the expense of the players themselves.

The case is not for individuals to delve into, it being a ridiculous argument, and I believe it is an occasion when the Board of Control might review the matter.

Probably when Larwood visits Australia in 1936 the crowd will express its opinion of his remarks. No crowd in the world understands cricket better than the Australians and none is more impartial.

Jack Fingleton said:

Larwood painted a pathetic picture of how he had been torn limb from limb by the Australian press and public, but there were no tears about him when he deliberately tried time after time to dislodge the Australian batsmen's heads from their shoulders.

Larwood and Voce tried to stave in the Australian players' ribs, while their team-mates, some of whom were as disgusted as the Australians at the tactics, were set on the leg side. Larwood appears to have thrown his mental balance to the winds. Every Australian player acknowledges his genius as a fast bowler, and there are legions of supporters in the game who pay him homage.

The veteran Australian Test umpire, Bob Crockett, said in the Melbourne *Sun-Pictorial* that my expressions were a breach of good form. He thought my remark that half the Board of Control members wouldn't even know the weight of a cricket ball to be particularly offensive. 'Larwood's chief objective in talking,' Mr Crockett said, 'seems to have been to show what a wonderful bowler he is.'

The *Sun-Pictorial* in an editorial urged that cricket must be saved from the critics. The latest eruption of the bodyline dispute was a much greater menace to the survival of cricket and the spirit of cricket than were the simple principles of leg theory themselves, the paper said. The dispute now in full blast in two countries has had as its fuel the opinions, expert and inexpert, of cricketers, ex-cricketers and near-cricketers on what had gone on in the minds of Jardine, Plum Warner and other members of the team in Australia. The paper said it could only hope that some Divine tactfulness would be breathed into the Board of Control, the MCC and all connected with the bodyline dispute.

Dr C. E. Dolling, one of the Australian selectors, said:

It is a great pity to see so magnificent a bowler as Harold Larwood sink to such depths as to speak in this manner. Larwood's confession of pre-arranged methods of attack showed us that the Australian attitude towards bodyline bowling was entirely justified. Larwood would be well advised to use less presumption and to refrain from criticizing such fine sportsmen as Woodfull and Bradman.

Victor Richardson said:

If Marylebone Cricket Club could have witnessed the bodyline bowling in Australia I am convinced that they would have been entirely in agreement with 99 per cent of the Australian public, which is behind the Board of Control in its attempt to stamp out this type of bowling. There is no doubt that England attained her victory by means of bodyline bowling. To say that Australian crowds know nothing about cricket is a libel on hundreds of thousands of keen followers of the game.

Writing in the *Sunday Dispatch*, V. W. C. Jupp, the Northants captain, said that although the best authorities declared Bradman was as technically fine a batsman as ever, the Test movies in slow-motion showed that I definitely frightened him. Jupp said that if Jardine's tactics were ill advised, which he did not admit, the Marylebone selectors must share the responsibility as they knew the methods of Voce and me.

Jupp said I was the first bowler to make the ball lift effectively in Australia because Bulli soil no longer supplied a soft cushion. If Australia could not treat the Englishmen more sportingly, he would like to see Marylebone cease sending teams until a better understanding existed.

Bill Ferguson, the scorer, said in the *Sunday Dispatch* the British public could rest assured there had been no violence shown the English players in Australia. There had been no public insulting of the players or dissension in the team, spectators did not throw anything at Larwood, I was treated as a friend, there had been no ban on beer drinking in the team, no beer glass had been thrown at anybody. There had been no bad blood between the distinguished tourists, and no Australian newspaper had reflected discredit on the Englishmen either as players or socially!

George Duckworth, the wicketkeeper, said in an interview which was cabled to Australia: 'The whole thing boils down to the simple fact that some of the Australian wizards were frightened to death of Larwood.'

Even my aged mother was quoted. In the *Daily Express* she said:

It is as plain as a pikestaff. Bradman disappointed them. They did not like the way we placed the field. Harold was too swift and our batsmen were not up to standard, leaving more for the bowlers, and they can't bear to think that we should win on our bowling. Harold did not seem to mind their barracking, and that made them worse. It was good cricket, but they can't take it, and that is all there is to it.

The *Daily Telegraph* correspondent, Thomas Moult, had this to say:

The behaviour of the crowd during the Tests was sometimes nightmarish and frightening. There were moments when the players felt that thousands would break the fences and pour into the field. A more friendly atmosphere returned towards the close of the tour when the Australian Board of Control realized that their bodyline protest was ill timed. There was little to fear regarding the cancellation of the tours unless the MCC cancelled them. Every player above all emphasized Jardine's strength of character and his utter fearlessness in the most trying situation that a cricket team has ever had to face.

Every player expressed his willingness to go to Australia again. Jardine alone hinted that this was his last tour. Several players I imagine would argue against the leg-theory bowling as a principle, but when the Tests had reached a critical stage it became vitally important for Jardine to continue to have the team behind him. In continuing to use Larwood, the approval of every player was unhesitating. We in England have been given no idea of the intimidation that they endured.

The Test crowd went much further than throwing oranges onto the field and counting Larwood's strides in chorus. Forty thousand out of 60,000 spectators stood and unanimously roared an offensive epithet of two syllables repeatedly till they were hoarse. Doubtless it was to this that Jardine wittily referred in New Zealand, when he said, 'We have just come from a country where our parentage is regarded as doubtful: our ultimate destination is absolutely certain.'

Jardine on the team's return to England avoided controversy but paid high tribute to the team's loyalty and support. They went and returned a happy and united team, he said. They made themselves a great side in spite of difficulties which quite excusably might have broken up most sides and undoubtedly would have bent almost any side. 'England should be as proud of them as I am,' he said.

Thousands met the team on its return to London, greeting the captain with shouts of, 'Good old Jardine.' He became the centre of a cheering, back-slapping crowd which swept his parents aside and tried to shoulder him. But he escaped to a hotel where, in response to repeated demands, he appeared at a window and acknowledged his welcome.

Most of the team had little or nothing to say, maintaining that they were committed to silence. The reason was simple: nobody wanted to risk losing their bonus from the tour. The MCC made about £30,000 from the tour.

At a celebrated banquet in London for the conquering heroes, Lord Hailsham declared: 'Jardine is probably the best captain in the world today, and his gallant band of sportsmen have worthily upheld England's reputation.'

The Sydney paper, *Smith's Weekly*, wrote a memo to the editors of the *Sydney Morning Herald* and other morning newspapers:

Dear Sirs, Did it ever occur to you that in publishing Larwood's poisonous libel on Bradman that you were doing something as viciously evil as Larwood? For him to defame Bradman by impugning his courage was clearly that he might make some money. Obviously the more sensational his assault on Bradman the larger his fee. But you have no such excuse if excuse it be. You print a lying slander and by so doing bring your paper within the Defamation Act if Bradman decides to vindicate his manhood.

Sydney *Truth*, although owned by the same proprietor as Melbourne *Truth*, must have had a different editor. It came out with this story, of which the following are extracts:

The cricket dog fight has broken out again. Writers and players who have howled against Larwood are again trying to justify themselves with brave talk of sending a delegation to England to discuss so-called bodyline bowling with the MCC. It would be a nice trip, but let us forget it. Most people are sick of the whole affair, and only cricket writers, players and Board of Control members who 'squeak' so childishly against Larwood are still wailing.

Be fair and honest. The crowd is not against bodyline, leg theory or any other kind of bowling. It is against Larwood. He proved his superiority over our batsmen and carried off the Ashes. Now, like petulant schoolboys, legislators and players want him barred so that this will not happen again. What absurdity!

Well and truly licked on the cricket field, our cricket legislators have been well beaten in the controversy with the MCC and should lose no time in resigning. The Board of Control, by its ridiculous attitude and its equally ludicrous cables, has put a stigma on Australians generally; branded them as a pack of squealers who cannot take a defeat in the proper spirit.

This opinion appears to have become general in England and the cricket Board of Control could help to dispel it by resigning in a body, for it has forfeited the confidence of the public, and give a chance to a new set of cricket legislators to rehabilitate Australian cricket in the esteem of Britishers generally. Talk that unless 'bodyline' bowling is discontinued there will be no further Tests for the time being is real baby prattle . . . Legislation to assist bowlers has been forgotten since Larwood unleashed his attack. For years bowlers had been belted and bowled to a standstill against batsmen who refused to play cricket as it was meant to be played, but used their pads and their bats purely in defence. Batsmen refused to take risks.

To put it bluntly they had a long innings of sublime quiet at the expense of the bowler. Larwood made them squeal, when he forced them either to hit out, get hit or get out. We had the humiliating spectacle of our leading batsmen ducking balls from Larwood that were only stump high and nearly bowled them, and we had the spectacle of the same batsmen running away from straight balls and being clean bowled by the same bowler. Let the Board of Control and our batsmen forget their tears of chagrin. It is not cricket to squeal.

Gregory and McDonald, the two fastest bowlers in the world at that time, had England's batsmen in a blue funk on the Australian tour of England in 1921. These fast bowlers struck terror in two counties. They battered and bruised and knocked out some of England's star batsmen. They curled up against their willing attack. England suffered in silence. Larwood is the answer . . . Admittedly Gregory and McDonald did not use leg theory or alleged 'bodyline' methods as far as the placing of the field is concerned, but as terror merchants they were just as effective as Larwood. But (let us say in *sotto voce* and shamefacedly) England did not cable us to call off our fast bowlers.

Truth blamed Jardine for most of the barracking:

Financially neither England nor Australia can afford to drop the Tests. There may be a few abusive barrackers in Australia, but in crowds of 30,000 or 50,000, such as attended the last series of Tests in Australia, there must be a certain unruly element and that players or anyone else should take notice of it shows a lack of perspective, and the childish working of minds that appeared to be more or less filled with a sense of importance entirely unwarranted . . .

If there were no large crowds at the Test matches there would be no Tests. It is humorous to talk of cutting out the Tests because of the barrackers. Without the barrackers the Test matches would automatically cut themselves out. The barrackers provide the wherewithal – in horrid slang, the cash – that keeps international cricket going. The Board of Control and MCC seemed to have overlooked this little fact . . .

If the MCC leaves Douglas Jardine at home next tour, the barracking to which he has evidently taken such objection will disappear. Jardine showed himself to be a great cricket leader, a real gentleman, but absolutely devoid of humour – just a cricket automaton. He came out here to win the Ashes, and won them. He didn't give a hang what the crowds or anyone else thought of him. The crowds did not like him. He was not the type of captain to lead an English side on an Australian tour.

Jardine made just one public statement about the tour in an exclusive article in the Nottingham *Evening News* of Monday, 22 May 1933, in which, among other things, he said:

To me I confess the term 'bodyline bowling' is meaningless. What is the bodyline? That term was coined by a sensational press to explain or excuse defeat and would have died a natural and speedy death had it not been adopted by the Australian Board of Control in its lamentable wire to the MCC.

As long as we were in Australia, we kept a strict silence. Rightly or wrongly it seemed to be that it was conceivable that people might take the view that we were in a position of guests and, as such, we should be lacking in courtesy to our hosts, whether they were the Australian Board of Control or the people of Australia, if we opened our mouths in comment, complaint or criticism, as long as we were in that position. This forbearance on our part did not, however, call forth any reciprocal forbearance from our hosts!

My own experience of leg theory is limited. The first time I played against it it was bowled – and well bowled – by McDonald, the Australian–Lancastrian. The next time I saw it was in Australia in 1928 when J. Scott, the South Australian fast bowler, bowled it to a field with only two or sometimes three men on the off side, under the captaincy of V. Richardson.

There were no complaints from us, nor I gathered from the Australian states against which Scott used to play. Leg theory wasn't much of a success! Larwood tried it in 1928–29 without placing a full leg side field for it and did not find it a very paying proposition. Had Larwood been an Australian, he would have out-rivalled Bradman in popularity and popular esteem. No fast bowler, England or Australian, can show a fairer or more convincing record.

For years the cry has gone up that the bat has been too much on top of the ball. It need not be imagined that leg theory is any permanent solution to the bat's mastery of the ball; far from it – so very, very few can hope to bowl it with success.

The Marylebone Cricket Club paid Australia the compliment of sending out the best team possible. We on our part paid our opponents the compliment of playing our best. For the Marylebone Club or ourselves to have done less would have been a very poor compliment to Australia, though in some quarters this was apparently not appreciated as it might have been.

The Australian Board of Control could have helped a great deal. Rightly or wrongly these rulers of cricket in the Dominion did not see their way to do so. Though controlling cricket and cricketers with a hand far heavier and more autocratic than that with which say the Football Association in England controls football and footballers, on this occasion they failed to control even themselves, just as on this and previous tours they have failed to control their crowds. In the eyes of many Australians, the board let Australia down. It will be a thousand pities if any controversy is allowed to distract the board's attention from the matter of controlling the crowds who watch cricket matches.

When all is said and done cricket is a game for eleven a side. For 20,000 or 30,000 people to participate by counting out a bowler or yelling 'no ball' or barracking the umpire is neither sporting nor funny. In the long run and if it is not checked I feel that barracking may kill most of the joy of the game. This is a question which affects cricket and cricketers the world over. Be it said in fairness that there is a percentage of Australians blushing for the actions of their crowds, but blushing isn't enough.

It is a pleasure to turn and pay a tribute to the members of the MCC team. The greatest tribute that one could pay them would be to say that they were worthy representatives of the great club they represented. Personally I cannot praise them sufficiently. Proud indeed ought any captain to be to lead such indomitables.

A captain cannot make a bad side into a good one, but a great side can make an indifferent captain into a moderate one. As for me, the knowledge that I have been privileged to lead this band of good men and true to victory and have gained their loyal friendship in the process will be treasured all my cricketing life and beyond.

Throughout the 1933 English season I hardly bowled at all but returned to the side towards the end of the season after having an operation for a fractured sesamoid bone in my foot. Notts decided to keep me on mainly as a batsman.

With the £800 I got from the Australian tour and the £400 from a shilling fund, which Notts supporters raised for Bill Voce and me, I wanted to do something for my father. He was about fifty and still down the mine, and I was anxious to get him out. I extended my chicken farm and made it into a market garden, which we gradually developed into a small horticultural farm.

There came a day in 1933 during a Notts–Surrey match when I received an unexpected presentation. Jack Hobbs and Jardine were playing. Out in the middle Jardine made a speech over a microphone telling the crowd of at least 20,000 that I had been the reason why England won the Ashes. Jardine then presented me with a silver ashtray which had inscribed on it these words:

'To Harold for the Ashes. 1932–33. From a grateful Skipper.'

CHAPTER EIGHTEEN

'I'm an Englishman'

I listened till I had my fill:
And as I mounted up the hill,
The music in my heart I bore
Long after it was heard no more.

WORDSWORTH's *The Reaper*

ANY JURIST or learned individual will tell you that the greatest gift Britain has given to the world is her system of justice. It is the envy of every country in the Western world outside the British Commonwealth. Nowhere can a man, especially one who is poor, find the same opportunities to establish his innocence. British justice is founded on this function of the law whatever the nature of the evidence against the accused.

But in my case traditional British justice was not to be applied. The full committee of the MCC met at Lord's in May 1933, while a Lancashire v. Middlesex match was in progress, and appointed a subcommittee to investigate bodyline bowling and to make a report on it. Jardine and the co-manager Palairet were the first to appear before the MCC regarding the events leading up to Australia's protest against bodyline bowling, and Plum Warner was also called. I believe some of the players had been invited, including vice-captain Wyatt, Allen and Hammond.

I didn't know it at the time but Allen and Wyatt, after being told they would be required as witnesses, were later informed that they would not be needed. The tribunal, comprising Lord Hailsham, four other lords and two knights, obviously did not wish to hear anything against bodyline, and it was felt that Allen and Wyatt might be critical.

The only misgivings expressed came from Warner, but this only canvassed the reaction in England if bodyline were to be bowled there in the coming season. The assembled peers confidently told Warner that he had 'got the wrong perspective on bodyline'.

Newspapers indicated that Jardine and Palairet spoke in favour of bodyline and Plum Warner against it.

But the star witness was not asked to attend. I doubt if I would have gone had the request been made. I had been under the captain's instructions, had not bowled to injure anyone and, in any case, the members of the selection committee could not but have been aware that Australia was to receive a burst of leg theory when they selected four fast bowlers, the last one, Bowes, a few days before the team sailed.

At the end of April the Australian Board of Control framed a new rule, which was to apply to all Australian cricket from the ensuing season, and which made 'thought readers' of the umpires. The board forwarded its rule to the MCC in the hope that it would be adopted in all cricket under the aegis of the MCC.

The rule read:

Any ball delivered which, in the opinion of the umpire, at the bowler's end was bowled at the batsman with intent to intimidate or injure him shall be considered unfair and no-ball shall be called, and the bowler notified of the reason. If the offence be repeated by the same bowler in the same innings he shall immediately be instructed by the umpire to cease bowling and the over shall be regarded as completed. Such bowler shall not again be permitted to bowl in the course of the innings then in progress.

Cricket a batsman's game? Victor Richardson, a member of the Australian committee and a prime mover behind the rule, must have had some second thoughts on my field placings. For, in the Brisbane *Sunday Mail* of 2 December 1934, I see that he used a similar field. In a match between

South Australia and Queensland the *Mail* reported:

Richardson, the visitors' captain, had adopted drastic measures to bottle up the on side brilliancy of Hansen, swinging in a close-in cordon after the style employed by Larwood in his much debated bodyline attack. The move was successful in curbing the South Brisbane man but he artfully picked his spots and continued to score steadily.

After its investigations, the MCC tribunal came down firmly on Jardine's side. In June 1933, they sent a further telegram to Australia saying bodyline was being confused with 'leg theory', which was bowling at the leg stump but without intent to hit or intimidate the batsman.

Don Bradman, no doubt with the 1934 tour of England in mind, had applied himself to seeing what could be done about bodyline. In an article he wrote in August 1933, urging the Board of Control not to delay unduly, Bradman said: 'After all, it is the players who have to face the music, not the members of the board.'

The English team had a real taste of bodyline during the 1933 season. Manny Martindale and Leary Constantine, the two speed merchants of the West Indies team, unleashed bodyline at full pressure against England's batsmen in the second Test at Old Trafford. Jardine, who captained England in her first two Tests against the West Indies, defied the attack and scored his first Test century of 127. Jardine didn't flinch. He wasn't afraid. But he had, owing to injury, to stand down in favour of Wyatt in the last Test.

One result of the Manchester Test was that Wally Hammond received a nasty blow on the chin, laying it open. Hammond reportedly said he would get out of first-class cricket if that type of bowling continued. This was the Hammond who repeatedly encouraged me to bowl bodyline at the Australians. He was all for it, as was every other member of the team, except Allen and Wyatt, because they could see it would beat Australia. But Wally didn't like them flying around his own ears. Still, who does?

Voce, Bowes, Clark and several other fast bowlers used leg theory extensively and some counties, mostly those who didn't possess a fast bowler, were very unhappy about it. The MCC did not make any of its investigations public and made no charges against me. But it decided to legislate against intimidatory bowling at a meeting at Lord's in November 1933 of the Advisory County Cricket Committee and the Board of Control of Test Matches at home. That was only after a lengthy exchange of cables between the MCC and the Australian Board of Control, in which the MCC stood firm, declaring the term 'bodyline' to be unfair and improper and refusing to give a definite assurance that the type of bowling used in Australia would not be repeated. This, of course, was before the politicians intervened.

Jardine had taken the MCC side to India as captain in 1933–34 and, in the prevailing atmosphere of change, the knives were being sharpened for him in the Lord's Long Room. By now the aristocracy of cricket was turning on the bodyline issue.

Lord Hawke, a strong supporter of Jardine in 1932, and an elder statesman of the cricket hierarchy, was asking friends in influential circles how bodyline could be prevented from happening again 'without letting Douglas down too badly'.

Warner, who had written to the *Daily Telegraph* in London following the counties bodyline onslaught, saying that bodyline was causing 'anger, hatred and malice', had received a letter from Governor Hore-Ruthven in Adelaide declaring: 'Keep Jardine out of the picture on any plea you can find . . . some excuse must be found for leaving him out (of the 1934 England-Australia series).'

Finally, Jardine solved a delicate situation and brought about his own demise. From India he sent a telegram announcing he would not be available for the 1934 Tests against Australia. (Percy Fender condemned the Lord's attitude towards Jardine, saying they had rejected a man with the character and vision to play for victory.)

The MCC decided that any form of bowling would be an

offence against the spirit of the game which was obviously a direct attack by the bowler upon the batsman. The matter was to be left to the captains, a principle which was affirmed by the Imperial Cricket Conference in July 1934.

Meanwhile the Australian Board of Control was still desperately trying to gain an assurance from the MCC before deciding to send a team to England in 1934 that the bodyline form of attack would not be used again. In London the Australian board's representative, Dr Robert Macdonald, conferred with the new MCC president, Lord Hailsham, and then met a subcommittee which included Lord Hawke, Lord Lewisham, Sir Stanley Jackson and MCC secretary W. Findlay. These talks were described by Macdonald in what became known as the 'Secret Letter Case'.

The board members decided that the contents of the letter should not be disclosed even to State Cricket Association delegates who had elected them. Dr Macdonald said in the letter that the MCC subcommittee wanted to leave the matter until the Australian team reached England, when the captain, manager and any board member accompanying the team could take part in talks. He maintained that the board was entitled to know before the Australian team was selected in case Australia should think it necessary to maintain a shock attack from both ends in the Test matches.

Lord Hawke: 'Reprisals, by gad!'

Dr Macdonald: 'Not reprisals – reciprocity. Action and reaction on a mutual basis.'

The committee members told Dr Macdonald they could give no definite assurance that the same tactics would not be used and would not go beyond saying that cricket would be played in the same spirit as in the past should an Australian team be sent. They did affirm, however, that a direct attack by a bowler on a batsman would be against the spirit of the game, but they would not agree that bodyline was different from leg theory.

After the board cabled that it would send a team only on an assurance that bodyline would not be used, the MCC on

12 December 1933, cabled: 'We cannot go beyond the assurance therein given (that cricket would be played in the same spirit). We shall welcome Australian cricketers who come to play with us next year. If however your Board of Control decides that such games should be deferred, we shall regret their decision . . .'

Faced with a deadlock, the Australian board backed down and, within a day or so of Dr Macdonald's meeting with the committee, the Australian board cabled that it would send a team. But it was only by a narrow decision that the tour was not abandoned. The decision to send a team was made before five of the thirteen members, including J. S. Hutcheon and Roger Hartigan, had voted. Hutcheon and Hartigan protested later at the chairman's hurried acceptance.

The politicians had been busy. I didn't know at the time, but in Whitehall J. H. Thomas, the Secretary for the Dominions, had been conferring with MCC officials; everything was done behind the scenes. A scapegoat had to be found to seal the rift in the Empire and placate the noisy protests from Australia.

Whitehall, perhaps, could foresee Australia refusing to have another English Governor-General, thereby cutting off a direct link with the Monarch. The bonds of Empire had to be cemented at any cost. Jardine's story to the MCC committee could not be faulted: I could imagine him being magnificent in defence. Even had he cracked he would not have been sacrificed. He was a gentleman.

The gentlemen of the MCC did not show their hand until early in the 1934 season, and I was certainly not prepared for the devious approach that was made.

We were playing a match in Nottingham at the private ground owned by Sir Julien Cahn, who had been president of Nottinghamshire in 1931. He was a wealthy man, a patron of the club, a gentleman, a big businessman who rode in a chauffeured Rolls Royce. During the match I was asked to go and see him.

He talked for a few minutes, and I knew he was buttering me up for something. Finally he said: 'Harold, I'm afraid you'll have to apologize to the MCC.'

Harold! Usually I got called plain Larwood.

'Apologize, sir? What for?'

'For your bowling, Harold.'

'I have nothing to apologize for, sir.'

'Oh, but you must Harold. You must apologize to the MCC for your bowling, and you must agree to bowl legitimately in future. If you do, you will be picked in the Tests against Australia. But unless I have your word, I'm afraid you will not be considered at all.'

Sir Julien was the man who would not have anything said against me because I was a member of his club. Remember? That was before Whitehall intervened.

I couldn't believe what I had been told, and my stomach turned over. I thought of how I had bowled myself to a standstill in Australia, at the captain's orders, how I had bowled till my side ached, bowled till my toes bled. I thought how my stomach had revolted against food because of the strain of bowling. I thought of how I had bowled long spells until I was weary, only to have Jardine come across and say, 'Try one more, Harold.'

I thought of the cables the MCC had sent me in Australia. There were three of them, all signed Marylebone. The first, addressed to me at the Hotel Australia, Sydney, during the first Test, said: 'Well bowled Notts.' The second, during the Brisbane Test: 'Well bowled, congratulations.' The third one, during the last Test: 'Bravo.'

After a while I said to Sir Julien Cahn: 'I'm an Englishman – I will never apologize.'

Bill Voce was approached in the same way, and I think he apologized at the time. I know we had an argument about it.

Having failed to put me on the chopping-block, the MCC tried again. We were playing Lancashire at Old Trafford. Before the match Arthur Carr came up to Bill Voce and me and said, 'Well boys, I don't know what's going to happen in this match, but there's going to be a protest.'

'What's it all about?' I asked.

'It's a protest against you and Bill.'

'What?' we said together. 'Yes,' said Carr. 'I've got the inside information. There's going to be a protest all right.'

'Look, I'm refusing to play, Skipper,' I said.

'No, you're going to play.'

'Well then, I'm only going to bowl half-pace.'

'That's up to you, Harold.'

Bill Voce and I played, and it was an easy wicket. Several players ducked and drew away on purpose. Operating on a shortened run, I was not quite as fast as in Australia, but I was still the fastest bowler in England. In this match, however, I bowled nowhere near my customary speed. I don't think I hit anybody, but Bill bowled some leg theory and hit one or two batsmen a few times.

It was such a farce, at least as far as I was concerned, that George Duckworth got 50–odd runs against us, and he was one of the last in. If George broke his duck, he was considered to be in exceptional form. I'm sure I didn't hit him because I didn't drop any short. But Bill hit him around the thighs a few times.

Next day the papers were agog with the news that Lancashire had protested to the Notts club about our bowling and would not play against us in county cricket again unless no more leg theory was bowled. There were pictures of Duckworth who had sustained some bruising.

I went straight up to Duckworth that day and said, 'What the hell have you been up to?'

'Nothing,' said Duckworth. 'I just protested about your bowling.'

Later that day he came to see me and said the president of his club wanted to see me. 'Look, George,' I said, 'if he wants to see me let him come and ask me and not send a little —— like you to tell me.'

That day the crowd cheered me as I bowled. They wanted to let me know that I had their sympathies.

It was easy to see how the minds of the MCC gentlemen worked. The president of the Lancashire Club was T.A. Higson. Remember he was on the selection committee for the 1932 tour? He must have known Australia was to get a feast of leg theory; he helped select us. With regard to George Duckworth, I can only say that when he returned from the tour he gave lectures on bodyline, saying it was all fair and above-board. The ironic thing was I wasn't bowling leg theory in the 1934 season. I may have tried it once or twice but, soon after the season began, Carr and I decided I should not bowl it. I could swing the ball in England and didn't need leg theory.

The writing was on the wall for me. Arthur Carr said he had learned from Sir Julien Cahn that J. H. Thomas had told him I must not be taken on tour again or represent England unless I apologized. I was in two minds anyway about the Tests against the Australians; I didn't want to play against them if it meant I was going to be hit all over the field, and I wasn't quite as fast as I was in Australia. I had humbled them on their own pitches, and I didn't want them to humble me in England, especially as they had said I was unfair. Nevertheless, I think I might have played if I had been selected without having to apologize, but to give myself an easy let-out with the public in case I was passed over for the Tests, I told the Nottingham officials that I didn't think I was 100 per cent fit. I was deeply hurt to think that my own club had turned against me, and I think I said that more or less as a sop to my pride. It wounded me to find that they now implied I had been unfair.

I was given the go-by for the first Test which began at Trent Bridge on 8 June, and I saw clearly what was intended. In short, the game was up, and I knew I could not beat the establishment. I was to be sacrificed, and I promptly hit out.

In the *Sunday Dispatch* of 17 June 1934, I explained my reasons for refusing to play in any more Tests. I said:

It is time the public knew the truth. England's selectors meet tomorrow to choose a team for the second Test match. My friends tell me I am certain to be asked to play. It will not matter.

I have definitely made up my mind not to play against the Australians in this or any of the Tests. I doubt if I shall ever play against them again – at least in big cricket.

Some people in authority have conveniently short memories. I have not forgotten that two years ago in Australia Woodfull said: 'There are two teams playing and one of them is not playing cricket.' He has never taken back that statement, which was a direct thrust at Mr Jardine and myself. I am unrepentant about leg theory. There is a big hush-hush campaign to bury leg theory and brand me as a dangerous and unfair bowler . . .

In that declaration I locked myself out from Test match play for all time. The bodyline row flared up again, but this time I brought the politicians into the open. J. H. Thomas vigorously denied my claim that he had put pressure on the MCC to squeeze me out. 'There is not a vestige of truth in the statement,' he said blandly. 'Neither directly nor indirectly have any discussions taken place with politicians with regard to Larwood either in Australia or here.' He advised me to stick to cricket. Years later he was to admit that bodyline had caused him more trouble than any other issue introduced into politics in the British Empire.

Viscount Hailsham, the MCC president who was also Secretary of State for War, was equally vehement in his denials. 'It is the most extraordinary moonshine I have ever heard of,' he said. 'I must know if any influence, political or otherwise, worked against Larwood. I cannot understand what he means. Whose is this political influence and what is it supposed to do? It is unfortunate that Larwood has dragged politicians into his grievance against somebody.'

Arthur Carr came to my support then and even after the end of 1934 when he was sacked from the captaincy of Notts for publicly defending me and letting Bill Voce bowl leg theory. A man who had given his heart and soul to the county team, he was simply notified by letter that he would no longer be captain. Before that happened his defence of me appeared even in Irish newspapers:

I believe Larwood is right in not playing for England when the rulers of the game have so completely deserted him.

In several matches Larwood has proved without a shadow of a doubt that batsmen cannot play fast bowling. That is why they shout so much about the leg side field to catch the palsied stroke. I have been told that it may be advisable that Larwood should give up leg theory in county cricket, but I shall give no orders to Larwood. I am not going to dictate to my bowlers. If we happen to have the two best fast bowlers in the world, Larwood and Voce, that is not our fault. For years our bats-men have been using their pads and their bodies as a shield. It is about time it was stopped.

Carr went on to say that Lord's should stop trying to run with the fox and hunt with the hounds and give a clear ruling on whether my bowling was unfair. Carr's support was all the more courageous because it was unnecessary: I was not bowling leg theory, and my fight with the MCC was not his. He could have kept out of trouble by remaining silent. But Carr was a forthright man who fought for what he felt was right.

Cartoonists made light of the intervention of politicians into the game of cricket. I remember one cartoon of the Dominion Secretary holding up a copy of a newspaper with the headlines, 'England routs Australia. Verity delivers the body blow,' and Verity the slow bowler standing nervously on the carpet, cap in hand, saying, 'I can't tell a lie, Jimmie – I DID IT!'

The *New Statesman and Nation* ran this rhyme:

BOWLERS AND BARGAINS
Some folks seem to be astonished but it doesn't startle
    me
To discover Jimmie Thomas chatting with the MCC;
For an Empire builder's duty is by any means to seek
Fresh and up-to-date improvements in Imperial
    technique.
Now we know that Larwood's bowling may affect the
    fate of nations,
And that leg traps may imperil our Imperial relations,
He, our master hand at bargains, must be hungering to
    wield
All the diplomatic assets lurking in the cricket field.
Dimly one can see the process – say that British

exports fall:
'If you'll give us further preference, Larwood shall not
    bowl at all.'
While if meat should be in question then experience
    suggests
An increased Australian quota, in return for four-day
    Tests.
But while thus employing cricket to cement the
    Commonwealth,
We shall make it clear that Britons don't play cricket
    for their health;
If a Test match should be cancelled we shall tax at
    higher rate
All Australia has to send us, to recoup the vanished
    'gate'.
So the weapons that have banished unemployment
    from our land
And impressed the Irish voter with the weight of
    Britain's hand
Shall be sharpened and perfected – that is how it seems
    to me –
By the aid of Jimmie Thomas, Larwood and the MCC.

The former Australian batsman, Warren Bardsley, in the
Star, supported me in my demand to have the air cleared.
He wrote:

Larwood has practically been forced out of Test cricket. While
it is extremely regrettable that he has decided not to play for
England, there is something to be said for his side of the case. I
played against Larwood in his first two Tests at Lord's and the
Oval in 1926 and also at Nottingham against his county, and
Folkestone against an England XI.

The next time I saw him was on the Melbourne Cricket
Ground under Chapman, when he took seven Victorian
wickets for 51. I saw first-class batsmen running away from
him. That was before the term 'bodyline' had been invented.
In the Test series against Jardine eighteen months ago Larwood bowled quite in accordance with the laws of the game.
He had a right to place his field as he liked. We will be

interfering with cricket when we say that a bowler cannot place a leg field to defeat a batsman's stroke play.

But the case is deeper than that. The MCC refused to admit that Larwood's bowling was unsportsmanlike throughout the controversy with our Board of Control. If the MCC had thought that Larwood's tactics were contrary to ethics of cricket, I feel sure they would have admitted it. Marylebone, however, has failed to clear the air as a result of its passive attitude. Larwood's case now is that by inference his bowling is regarded as unfair unless he relies entirely on orthodox bowling to an off-theory field.

The MCC may have been actuated by the desire to placate Australian feeling, but Larwood is legitimately entitled to feel that his sportsmanship has not been vindicated. It is just ridiculous to say that he would not have been bowling under a cloud of suspicion if he had played in the Test only on condition that his field placing was restricted.

I go farther. I am positive that Larwood would not have been hounded the way he was if he had been punished again in the way McCabe trounced him all over the field in the first Test in Australia. Furthermore, Larwood is justified in regarding Woodfull's statement in Adelaide that only one side was playing cricket as a personal reflection on his fairness. That remark has never been withdrawn.

Is not Larwood entitled to believe that the implication still exists? I can sympathize with Woodfull. No doubt the remark was made on the spur of the moment, for no one has ever found him otherwise than a first-class sportsman.

Whether the MCC has handled the matter diplomatically or not is beside the point. In my view there has been too much diplomacy, just as there was too much howling condemnation of Larwood's bowling when our batsmen definitely had an inferiority complex.

To those who say that Larwood relied for his wickets on intimidation I reply that others have done so long before him – Australian bowlers as well as English. I think Larwood is the best bowler in the world today. The storm broke about him because of the very excellence and accuracy of his pace.

I didn't play in the Notts match against the Australians in

August. I might have if Bill Woodfull had made a gesture that would have gone a long way towards bringing the old conflict to a swift end. But he chose to remain aloof. The situation in county cricket had become farcical. It seemed I was the only bowler who couldn't bowl leg theory. I had to look on while other bowlers like Bowes packed the leg side. What was meat for other counties was poison for Notts because if I had used our leg side field placing the cry, 'unfair', would have gone up.

As a professional I could not dictate. If selected against the Australians I would have had to play, but I asked to be stood down, and the committee reluctantly agreed. Bill Voce played and bowled leg theory, taking 8 for 66 in the first innings. He mysteriously didn't appear in the second innings, the official reason being that he had a 'strained muscle'. Strained relations was more like it. The Australians complained, and Voce was diplomatically withdrawn. The crowd sensed this and barracked the Australians. Later the Australian manager, Mr H. Bushby, complained to the MCC in writing that Voce's bowling was 'certainly intimidatory and a direct attack on our batsmen'.

On 5 October the president of the Middlesex Club, Mr A. J. Webbe, complained to the Notts chairman about Voce's bowling. Webbe was a member of the full MCC committee which investigated bodyline.

Middlesex was also Plum Warner's club: he was one of the first to squeal. He was knighted in 1937 for his services to cricket, became president of the MCC and later its first life vice-president. *Wisden* wrote after his death: 'He was completely opposed to this type of bowling; indeed he had objected to it as long ago as 1910 when W.B. Burns bowled it for a few overs for Worcestershire against Middlesex at Lord's, but he never allowed his opposition to interfere with his admiration for Jardine as a man and as a leader.' *Wisden* did not mention that Warner raised no objections when the Australians had to face bodyline!

In December the Notts committee sacked Carr, appointing two players in his place as joint captains. But before then, in November, the MCC declared that 'as a result of their own observations and from reports received the MCC committee consider that there is evidence that cases of the bowler making a direct attack upon the batsmen have on occasions taken place during the last cricket season'.

The MCC committee did not see exactly eye to eye with the Australian rule, nor did it legislate against leg theory entirely, but it passed a new rule which had the effect of banning leg-theory bowling. It ruled that 'the type of bowling regarded as a direct attack by the bowler upon the batsman and therefore unfair consists in persistent and systematic bowling of fast short-pitched balls at the batsman standing clear of his wicket'.

My protest had not been entirely in vain. If the Australian rule had been adopted, cricket would overnight have become even less of a manly game than it is today. As it was, the bodyline ogre was so much out of perspective that one bumper was enough to brand a bowler intimidatory in the eyes of many people.

What a game for softies it has become with today's modified rule! 'The persistent bowling of fast short-pitched balls at the batsman is unfair if, in the opinion of the umpire at the bowler's end, it constitutes a systematic attempt at intimidation.'

The Brisbane *Courier Mail* summed up my demise from cricket in an editorial under the heading of Larwood Versus The Rest:

Larwood has retired of his own volution from Anglo-Australian Test cricket. In doing so he has bowled the last ball – a controversial one – which must have set many heads ducking. So far as Test cricket is concerned he has not only burned his boats, to use his own metaphor, but has made a spectacular bonfire of them. In this performance there is a queer mixture of egotism; of loyalty to his old captain Jardine and his county captain Carr; of genuine conviction that in defending his exploitation of 'leg theory' he is fighting for a sound principle; and of bitter personal resentment against Australian cricketers and critics and against Woodfull in particular.

Larwood's defiant apologia, however, is not solely inspired by memories of his treatment in Australia. It voices a spirit of angry grievances against those English counties which also object to the manner in which he employed his undoubted bowling skill, and against the MCC, which with some logic he assails for not definitely declaring whether or not the bowling tactics he used in Australia and which he would use again are sanctioned by the laws of cricket, written or unwritten . . .

I felt bewildered, crushed, that the MCC should have silently condemned me, leaving a stigma that I bowled to maim the man: a stigma that still lives today.

So many letters poured into my home in the village of Annesley Woodhouse that it came to look like a sorting office. Hundreds of my countrymen abused me for refusing to play for England. It was a bitter pill to swallow, but I realized later their anger reflected their keen desire to see the Australians beaten. I don't want to suggest, however, that I was friendless, far from it. An impressive number of pro-Larwood cricket fans took the trouble to write to me and the following letter from the Reverend A. F. Smith of Tothill Rectory, Alford, Lincolnshire, on 20 June 1934 is one of many similar messages I received during the controversy:

I admire your courage over the Test (?) cricket, and I am sure you will have the support of thousands of cricket enthusiasts in this country and also throughout the Empire. Stick to your guns and let Woodfull and Bradman play marbles.

I hope you will leave the so-called test matches alone; with the world's best bowler out of them they will be poor 'tests' but it will please the Australians and that seems the principal thing according to our newspapers. Long before the Australians arrived in England there was an undercurrent in nearly all our newspaper articles which clearly meant, 'Please do not be unkind to our visitors; bowlers must not try to bowl the unbowlable Woodfull; and Bradman must always be allowed to score a century.' Not only our newspapers but also our public men voiced the same feeling. The Australians must be treated like spoiled children or they won't play.

A friend has offered to pay all my expenses to go and see the next Test (?) match in London but I have refused and have suggested the money should be sent to you instead.

For the courageous stand you have taken ... and for bringing back the Ashes to England you are worthy of a national testimonial. I have never met you but I am proud of you as a cricketer and an Englishman.

I was not chosen for the 1936 tour of Australia, although there was a good deal of newspaper support in my favour because of my bowling performances that year. I topped England's bowling averages, taking 119 wickets for 12 runs apiece. I had finished second in 1934 with 82 wickets, and in 1935 bagged more than 100 wickets. I remained one of the leading wicket-takers in 1937 and got my share in 1938. In all, I was at the top of England's bowling averages in 1927, 1928, 1931, 1932 and 1936. My idea after 1934 was to play county cricket only until I retired. Test cricket in which the thrills had gone did not interest me.

To give some idea of how I was bowling in 1936 here are some of my performances: 5 for 65 v. Gloucestershire, 6 for 55 and 5 for 40 *v.* Middlesex, 4 for 47 and 5 for 30 *v.* Essex, 2 for 39 and 6 for 34 *v.* Kent, 5 for 27 and 5 for 35 *v.* Lancashire, 5 for 50 *v.* Middlesex, 4 for 81 and 6 for 64 *v.* Kent, and 6 for 38 and 6 for 42 *v.* Surrey.

A cricket commentator asked Sir Stanley Jackson, chairman of the Cricket Committee of the MCC if Bill Voce and I would be picked for the Australian tour. Jackson was reported as saying: 'This is a matter of some difficulty. I must be excused from discussing it now. Obviously we are aware, as everybody is, of their bowling form this season; beyond that I can say nothing.'

It was a ticklish situation for the MCC. I had written indiscreetly and had declared I would never play for England again – the greatest honour in English cricket. No doubt the MCC felt I should not be coaxed into playing, as too great a price can be paid for any man's services – even for victory. And besides, they might be further embar-rassed if I refused to play. They were right. I would not have played. Bill Voce went to Australia and bowled well under the captaincy of Gubby Allen, the Australian-born Englishman who was popular in Australia and who was no doubt appointed captain in an attempt to bury the bodyline hatchet with Australia.

Before the beginning of that Test series, which Australia won three matches to two, Sydney *Truth* said in an editorial:

It is safe to say that if the critics had taken no notice of the last bodyline controversy nothing would have been heard of it. Our batsmen were frightened stiff by Larwood and his expresses. Frankly they did not know how to play him and the squeals that they sent up, supported by namby-pamby critics, who think that cricket should be a cottonwool game, resulted in England not playing her best bowler during the last series of Tests in England.

Australia won the series but there was little glory in it; for England did not put her strongest side into the field. The coming English side may develop into a devastating combination, and win back the Ashes. Whether it does or not, in the opinion of *Truth* it is not England's best team.

Occasionally other echoes of bodyline were heard. C. B. Fry reported in the Adelaide *News* on the second Test in 1936:

McCormick (Australia) began bowling in the Test today with the fastest leg theory he could muster. In fact, the difference between this and bodyline bowling consists in nothing but a difference of speed and accuracy. Few critics will dare tell you this, but I do so. McCormick is simply bowling to bump the batsmen out by leg side short stuff. He is scarcely good enough to succeed.

George Hele, one of the 1932–33 Test umpires, wrote of his observations from behind the stumps. In the course of saying that I did not bowl to hit the batsmen but certainly to intimidate and rattle them, he said:

Larwood that day, not only surprised me, but frightened me. His pace was terrific, his accuracy flawless. I have never seen Larwood or any other fast bowler attain such speed. But he frightened me when he switched to a leg side field. I watched every ball at close quarters. The thought kept recurring in my mind, 'If this cove hits a batsman, that man is going to be seriously injured.'

In 1938 in the Perth *Sunday Times*, I was to read a defence of bodyline by Clarrie Grimmett, the slow bowler, who said it was not unfair, and that batsmen were solely to blame because slow footwork made them more or less helpless against Voce and me.

While the English team was battling for the Ashes in Australia in 1936, I took a coaching job in India. The Maharajah of Cooch Behar had signed me up in London to coach for the Maharajah of Patiala, one of the world's wealthiest men and a great patron of the game in India. Two or three newspapers had wanted me to cover the Australian tour for them, with a 'ghost' at my elbow, but I declined and took the coaching job. I was to receive £250. But it was a failure: I didn't receive a penny apart from a few incidental expenses and got back to England flat broke.

That was an experience I will never forget. It took me three days and nights to reach Patiala, near Hyderabad and the only white man I saw on the journey among millions of people was a stationmaster. I was at Patiala for three weeks without receiving any money, and the only time I saw the Maharajah was once when he appeared in the distance riding a magnificently bedecked elephant.

I was to play in Bombay for a team of Europeans against an all-Indian team. I didn't have enough money to get there and, in trying to secure an appointment with the Maharajah, I waited in the hall of his palace from early in the morning until seven o'clock at night, before his tur-banned son noticed me. He asked me if I had had anything to eat and when I said no he clapped his hands, servants seemed to spring from everywhere, and I was dining in a matter of a couple of minutes.

I played in the Bombay match in about 105 degrees, suffered sunstroke, and decided I had had enough. My return passage had already been booked to England for three months ahead, but I persuaded the shipping company to bring it forward, and I left soon after on the *Strathaird*, lighter in pocket but wiser for my experience. The Maharajah's solicitors threatened to sue me for breach of contract, but when I wrote and told them what a poor deal I'd got I heard no more.

The following season I had my benefit match, against Yorkshire, and the *Sunday Express* had this to say:

Larwood is a fast bowler of genius, and in the last ten years he has thrilled millions both in England and Australia with the beautiful controlled fury of his action and deadly speed.

His poise at the moment of delivery is like that of a Greek sculpture, and his accuracy flows from his perfect balance. His break-back, too, is a thing to make one gasp at even from the ring. Small wonder that he has inspired counties – nations even – to extremes of hero worship and hate. Larwood has given up bowling at his fastest, for his injured foot might not stand the terrific strain of that stamp on the ground every time he loosed the ball.

He is still fast enough though, to make the wicketkeeper stand well back, and his accuracy is as marvellous as ever. Larwood should be filmed and shown to schools and county ground staffs all over the land.

He deserved brilliant sunshine and a fast bowler's wicket for his benefit match against Yorkshire instead of grey skies, half a gale of wind and intermittent rain. Yet there were nearly 15,000 people on the ground for the first day, and they did not fail to make their presence known when Larwood took a wicket. He bowled for the first hour from the pavilion end with the wind and got rid of Yorkshire's opening pair before the crowd had lost patience with them. Hutton was yorked off-stump at 9; and when 16 laborious singles had been scored in three-quarters of an hour Larwood gave Sutcliffe his break-back. For years and years Sutcliffe has presented two good Yorkshire pads to this ball; habit asserted itself and he was LBW under the new rule . . :

I still have the letter from the secretary of Notts Cricket Club, dated 6 December 1937, replying to my request to be relieved from the match against the Australians on their

1938 tour. The secretary, H. A. Brown, said: 'The committee agree to this, but they feel that it would redound to your credit if you did play.'

In 1938 Ted McDonald, then a professional coach at Blackpool, was killed in Lancashire when a car struck him on the roadside. I obtained my release from Nottinghamshire and took his place. When the war broke out in 1939 I retired from cricket for good and concentrated on growing vegetables and flowers in Nottingham.

In 1946 I bought a confectionery business in a side street in Blackpool. You wouldn't find my name over the door. A recluse never advertises. I just wanted to lead a quiet future and not to rekindle the past. Soccer became my only interest outside my family. If it hadn't been for the game, I would hardly have left the shop.

Nobody took a second look at the bespectacled man on Blackpool sands who sometimes bowled a rubber ball to the younger ones among his five daughters swinging a bat their father had carved for them out of an old piece of boxwood.

CHAPTER NINETEEN

Second Thoughts

WAS MY BODYLINE bowling 'unfair'? If I could have seen my own bowling I might have thought it so. Not because of any malevolence on my part but because of what the batsmen had to put up with.

I thought I was pretty fair, though. I believe I could have hit Bill Woodfull almost any time I liked, probably two or three times an over. All I needed to do was bowl ordinary pace and then slip in my extra-fast one just short of a length and breaking back. And yet I hit Bill seriously only twice, neither time on the head. I didn't mean to hit him on either occasion. You can discount hits on the thigh as being intentional because he would have been hit there occasionally anyway. I also think I could have seriously hit Bill Ponsford and Jack Fingleton fairly regularly had I been trying.

I never bowled to injure a man in my life. Frighten them, intimidate them, yes. I had a very unspectacular record of causing serious injuries to batsmen. Apart from Oldfield, the only others that I can remember were H. B. Cameron, the South African wicketkeeper, Patsy Hendren, and R. A. Sinfield the Gloucester opener. Cameron was carried off when I struck him on the head at Lord's in July 1929. He tried to hook a ball and missed. I have a picture of that incident and, as Cameron was being carried off, I had my hands on my head in genuine anxiety.

In 1931 when playing against Middlesex, I met Patsy Hendren and Mrs Hendren outside Lord's. 'Don't you hit my Patsy today,' chided Mrs Hendren. 'I'll knock his block off,' I said jokingly. I dropped one short to Patsy in the match, he shaped to hook, missed, and was struck on the head. He was taken to hospital, and I was horrified when I thought of what I'd said to Mrs Hendren. I wasn't game to face her for some time. When I went to the hospital, I found Patsy was all right, and he assured me it wasn't my fault.

In June 1934, about the time of the second Test against the Australians, I hit Sinfield on the head in a county match. He had been batting for almost four hours and was laid out for more than an hour. He stood up to me for another four hours in the second innings.

Sinfield said in a newspaper article published a fortnight later:

Probably I am better qualified than most to say whether Larwood's bowling is fair. In my opinion he is the straightest fast bowler in the game. His success is entirely due to his amazing accuracy and speed. He can pitch a ball with as much precision as any slow spin bowler and is at least two yards faster than any other man in the country. I remember playing against him at Nottingham where he was taking advantage of a worn pitch. For over after over every ball landed on that tiny circle.

If Larwood wanted to hit anyone he is so accurate he could do it every time. Actually his casualty list is one of the lowest in first-class cricket. The real trouble is that most batsmen are beaten before the ball leaves his hand. They are so demoralized that when he starts to run they start to back away from the crease. Larwood told me the other day he now gets threatening letters – unsigned – from his opponents . . .

The Australian Broadcasting Commission even published a book of statistics called *Cricket Casualties*, in which they listed the batsmen who had been struck and the bowlers who struck them. I headed the list with thirty-four 'victims', but I am sure I hit batsmen about the body more often than that in all the Tests I played. Herbert Sutcliffe headed the victims' list with eighteen blows, followed by Woodfull, eleven. The booklet pointed out that during the bodyline tour some of the batsmen including Woodfull were hit on the back and between the shoulder blades while ducking.

Bodyline could not be considered unfair in the broad meaning because it was perfectly within the rules. If it was unfair it was only because of my speed. That's what the batsmen didn't like, and that's what confused them. Bodyline, in theory, was no different from leg theory. It was the speed that made the difference. I was no more trying to hit the batsman than was Warwick Armstrong when he bowled slow leg theory. But I am not pretending that bodyline was not intended to intimidate the batsmen. I bowled to intimidate them, I didn't shed any crocodile tears if a batsman was hit on the thigh, and I am still bewildered at the success I had.

Was bodyline against the spirit of cricket? I have asked myself that question hundreds of times over the years. I am still not satisfied that it was. I have come to realize that bodyline was against the spirit of the game as applied to lower grades of cricket. On rough or uneven pitches against batsmen unskilled in the hook shot, it was palpably dangerous. It probably would have harmed the game if it had continued unabated in junior and social ranks. But you do not expect Test batsmen to have any weaknesses. If they have, the bowler has a right to exploit them.

I found a weakness among the Australian batsmen. Some of them did not show the traditional spirit of standing up and taking the bowler on. They put up the cry that batsmen facing bodyline had to either get hit or get out. That was not so: they could have used their bats to hit the ball. By drawing away from me they showed they didn't like it, and that encouraged me to send them down all the harder.

Stan McCabe proved bodyline could be played when he got his 187 not out. He made his runs by playing his natural game – hooking the rising balls and not letting the leg–side fieldsmen play on his mind. A batsman cannot place a hook shot precisely where he wants it, but he can hit it roughly in the direction he wants. I left plenty of open field for those who wanted to accept the challenge. Stan accepted it and thrashed me. Vic Richardson did the same thing to a lesser extent several times. The only time they got hit was when they didn't play their natural game and used their bats as a shield.

Stan was supposed to have received such a battering and become intimidated to such a degree that he didn't make any more runs after he got that 187. I think he was out of luck for a time, and also that instead of attacking the bowling on the leg side he adopted some of the methods of his team-mates of ducking.

The Australians helped to beat themselves. It wasn't until years later when I met some of them again that I learned why. They had elected not to hook in order to keep their wickets intact, believeing they would go cheaply to the leg-side fieldsmen if they did. This explains why we all thought the Australians were frightened. It was extraordinary to see them ducking and weaving, making the bowling look murderous stuff and giving the crowd the impression that Voce and I were out to kill them. It was a bad mistake. Had they stood up and used their bats to hit the ball, they might have smothered bodyline. Instead, they were caught in two minds and as a result were always struggling for runs in that series.

Woodfull probably had a good deal to do with this decision. The Queensland fast bowler G. H. Thurlow and others have said that the bodyline row would not have occurred if Australia had had a more astute captain. Woodfull was at a disadvantage not being able to hook with his slow-footedness and crouching style, and probably he influenced the other players because of his own attitude. But I do not question Woodfull's courage or sincerity. A very correct man, he gave reporters the impression he would rather sacrifice the Ashes than retaliate, and the Board of Control members were no doubt influenced in not seeking retaliation for the simple reason they could not call upon a really fast bowler. In that respect bodyline was a stroke of genius: the Australians were beaten on tactics.

Woodfull ducked frequently, at times unnecessarily I thought, but he also stood up to me, preferring to take balls on the body rather than make a stroke. Ponsford, Fingleton and Richardson behaved in a similar way. They had guts. Fingleton was probably the most courageous man I ever bowled to.

Bradman's approach was different. He didn't want any knocks or to take risks. In some respects Bradman's and my career were similar. We both came from humble beginnings, cricket being the one thing which lifted us out of the crowd, and we achieved fame in the same era. I think that as Don looked down the wicket at me when I ran in to bowl, he could see his career flash in front of him: he was a national hero and making more money than he had thought possible. One error of timing could end the lot. I wish Don had shown more of the traditional spirit, just as I wish the bodyline row had never developed. But I do not blame him.

I believe that no criticism of Bradman can be valid because above all he did try to score runs. I felt he was always giving me a chance, and I preferred bowling to him and McCabe than any of the other Australians. I think bodyline erupted because it was felt that Don had failed the Australian crowds, yet he finished the series with an average of 56, just ahead of Hammond and Sutcliffe for England. But he didn't make the big scores the crowds expected of him. The alert Australians were quick to sense that bodyline had been hatched for his discomfort. It will be seen that I do not agree with my former skipper, who, after the Tests, wrote that he was sorry to disappoint anybody who imagined leg theory was evolved with the help of midnight oil and iced towels simply and solely for the purpose of combating Bradman's effectiveness as a scoring machine. Jardine said, 'However highly Bradman may have been rated, this view is exaggerated. It did, however, seem a reasonable assumption that a weakness in one of Australia's premier batsmen might find more than a replica in the play of a good many of his contemporaries, some of whom had doubtless modelled their play on his.'

Bodyline was devised for Don: it would never have been used if he had not drawn away at the Oval in 1930 to avoid being hit. He asserted later that he didn't think it could be mastered. I think it could, if a batsman was prepared to take risks.

Bodyline gave the crowd their money's worth. But it left a mark. For one thing it has killed off the hook shot. I think something psychological crept into the game after the bodyline controversy. Perhaps players think they cannot receive many short-pitched balls before the umpire cries 'unfair' and so they don't worry. It is a pity, and cricket is less a game because of it. Bodyline, because of its success, also ushered in an era when teams relied almost 90 per cent on fast bowling. It inspired the Lindwall–Miller combination and that of the Statham–Trueman–Tyson attack. There was a time when England opened with a slow bowler at one end.

Any attacking batsman who could hook and had a little luck could have handled bodyline. It's a pity we don't have a sampling of bodyline today to remind batsmen that their bat is there to hit the ball with and not merely to protect themselves; it would make them realize how spoon-fed they are.

Look how a game lives when the West Indians are at the crease. They give the bowler a chance, thrill the crowd and the match has character and interest.

Australia won the 1964 Test series in England, but what a colourless victory it was – four games drawn out of five. The batsmen of today shouldn't be any less skilful than they were thirty or forty years ago, but it seems that the standard has dropped. Certainly Australia has no Bradman or McCartney or Jackson or McCabe or a bowler like O'Reilly, and England has no Hobbs, Hammond, Sutcliffe, Leyland or Hendren, but I think the essential difference is in the batsmen's attitude – they do not have an attacking outlook today.

Legislators are repeatedly changing the rules to help the batsman. The rules should be left alone. The number of fieldsmen on the leg are now being restricted to five. Why? A few drops of rain fall, and the batsmen of today are convinced the wicket is bad. Trumper on the 1902 English tour scored eleven centuries in one of the wettest seasons in memory. What has the rule that a bowler must keep his front foot *behind* the popping crease done to brighten cricket? Nothing, only to make it harder for the bowler.

I doubt whether as many young people are taking up cricket today as they did formerly. Certainly they do not seem as keen as they were in my time. I think this is shown in Australia by the fact that if you look at the Melbourne district or the Sydney grade sides you will see veterans who have been batting and bowling for the past fifteen years. Countless thousands enjoy their weekend games in every country without a care for what has happened to standards, and will continue to do so. But is there another Bradman or a demon bowler in the house to fire young imaginations?

Bodyline cannot happen again. Quite apart from the rules, it could not happen without Jardine. It would have died in Australia without him. I thought Jardine was tough on me at the time – if he hadn't insisted on my bowling in the last Test I would not have broken down. But if he had wavered, discipline would have suffered, and the team could have gone to pieces.

It was suggested in some quarters that I was opposed to bodyline, and it is certainly true that towards the end of the tour I became heartily sick of the arguments it had stirred up and depressed and exasperated by the physical demands made on me, even when I had run myself into the ground. But at no time did I want to give up bodyline bowling because I thought it 'unfair'.

I accept responsibiity for all the trouble that was caused, but it should not be forgotten that Bill Voce was also involved. Had I refused to bowl bodyline there would not have been any row, but I did what I wanted. When the eruption came I kept quiet about how it all started. I didn't want to embarrass Jardine or Carr or any of my fellow-players. It sickened me later though to hear players who had supported bodyline in Australia speaking out against it in England. If everybody had stood firm, batsmen and bowlers would have worked out a solution to bodyline. I can't see myself doing anything different a second time, but if I had my whole life over again I wouldn't be a fast bowler: it's too much hard work.

I have heard it said many times that the Test wickets I took in 1932–33 were mainly tailenders. That is not so. Of the 33 wickets only 9 could be considered tailenders. Sixteen were bowled, 15 caught and 2 were out leg-before.

Those bowled were: Bradman (twice), Woodfull (twice), Ponsford (twice), O'Brien (once), Kippax (once), O'Reilly (four times), Ironmonger (twice), Fingleton (once), Nagel (once). Caught were: Bradman (twice), Richardson (three times), Ponsford (once), Fingleton (twice), Oldfield (twice), McCabe (once), Bromley (once), Grimmett (once), O'Reilly (once) and Woodfull (once). Leg-before were Kippax and Love.

Many years after the bodyline tour I read an article by Hugh Buggy, who saw every ball bowled in that series, and said:

Larwood was the fastest and most devastating bowler we've seen in Australia in the last forty years. His catapult deliveries made him a terror to batsmen whether he bowled to an off field or on the wicket or attacked the leg stump. But having seen a lot of Harold Larwood both on and off the field in that remarkable tour I am positive that at no time did he bowl with any malevolent intention of injuring a batsman. He bumped the ball to unsettle or intimidate the batsmen, certainly, but not with the idea of knocking them over.

Larwood's Nottingham team-mate Bill Voce and the rangy Yorkshireman Bill Bowes also bowled many short balls that blazed past the batsmen's shoulders. But for hostility, accuracy, pace and for morale-breaking, the bowling of Voce to that of Larwood was as flat as soda water is to champagne. Eliminate the Notts Express and those shock tactics at once lost 60 per cent of their hostility . . .

When I met Buggy again long afterwards I asked him, as an experienced and trained observer, to give me his final judgment on bodyline. I don't accept entirely what he wrote for me:

I think the bowling was dangerous. It was very dangerous to the slow-footed batsman. Larwood's great speed and accuracy was the point of danger. Any batsman at any moment could have walked into one of his deliveries and at that speed it was possible to fracture a man's skull and kill him on the spot. I think bodyline would have ruined cricket. Batsmen would have had to come out in armour and headguards if Larwood had been on. There was no doubt his pace was the decisive factor in the general hue and cry.

Stork Hendry, the international whom I battered in 1928, went on record later as saying:

Larwood was the fastest bowler I played against or saw since just before World War I. And I played against Tibby Cotter in 1912 when he was still at his top. I laugh today when I hear people talking about Lindwall and Tyson being faster. Larwood was yards faster. The modern-day crop of fast bowlers only *look* fast because the wicket-keeper stands right back. To get the ball up they have to drop it half-way down the wicket. The difference with Larwood was he used to make it rear at you from a good length.

When I retired I gave up watching cricket. I was disillusioned. There was an occasion, though, when I went to see Lancashire play the Australian Infantry Forces team. Wally Hammond saw me from a balcony and beckoned me to go up. I just shook my head. George Duckworth came down and took me to the dressing-room. The secretary asked me how I got into the ground.

'I paid.'

'You what?'

'I paid. I am not going to knock on anybody's door.'

'Look, Harold,' said the secretary. 'You're never to pay at this ground again. For what we owe you in cricket you shouldn't have to pay.'

'Thanks,' I said. But I never went back.

One day, in 1948, George Duckworth came to my confectionery shop. He had somebody with him. It was Jack Fingleton. It was the first time I had met any of the Australians since 1933. We went into the lounge and sat down, but conversation came slowly at first. Jack was a newspaperman on tour with the Australian team, and I didn't want to say anything he might use. We were talking about the sunshine in Australia. 'It wouldn't take me long to settle out there,' I said.

Two days later the newspapers announced that I was planning to emigrate to Australia. I began getting letters from Australia. Frank O'Keefe, the Mayor of Gunnedah in New South Wales, offered me a job and a house and so, too, did the Australian Paper Mills at Burnie in Tasmania. There were other letters, and I began to think I might be well received. But my wife wouldn't hear of it. Our five girls were always suffering from colds in the dank English climate, and I was concerned about their future. I had many happy memories of Australia. I knew it was a young country with a future and that plenty of jobs were available for those not afraid to work. England had lost some of its pull for me.

Just before the end of the 1948 tour I received an invitation from a London newspaper to a farewell luncheon for Bradman. I didn't know whether to accept or not. I wasn't sure how Don would react to meeting me again. I didn't want to reopen old wounds. I just wanted to forget. But my wife said I should go for the sake of the children. Then a letter arrived from George Duckworth asking me if I would accompany him. That decided me.

It was a wonderful occasion. When Don and I shook hands photographers were all around us. Don was very friendly, and we had a pleasant chat, but I think we skated round the bodyline days. We asked each other how we were getting on.

Conversation was much freer with other Australians I met there, including Jack Fingleton and Bill O'Reilly, and I sat at a table with Ray Lindwall, Arthur Morris, Keith Miller, Bill Johnson and one or two others. They made a fuss of me and I did so much talking I hardly ate a thing. It made me feel good.

Twelve months went by, and one morning I left the sweet-scales to tear open an envelope that helped heal a sixteen-year-old wound. It was an invitation to become an honorary member of the MCC. My name was on the first list of retired professionals to be recognized in this way.

My girls had always been a bit daft about Australia, ever since I brought back a koala, 'Billie Bluegum' for the eldest, June, in 1933. Billie, now a little the worse for wear with only one ear, and no eyes, had been handed down and was now the proud property of my youngest girl, three-year-old Sylvia.

June was engaged and wasn't keen on going to Australia, and the family was divided. I sold my shop to the man I promised it to for £5,000. I was glad to leave it – everything was on ration, I worked seven days a week, and it only returned little more than a living.

I rang the Orient Line in London but was told there was no passage for two years, but an agent in Blackpool fixed it up for me in six weeks. 'A good job your name was Larwood,' he said. I cabled Jack Fingleton asking him if he could find me a house temporarily, and he replied that he would.

We were to sail on 28 April 1950. June folded her trousseau away and greased her new sewing-machine for the voyage out. Mum bought clothes and schoolbooks for studies on the ship, and I took my cricketing pictures down from the walls and packed away my trophies. We booked in at a hotel in Bloomsbury for one last look round.

Jardine gave me a farewell luncheon at a London club. He had written to me earlier saying he wanted to do that. Herbert Sutcliffe was there and one or two others. Jardine made a speech and then gave me a pencil which Jack Hobbs had presented to him after scoring his hundredth century. An inscription on the pencil says, 'D. R. Jardine. From Jack Hobbs, 1925.' Jack had given every member of the Surrey team a pencil.

I asked Jardine what Hobbs would think of him giving me the pencil. 'Jack will be thrilled to know you have it,' he replied.

Sutcliffe and I went to see Jack Hobbs (he had not yet been knighted) at his Fleet Street sports store, but he wasn't in and we found him having lunch in a near-by club. 'This calls for champagne,' said Jack. I showed him the pencil and asked him what he thought of it. 'It's an honour to know you have it,' said the Master.

We had so much champagne I was ill. I didn't wake up till midnight and had the worst hangover the next morning I have ever had in my life.

John Arlott and a few pressmen saw me off. Nobody from the MCC came. Just as we were about to leave Tilbury, it started to snow, a rare occurrence in England in April. I marshalled the girls, and said, 'Have a good look at it. You probably won't see any more.'

From Tilbury we gradually slipped away from the dreary suburbs, the dingy factories blackened with the smoke of ages, the factory whistles, the hoot of tugs, the roar of the traffic fell behind. The sounds of London beat with a strong pulse. It was a wrench to leave England behind.

The *Orontes* brought back memories. It was the same ship that took me to Australia in 1932.

CHAPTER TWENTY

Fifty Years After

ALL WAS QUIET. The scene was as peaceful and tranquil as an old oil painting. Adelaide Oval was certainly not like this in 1933 the day I hit Bertie Oldfield.

The Board of Control secretary met me in Adelaide and took me on a tour of the city. I stood inside the cricket ground for several minutes, reliving the bodyline feud in silence.

In Melbourne quite a crowd had come to the ship to meet me. Someone asked me if I wanted to meet Bill Woodfull.

'I don't know,' I said. 'Does Bill Woodfull want to meet me?'

They said it had all been arranged. I was taken to Melbourne High School where Bill was headmaster, and we shook hands and had a pleasant talk. We buried the hatchet and became friends.

Jack Fingleton met me in Sydney, and I was mobbed by reporters there. One reporter asked, 'Have you come out here to retire, Harold?' 'My name's Larwood, not Bradman,' I said. I meant that Don had made all the money he needed out of cricket. The reporter scribbled furiously and Jack Fingleton stepped in. 'If you write that I'll skin you,' he said.

I was amazed at my reception. Many people came to the ship just to look at me, as they did in Melbourne.

Jack Fingleton had arranged accommodation for us at the Nine Ways Hotel at Kingsford, a few miles out of the city. There were eight of us, including June's fiancé, Cyril Roper, and I was surprised how cheap the accommodation was – £16 a week. They even had new furniture in the rooms. I hadn't realized until then that Jack lived in Canberra, 200 miles from Sydney, and that I had put him to a great deal of inconvenience, but he didn't mind in the least. Six weeks later we bought a house in Kingsford and my family settled down to life 'Down Under'.

Bert Oldfield took us all to dinner at Sydney's Hotel Australia and several of the old Australian players, including Stork Hendry, entertained us in their homes. I met Bill O'Reilly, Stan McCabe and most of the boys again.

Early in 1951 Jack Fingleton took me to Canberra because he said Ben Chifley wanted to meet me. Ben was the federal opposition Leader in the Australian Parliament and had previously been the Labour Prime Minister for a record period. The son of a blacksmith and a footplate philosopher for many years when he drove an engine for the New South Wales Railways, Chifley was one of the great Australians and a real democrat. He had a wry sense of humour and even as Prime Minister he always had trouble keeping an old curved stem pipe alight.

He had come up the hard way, was sacked from the railways in 1917 for taking part in a strike, was reinstated as a cleaner, and fought his way up through the depression and rowdy campaign meetings to become Prime Minister.

I was glad I met Chifley because he died a little later, on 13 June, 1951. He died as he lived – without overmuch fuss, his last evening spent working in an unpretentious hotel room for the Labor Party he loved. News of his death was announced while a glittering state ball was being held in Parliament House, Canberra, to celebrate the Commonwealth's centenary. Gaiety turned to gloom under the blazing chandeliers and genuine tears were shed that night.

It wasn't till after his death that Jack Fingleton told me Ben Chifley had paid half my hotel bill when I first came to Sydney and had asked him not to mention it to anybody. I understood then why the tariff was only £16.

While walking in Martin Place in Sydney one day in 1952, I bumped into Don Bradman. We stood there chatting and nobody recognized us.

'This is not like the old days, Don,' I said.

'How do you mean, Harold?'

'Thirty years ago there would have been hundreds around us by now.' Don just laughed.

I couldn't help thinking how Fate had treated us both. The game had been perhaps overkind to one, unkind to the other. Don was wealthy and was on the Board of Cricket Control. I was working for a living on the assembly line of a soft drink firm. And Don was the amateur.

But that is cricket. I expected no favours and didn't mind working hard for a living. Late in 1953 Douglas Jardine visited Australia. He was sent as a director of an English firm to inspect pastoral properties in North Australia because it was considered that he knew the situation in Australia. Arthur Mailey enquired in the *Daily Telegraph* in Sydney: 'Anybody knowing the whereabouts of Douglas Jardine who is believed to be in Australia please let him know that I would be prepared to invite him to lunch.' I think that as a result, a luncheon was arranged. Those present apart from Jardine and me were the Prime Minister Mr Menzies (not yet knighted), Charlie McCartney, Warren Bardsley, John Taylor, Bert Oldfield and Mailey.

We sat round at the Pickwick Club with Mr Menzies, one of the keenest of cricket observers, in the middle, and talking to each one of us in turn. He told me I was the fastest and one of the greatest fast bowlers he had seen since World War I. We all talked and laughed about bodyline.

McCartney declared that he would have belted the cover off bodyline balls. 'I'd have had a crack at you and it would have been you or me for it,' he said. Johnny Taylor reckoned he would have played me with a broomstick. I remember Mr Menzies showing his exceptional knowledge of the game by correcting somebody who mentioned Mailey's bowling averages in a Victoria–New South Wales match. The indiscreet member of the party said that 365 runs had been knocked off Mailey's bowling in the match when the world record score of 1,107 was made, and Mr Menzies said it was actually 362.

Mr Menzies told Bardsley he was one of the finest left-handers in the game. 'People will talk about you after I'm dead and gone,' said Mr Menzies. Bardsley died three days later.

Eventually, we strolled outside into the street and chatted with the Prime Minister for a few more minutes before he got into his car, and I thought what a remarkable place it was with people passing by not even giving a second look at their Prime Minister. In England they would have surrounded him. Australians are like that – they are not easily impressed.

An incident at the Sydney Cricket Ground about this time made me glad I had moved to Australia. The Master at Arms of the *Orontes* had brought out a bat from the Bishop of Chelmsford to have it autographed by the English team. I knocked on the door and explained the request to Trevor Bailey. 'I don't want the bat,' he told me bluntly. 'Well, I don't,' I said, and tossed it inside the dressing-room. It was retrieved later with the signatures on it. I was not made welcome in the English dressing-room, but I found Richie Benaud and the rest of his team pleased to see me when I dropped in and so, too, were the West Indies on a later occasion.

A correspondent who was introduced to Trevor Bailey at the Palace Hotel, Perth, on the tour told me that when he asked the Englishman what he thought of Australia, Bailey replied: 'Dee-lightful place you know – if it wasn't popu-lated.' I assume he was joking.

Not one unpleasant remark has been directed at me since I came to Australia. I like Australians, and I find them easy to get on with. It is my experience that, broadly speaking, there is no class distinction in Australia. The only notice-able distinction is that caused by degrees of wealth, and often that doesn't seem to matter.

Life is much more egalitarian in Australia. Even in the hotels people of different background and social status mingle closely. In England there is one room for the workers, one for the middle class and another for the 'better' class. Out here there is a fair living for everyone who wants to work, and the climate is marvellous.

We have absolutely no regrets about coming to Australia, where at one time I thought I was hated. To all of us Australians have been a warm and friendly people. In those first few years some members of the family had an occasional yearning for England, and for many years Mum expressed homesickness for the English spring. In 1952, June and Cyril Roper returned to England, planning to stay two years – but they were back in Australia after nine months. None of us would ever return to England to live permanently.

All the girls love the sunshine, the open spaces, the cleanliness and the more relaxed way of life in Australia. The girls are all married with children, owning good homes with their husbands and enjoying all the trappings of a comfortable middle-class lifestyle, such as cars and swimming pools.

At the age of seventy-seven, just thirty-two years after migrating to Australia. I became a great-grandfather. There are thirteen grandchildren in the family. To realize that I have a daughter over fifty makes me feel very old indeed, but the wonderful gift of good health remained with me.

For many years after coming to Sydney I tended to live a quiet, somewhat monastic type of life, working in a printery to support the family and spending most of my leisure time at home. My real pleasures centred on family life.

I preferred not to meet any of the cricketers of my time, and to some extent I still feel the same even today. I would rather remember them as they were, just as I prefer to be remembered as I was.

I know my name in cricket history will be inseparable from the term 'bodyline', and I don't mind being remembered for bowling bodyline. I wish to remember the great cricketers I knew and played against as I see them when I look around the memorabilia in my living-room. And as I look around the walls, I live.

My fragile links with the momentous past included a Christmas card every year from George Duckworth until his death and the list of fixtures sent by the MCC. The walls of my living-room are lined with photographs, and my white mantelpiece is studded with trophies. A glass cabinet contains more of them. I have, mounted in silver and suitably inscribed, the ball which Stan McCabe hit so hard to score his 187. I have other cricket balls from stirring games, silver trays, rose bowls and cigarette boxes and illuminated addresses on the walls. One of my most treasured photographs is of Jack Gregory bowling his last ball in Test cricket to me – in attempting the catch in Brisbane in 1928, he injured a knee and his great career came to an end. I have a trunk full of newspaper clippings and several albums of photographs.

My home in the suburb of Kingsford is less than 3 miles from the Sydney Cricket Ground. Often I stood in my back garden when big sporting events were played on the SCG and sometimes, when the wind blew, I could hear the mob on the Hill roar . . . it brought back the memories. And that's the way I preferred it, reliving the past in this vicarious manner rather than through direct contact with old and present players. I even avoided the English players when they came out, unless they contacted me, and did not watch cricket except on television.

In a way my attitude was based on fear – fear of re-opening the old wounds, of being hurt again and stirring up the old controversies. Also, it seemed far safer to dwell alone in the afterglow of events in which one soared with eagles, rather than run the risk of being dragged into some form of renewed bitterness.

But a gradual change came over me. The friendship of Australians, and my complete acceptance by them played a role; they made me feel at home, and over the years it became clear no rancour existed towards me. The publication of my autobiography in England in 1965 helped, too. It buried the hatchet in my mind by telling the English people how deeply I felt at my treatment by the establishment, who tried to make me the scapegoat over bodyline. It helped to put the record straight.

Well-wishers from all over the British Commonwealth

contacted me, and it was a good feeling to know I wasn't blamed any more. People in Sydney took to ringing me up or dropping around to my home for a chat, and the general feeling of warmth towards me did a lot to restore my confidence. Sydney Cricket Ground made me an honorary life member.

I am grateful for the friendship of many former cricketers, men like Keith Miller, Ginty Lush and Alan McGilvray, to numerous officials and businessmen such as Brian O'Connor, for the kind way they have treated me. Often I have been overwhelmed by the fuss sportsmen in Sydney have made of me. Sadly, though, my two best friends have died – Bertie Oldfield and Jack Fingleton.

I have been back to England three times on sponsored trips, and my reception was heart-warming, both from the MCC and my old club, Notts. I met many old mates, among them Bill Voce, former Notts opening bat Walter Keeting, Alf Gover and Andy Sandham – the great Surrey opener who was kept out of Test cricket by the partnership of Hobbs and Sutcliffe. My itinerary in England was jam-packed, and it was nice to see England and old friends again. But I had no wish to live there again.

In recent years I have taken to going to cricket matches again, but only for special occasions. I hesitated for months before accepting an official invitation from the Australian Board of Control to visit Melbourne for the centenary Test against England, and only after Jack Fingleton spoke to my wife Lois did I agree.

I felt a little frightened at that game. Cricket official Bob Parrish asked Bill Voce and me to walk out on to the ground in the luncheon adjournment so the crowd could acknowledge us. It was announced over the PA system, and I was extremely reluctant at first. Bodyline and the roar of those crowds of the time were still vividly with me.

Many changes have occurred in cricket since my move to Sydney. The greatest has been World Series play, and although I can appreciate the game needed a shake up, I can't say I really approve of this style of cricket, Media chief Kerry Packer must be thanked for gaining proper financial rewards for cricketers, but in my day it was enough to play for your country just for the thrill of it.

I don't like one-day limited over cricket. It's just not cricket to go out and slog. The standard of play suffers. I think there's too much cricket these days, the game loses its razor-sharp competitive edge, and players and the public tend to become jaded. I don't like those fancy colours. And as for all that hugging and kissing that goes on after a wicket falls – it's terrible. A bowler is there to take wickets, and he shouldn't need to be embraced frequently just for doing his job. That's probably an old-fashioned view, but I don't think exhibitionism adds anything to the quality of a game. I would accept a four-day World Series match, provided it was played in white. And without the kiss-in-the-ring.

I consider I was both lucky and unlucky in my career. Lucky to have bowled against such great batsmen, but unlucky because it was always a struggle to get their wickets. The greatest all-round-the-wicket batsmen of my time were Hobbs, Hammond, Hendren, George Gunn, Ernest Tyldesley and Percy Holmes.

For Australia, Don Bradman was in a class on his own for his prolific scoring, and Archie Jackson, Alan Kippax, McCartney, Ponsford and McCabe were superb all-round-the-wicket players.

You hear talk that modern-day batsmen like Greg Chappell are as good as Bradman, or at least compared with him. Chappell would not be in the same street, nor would any other Australian or batsman from any other country since the war. It can be difficult comparing players down the years when you have not competed against them, but I have no hesitation in saying Bradman is the greatest batsman in my lifetime. I doubt if there will ever be another like him.

Such an accolade as greatest batsman of all can only rest between Bradman and Hobbs. Jack Hobbs was the classical stylist, a polished performer who played on all types of wickets with an easy artistry. He was brought up on sticky wickets whereas Bradman played on concrete in his formative years. And yet there was nothing to fault about

Bradman's playing on unfamiliar pitches. When he failed, other batsmen failed too. Don was incredibly hard to get out on any kind of wicket. I believe that taking everything into account for sheer run-getting and crowd thrilling, I must give Don the edge over the beautiful stylist that was Hobbs. But Jack remains my idol.

Since the war I have not seen any batsmen from Australia or England who have equalled the all-round-the-wicket players I have mentioned. Post-war batsmen have not had to face fast bowling of the type that was to be met with before the war – and I include Lillee, Thomson and Lindwall and Miller in that comment. There have been no demons since the war to make 'em draw away.

In my era I put Bill Voce first among the English fast bowlers followed by Gubby Allen, Bill Bowes (in England) and Ken Farnes. Voce was always difficult to play, swinging the ball and coming up into the batsmen because of his height and aggressive delivery. Allen was particularly good when he had his tail up.

Jack Gregory I nominate still as the greatest among the Australian fast bowlers. There was little between him and Ted McDonald in regard to speed, but I think Jack was just a little bit ahead of his great opening partner because he was a man of more terrifying appearance. I admired Tim Wall for his great tenacity and big heart but he lacked the paralysing speed.

As for Dennis Lillee, the world record wicket holder, I place him alongside Ray Lindwall. In my opinion he is the equal of Lindwall, but not ahead of him.

Lillee has had the advantage of playing against many weak teams, such as Pakistan, India and New Zealand, and he also had more Tests than Lindwall, Gregory or McDonald. Ted McDonald had the most beautiful action of any fast bowler I ever saw. A pity he died early before completing his career.

Lindwall had to take his wickets against players of the calibre of Hutton, Edrich and Compton, whereas the toughest Lillee faced appears to be Geoff Boycott. Lindwall definitely faced better batsmen than Lillee, though a couple of the West Indian batsmen in Lillee's time have been class players.

There are obvious difficulties in comparing fast bowlers from different eras and to a large extent the judgment must be subjective. But as great as Lindwall and Lillee have been, I doubt if either would have got into a team ahead of Gregory and McDonald.

Jeff Thomson was too erratic to make any permanent impression. He was quick and could make the batsmen wince, but in my estimation he was not accurate enough to be a great bowler. The top batsmen of my era would simply have waited for the loose ones he so frequently let go and punished him. He wasted his efforts outside the off stump far too much.

Lindwall, on the other hand, was one of the most accurate of fast bowlers, and clever, but he lacked that little bit of fiery aggression which struck terror in the hearts of batsmen. Keith Miller had the dynamite, but it's a pity a lot of his efforts were needed for batting.

I liked the look of Freddie Truman, Frank Tyson, Brian Statham and Alan Davidson, though none matched the standard of Gregory and McDonald, or even Bill Voce or Gubby Allen or, in England, Bill Bowes, or on his day when his blood was up, Ken Farnes. Tyson was really quick for only one season in Australia. Wes Hall was quick and Michael Holding can be when he likes, but not consistently.

Wes Hall is still the nearest approach to a fast bowler I've seen since the war who could make batsmen and spectators sit up and take notice. Lillee can do the same, but I don't think either made the batsmen draw away from sheer fright.

I remember Maurice Tate as the greatest English medium-pacer, with George Geary behind him. Bill O'Reilly for Australia was in a class of his own, the best bowler of his kind I ever saw from any country. He was always on a length, attacking all the time, and could spin vicously with control.

Wilfred Rhodes was the best English slow bowler I saw,

followed by Charlie Parker, Titch Freeman and Hedley Verity. All these bowlers had superb control.

Grimmett was the best of the Australian slow bowlers ahead of Mailey and Bert Ironmonger. Mailey could bowl equally as good a ball as Grimmett but he put down some rubbish in between.

Bradman and Hobbs were two players who could do something with the ball and both could have been really good slow bowlers if they had not concentrated on batting.

Bert Oldfield was the greatest wicketkeeper I saw, with Duckworth next. I shall never forget Bradman and Hobbs at cover-point, Gregory or Hammond in the slips or Tommy Andrews or Percy Chapman close in.

Constantine was the world's best all-rounder of my time and Hammond not far behind. Leary Constantine must go down as the century's most dazzling fieldsman, fast bowler and hurricane hitter. He fully earned his nickname of 'Electric Heels' because he performed so many contortions on the field that his bones might have been made of rubber. He often snatched up a ball in the outfield while running towards the fence and threw it smack into the keeper's gloves without taking a sighting.

The crowd loved the antics of this born showman – kicking up his heels behind with the ball between them, flicking it over his head into his hands in front. Leary played for the love of the game and although his Test average was only 19 his cross-bat smites for sixes thrilled thousands. As Sir Leary, lawyer and diplomat, he became a champion of the coloured people.

I also have memories of the captains. Fender of Surrey was the shrewdest and most astute I ever encountered in county cricket, especially on slow wickets, and Carr next. Both could extract the utmost out of a situation and get the best out of their men. I would place Jardine after them in county play, but he was the best I ever played under in Tests.

Jardine was on the shy side and had a peculiar sense of humour, but he was a far stronger character and a better

captain than has been credited over the years. He understood me better than I realized at the time, though I thought
him too tough then. When he annoyed me in the last Test in
Sydney in 1933 by sending me in early to bat, and I came
off after scoring 98, Jardine surprised me with
unaccustomed friendliness by slapping me on the shoulder
and saying: 'You little bastard – I knew you could play.'

Patrician, aloof and irritating this Oxford-educated
lawyer and upper-class Englishman might have been, but
without his strength of character there would have been no
bodyline. It could not have survived the pressure. In that
respect it would not be unrealistic to regard the amateur
Jardine as the first cricketer who was fully professional, in
that he went on to the field with one thing in mind – to win
and to do so at any cost within the rules.

When he died in 1958 the MCC's flag flew at half-mast at
Lord's during an England–Australia Test game and *The
Times* said in an obituary: 'He always regarded cricket as
"only a game".'

A lifelong friend and past MCC president, Sir Hubert
Ashton, MP, said of Jardine in a memorial address in St
Michael's, London: 'He was courageous and single-minded
– an example to us all to play a better innings ourselves,
however bad the light and however broken the wicket.'

In spite of the bitterness of those bodyline days, cricket
has been kind to me. It enriched my life, enabling me to see
places I would never have seen and form friendships I
would otherwise never have enjoyed.

I met King George V, the Prince of Wales, various Prime
Ministers and a whole range of personalities, among them
Gladys Moncrieff in Australia. Down the mine I would not
have met anybody outside the local village.

Above all, cricket enabled me to find a new life for my
family, and I'm happy in the land of my adoption. I'm an
Aussie now. We're all Aussies.

More than fifty years after all that tumult, bodyline
seems a long way off. But the memories are vivid. I still
remember every detail of those torrid Tests. I look back
with excitement and a feeling of exhilaration, knowing the

sporting combat of those bodyline Tests was played out to the highest pinnacle of emotion and ability, to the ultimate pitch of achievement that mind and muscle could command.

The personal wounds I felt so deeply after that bodyline tour have healed, the bitterness melted. But when I think seriously about it I still carry a slight resentment towards the MCC for their weakness in trying to blame me for all the trouble that erupted; I know that if I had agreed to be the bunny by accepting the blame, the interfering politicians of Whitehall would have been appeased, the honour of all those gentlemen from the MCC who sent me bravo cables for my bowling would have been upheld, and I would have played for England again.

And I still feel a tinge of disappointment with the officials of my old club for the coolness they showed towards me after bodyline. When finally in 1938, after a disagreement, I applied for my contract to be terminated so I could play for Blackpool, the Notts committee sent me a terse letter 'graciously granting' my request. Nothing else. Not a word of thanks for my long years of service.

But, fifty years and more after bodyline, none of that seems at all vital any more.

Except for one thing. I'm still glad to this day that I never apologized.

Appendix A 125th Test

AT SYDNEY, 2, 3, 4, 5, 6, 7 December 1932
England won by 10 wickets

AUSTRALIA

	1st Innings		2nd Innings	
W. M. Woodfull	c. Ames b. Voce	7	b. Larwood	0
W. H. Ponsford	b. Larwood	32	b. Voce	2
J. H. Fingleton	c. Allen b. Larwood	26	c. Voce b. Larwood	40
A. F. Kippax	lbw b. Larwood	8	b. Larwood	19
S. J. McCabe	not out	187	lbw b. Hammond	32
V. Y. Richardson	c. Hammond b. Voce	49	c. Voce b. Hammond	0
W. A. Oldfield	c. Ames b. Larwood	4	c. Leyland b. Larwood	1
C. V. Grimmett	c. Ames b. Voce	19	c. Allen b. Larwood	5
L. Nagel	b. Larwood	0	not out	21
W. J. O'Reilly	b. Voce	4	b. Voce	7
T. W. Wall	c. Allen b. Hammond	4	c. Ames b. Allen	20
	Byes, 12; l-b, 4; n-b, 4	20	Byes, 12; l-b, 2; wides, 1; n-b, 2	17
	Total	360	Total	164

	O.	M.	R.	W.	O.	M.	R.	W.
Larwood	31	5	96	5	18	4	28	5
Voce	29	4	110	4	17.3	5	54	2
Allen	15	1	65	0	9	5	13	1
Verity	13	4	35	0	4	1	15	0
Hammond	14.2	0	34	1	15	6	37	2

ENGLAND

H. Sutcliffe	lbw b. Wall	194	not out	1
R. E. S. Wyatt	lbw b. Grimmett	38	not out	0
W. R. Hammond	c. Grimmett b. Nagel	112		
The Nawab of Pataudi	b. Nagel	102		
M. Leyland	c. Oldfield b. Wall	0		
D. R. Jardine	c. Oldfield b. McCabe	27		
H. Verity	lbw b. Wall	2		
G. O. Allen	c. and b. O'Reilly	19		
L. E. G. Ames	c. McCabe b. O'Reilly	0		
H. Larwood	lbw b. O'Reilly	0		
W. Voce	not out	0		
	Byes, 7; l-b, 17; n-b, 6	30		
	Total	524	Total	0 for 1

	O.	M.	R.	W.	O.	M.	R.	W.
Wall	38	4	104	3	—	—	—	—
Nagel	43.4	9	110	2	—	—	—	—
O'Reilly	67	32	117	3	—	—	—	—
Grimmett	64	22	118	1	—	—	—	—
McCabe	15	2	42	1	0.1	0	1	0
Kippax	2	1	3	0	—	—	—	—

Appendix B 126th Test

AT MELBOURNE 30, 31 December, 2, 3 January 1932–33
Australia won by 111 runs

AUSTRALIA

	1st Innings		2nd Innings	
J. H. Fingleton	*b.* Allen	83	*c.* Ames *b.* Allen	1
W. M. Woodfull	*b.* Allen	10	*c.* Allen *b.* Larwood	26
L. P. O'Brien	*run out*	10	*b.* Larwood	11
D. G. Bradman	*b.* Bowes	0	*not out*	103
S. J. McCabe	*c.* Jardine *b.* Voce	32	*b.* Allen	0
V. Y. Richardson	*c.* Hammond *b.* Voce	34	*lbw b.* Hammond	32
W. A. Oldfield	*not out*	27	*b.* Voce	6
C. V. Grimmett	*c.* Sutcliffe *b.* Voce	2	*b.* Voce	3
T. Wall	*run out*	1	*lbw b.* Hammond	0
W. J. O'Reilly	*b.* Larwood	15	*c.* Ames *b.* Hammond	0
H. Ironmonger	*b.* Larwood	4	*run out*	0
	Byes, 5; *l-b*, 1; *wides*, 2; *n-b*, 2	10	Byes, 3; *l-b*, 1; *wides*, 4; *n-b*, 1	9
	Total	228	Total	191

	O.	M.	R.	W.	O.	M.	R.	W.
Larwood	20.3	1	52	2	15	2	50	2
Voce	20	3	54	3	15	2	47	2
Allen	17	3	41	2	12	1	44	2
Hammond	10	3	21	0	10.5	2	21	3
Bowes	19	2	50	1	4	0	20	0

ENGLAND

H. Sutcliffe	*c.* Richardson *b.* Wall	52	*b.* O'Reilly	33
R. E. S. Wyatt	*lbw b.* O'Reilly	13	*lbw b.* O'Reilly	25
W. R. Hammond	*b.* Wall	8	*c.* O'Brien *b.* O'Reilly	23
The Nawab of Pataudi	*b.* O'Reilly	15	*c.* Fingleton *b.* Ironmonger	5
M. Leyland	*b.* O'Reilly	22	*b.* Wall	19
D. R. Jardine	*c.* Oldfield *b.* Wall	1	*c.* McCabe *b.* Ironmonger	0
L. E. G. Ames	*b.* Wall	4	*c.* Fingleton *b.* O'Reilly	2
G. O. Allen	*c.* Richardson *b.* O'Reilly	30	*st.* Oldfield *b.* Ironmonger	23
H. Larwood	*b.* O'Reilly	9	*c.* Wall *b.* Ironmonger	4
W. Voce	*c.* McCabe *b.* Grimmett	6	*c.* O'Brien *b.* O'Reilly	0
W. E. Bowes	*not out*	4	*not out*	0
	Byes, 1; *l-b*, 2; *n-b*, 2	5	*l-b*, 4; *n-b*, 1	5
	Total	169	Total	139

	O.	M.	R.	W.	O.	M.	R.	W.
Wall	21	4	52	4	8	2	23	1
O'Reilly	34.3	17	63	5	24	5	66	5
Grimmett	16	4	21	1	4	0	19	0
Ironmonger	14	4	28	0	19.1	8	26	4

Appendix C 127th Test

AT ADELAIDE, 13, 14, 16, 17, 18, 19 January 1933
England won by 338 runs

ENGLAND

	1st Innings			2nd Innings	
H. Sutcliffe	c. Wall b. O'Reilly	9		c. sub (O'Brien) b. Wall	7
D. R. Jardine	b. Wall	3		lbw b. Ironmonger	56
W. R. Hammond	c. Oldfield b. Wall	2		b. Bradman	85
L. E. G. Ames	b. Ironmonger	3		b. O'Reilly	69
M. Leyland	b. O'Reilly	83		c. Wall b. Ironmonger	42
R. E. S. Wyatt	c. Richardson b. Grimmett	78		c. Wall b. O'Reilly	49
E. Paynter	c. Fingleton b. Wall	77		not out	1
G. O. Allen	lbw b. Grimmett	15		lbw b. Grimmett	15
H. Verity	c. Richardson b. Wall	45		lbw b. O'Reilly	40
W. Voce	b. Wall	8		b. O'Reilly	8
H. Larwood	not out	3		c. Bradman b. Ironmonger	8
	Byes, 1; l-b, 7; n-b, 7	15		Byes, 17; l-b, 11; n-b, 4	32
	Total	341		Total	412

	O.	M.	R.	W.	O.	M.	R.	W.
Wall	34.1	10	72	5	29	6	75	1
O'Reilly	50	19	82	2	50.3	21	79	4
Ironmonger	20	6	50	1	57	21	87	3
Grimmett	28	6	94	2	35	9	74	1
McCabe	14	3	28	0	16	0	42	0
Bradman	—	—	—	—	4	0	23	1

AUSTRALIA

	1st Innings			2nd Innings	
W. M. Woodfull	b. Allen	22		not out	73
J. Fingleton	c. Ames b. Allen	0		b. Larwood	0
D. G. Bradman	c. Allen b. Larwood	8		c. and b. Verity	66
S. McCabe	c. Jardine b. Larwood	8		c. Leyland b. Allen	7
W. H. Ponsford	b. Voce	85		c. Jardine b. Larwood	3
V. Y. Richardson	b. Allen	28		c. Allen b. Larwood	21
W. A. Oldfield	retired hurt	41		absent hurt	0
C. V. Grimmett	c. Voce b. Allen	10		b. Allen	6
T. W. Wall	b. Hammond	6		b. Allen	0
W. J. O'Reilly	b. Larwood	0		b. Larwood	5
H. Ironmonger	not out	0		b. Allen	0
	Byes, 2; l-b, 11; n-b, 1	14		Byes, 4; l-b, 2; n-b, 5; wides, 1	12
	Total	222		Total	193

	O.	M.	R.	W.	O.	M.	R.	W.
Larwood	25	6	55	3	19	3	71	4
Allen	23	4	71	4	17.2	5	50	4
Hammond	17.4	4	30	1	9	3	27	0
Voce	14	5	21	1	4	1	7	0
Verity	16	7	31	0	20	12	26	1

Appendix D 128th Test

AT BRISBANE 10, 11, 13, 14, 15, 16 February 1933
England won by 6 wickets

AUSTRALIA

	1st Innings		2nd Innings	
V. Y. Richardson	*st.* Ames *b.* Hammond	83	*c.* Jardine *b.* Verity	32
W. M. Woodfull	*b.* Mitchell	67	*c.* Hammond *b.* Mitchell	19
D. G. Bradman	*b.* Larwood	76	*c.* Mitchell *b.* Larwood	24
S. J. McCabe	*c.* Jardine *b.* Allen	20	*b.* Verity	22
W. H. Ponsford	*b.* Larwood	19	*c.* Larwood *b.* Allen	0
L. Darling	*c.* Ames *b.* Allen	17	*run out*	39
E. H. Bromley	*c.* Verity *b.* Larwood	26	*c.* Hammond *b.* Allen	7
H. S. Love	*lbw b.* Mitchell	5	*lbw b.* Larwood	3
T. Wall	*not out*	6	*c.* Jardine *b.* Allen	2
W. J. O'Reilly	*c.* Hammond *b.* Larwood	6	*b.* Larwood	4
H. Ironmonger	*st.* Ames *b.* Hammond	8	*not out*	0
	Byes, 5; *l-b,* 1; *n-b,* 1	7	*Byes,* 13; *l-b,* 9; *n-b,* 1	23
	Total	340	Total	175

	O.	M.	R.	W.	O.	M.	R.	W.
Larwood	31	7	101	4	17.3	3	49	3
Allen	24	4	83	2	17	3	44	3
Hammond	23	5	61	2	10	4	18	0
Mitchell	16	5	49	2	5	0	11	1
Verity	27	12	39	0	19	6	30	2

ENGLAND

	1st Innings		2nd Innings	
D. R. Jardine	*c.* Love *b.* O'Reilly	46	*lbw b.* Ironmonger	24
H. Sutcliffe	*lbw b.* O'Reilly	86	*c.* Darling *b.* Wall	2
W. R. Hammond	*b.* McCabe	20	*c.* Bromley *b.* Ironmonger	14
R. E. S. Wyatt	*c.* Love *b.* Ironmonger	12		
M. Leyland	*c.* Bradman *b.* O'Reilly	12	*c.* McCabe *b.* O'Reilly	86
L. E. G. Ames	*c.* Darling *b.* Ironmonger	17	*not out*	14
G. O. Allen	*c.* Love *b.* Wall	13		
E. Paynter	*c.* Richardson *b.* Ironmonger	83	*not out*	14
H. Larwood	*b.* McCabe	23		
H. Verity	*not out*	23		
T. B. Mitchell	*lbw b.* O'Reilly	0		
	Byes, 6; *l-b,* 12; *n-b,* 3	21	*Byes,* 2; *l-b,* 4; *n-b,* 2; *wides,* 1	9
	Total	356	Total	4 for 163

	O.	M.	R.	W.	O.	M.	R.	W.
Wall	33	6	66	1	7	1	17	1
O'Reilly	67.4	26	120	4	30	11	65	1
Ironmonger	43	19	69	3	35	13	47	2
McCabe	23	7	40	2	7.4	2	25	0
Bromley	10	4	19	0	—	—	—	—
Bradman	7	1	17	0	—	—	—	—
Darling	2	0	4	0	—	—	—	—

Appendix E 129th Test

AT SYDNEY, 23, 24, 25, 27, 28 February 1933
England won by 8 wickets

AUSTRALIA

	1st Innings		2nd Innings	
V. Y. Richardson	c. Jardine b. Larwood	0	c. Allen b. Larwood	0
W. M. Woodfull	b. Larwood	14	b. Allen	67
D. G. Bradman	b. Larwood	48	b. Verity	71
L. P. O'Brien	c. Larwood b. Voce	61	c. Verity b. Voce	5
S. J. McCabe	c. Hammond b. Verity	73	c. Jardine b. Voce	4
L. Darling	b. Verity	85	c. Wyatt b. Verity	7
W. A. Oldfield	run out	52	c. Wyatt b. Verity	5
P. K. Lee	c. Jardine b. Verity	42	b. Allen	15
W. J. O'Reilly	b. Allen	19	b. Verity	1
H. H. Alexander	not out	17	lbw b. Verity	0
H. Ironmonger	b. Larwood	1	not out	0
	Byes, 13; l-b, 9; wides, 1	23	Byes, 4; n-b, 3	7
	Total	435	Total	182

	O.	M.	R.	W.	O.	M.	R.	W.
Larwood	32.2	10	98	4	11	0	44	1
Voce	24	4	80	1	10	0	34	2
Allen	25	1	128	1	11.4	2	54	2
Verity	17	8	62	3	19	9	33	5
Hammond	8	0	32	0	3	0	10	0
Wyatt	2	0	12	0	—	—	—	—

ENGLAND

	1st Innings		2nd Innings	
H. Sutcliffe	c. Richardson b. O'Reilly	56		
D. R. Jardine	c. Oldfield b. O'Reilly	18	c. Richardson b. Ironmonger	24
W. R. Hammond	lbw b. Lee	101	not out	75
H. Larwood	c. Ironmonger b. Lee	98		
M. Leyland	run out	42	b. Ironmonger	0
R. E. S. Wyatt	c. Ironmonger b. O'Reilly	51	not out	61
L. E. G. Ames	run out	4		
E. Paynter	b. Lee	9		
G. O. Allen	c. Bradman b. Lee	48		
H. Verity	c. Oldfield b. Alexander	4		
W. Voce	not out	7		
	Byes, 7; l-b, 7; n-b, 2	16	Byes, 6; l-b, 1; n-b, 1	8
	Total	454	Total	2 for 168

	O.	M.	R.	W.	O.	M.	R.	W.
Alexander	35	1	129	1	11	2	25	0
McCabe	12	1	27	0	5	2	10	0
O'Reilly	45	7	100	3	15	5	32	0
Ironmonger	31	13	64	0	26	12	34	2
Lee	40.2	11	111	4	12.2	3	52	0
Darling	7	5	3	0	2	0	7	0
Bradman	1	0	4	0	—	—	—	—

Index

MORE ABOUT PENGUINS, PELICANS
AND PUFFINS

For further information about books available from Penguins please write to Dept EP, Penguin Books Ltd, Harmondsworth, Middlesex UB7 0DA.

In the U.S.A.: For a complete list of books available from Penguins in the United States write to Dept DG, Penguin Books, 299 Murray Hill Parkway, East Rutherford, New Jersey 07073.

In Canada: For a complete list of books available from Penguins in Canada write to Penguin Books Canada Ltd, 2801 John Street, Markham, Ontario L3R 1B4.

In Australia: For a complete list of books available from Penguins in Australia write to the Marketing Department, Penguin Books Australia Ltd, P.O. Box 257, Ringwood, Victoria 3134.

In New Zealand: For a complete list of books available from Penguins in New Zealand write to the Marketing Department, Penguin Books (N.Z.) Ltd, Private Bag, Takapuna, Auckland 9.

In India: For a complete list of books available from Penguins in India write to Penguin Overseas Ltd, 706 Eros Apartments, 56 Nehru Place, New Delhi 110019.

A CHOICE OF PENGUINS

☐ *Further Chronicles of Fairacre* 'Miss Read'   £3.95

Full of humour, warmth and charm, these four novels – *Miss Clare Remembers, Over the Gate, The Fairacre Festival* and *Emily Davis* – make up an unforgettable picture of English village life.

☐ *Callanish* **William Horwood**   £1.95

From the acclaimed author of *Duncton Wood*, this is the haunting story of Creggan, the captured golden eagle, and his struggle to be free.

☐ *Act of Darkness* **Francis King**   £2.50

Anglo-India in the 1930s, where a peculiarly vicious murder triggers 'A terrific mystery story . . . a darkly luminous parable about innocence and evil' – *The New York Times*. 'Brilliantly successful' – *Daily Mail*. 'Unputdownable' – *Standard*

☐ *Death in Cyprus* **M. M. Kaye**   £1.95

Holidaying on Aphrodite's beautiful island, Amanda finds herself caught up in a murder mystery in which no one, not even the attractive painter Steven Howard, is quite what they seem . . .

☐ *Lace* **Shirley Conran**   £2.95

Lace is, quite simply, a publishing sensation: the story of Judy, Kate, Pagan and Maxine; the bestselling novel that teaches men about women, and women about themselves. 'Riches, bitches, sex and jetsetters' locations – they're all there' – *Sunday Express*

A CHOICE OF PENGUINS

☐ **Small World** David Lodge   £2.50

A jet-propelled academic romance, sequel to *Changing Places.* 'A new comic débâcle on every page' – *The Times.* 'Here is everything one expects from Lodge but three times as entertaining as anything he has written before' – *Sunday Telegraph*

☐ **The Neverending Story** Michael Ende   £3.50

The international bestseller, now a major film: 'A tale of magical adventure, pursuit and delay, danger, suspense, triumph' – *The Times Literary Supplement*

☐ **The Sword of Honour Trilogy** Evelyn Waugh   £3.95

Containing *Men at Arms, Officers and Gentlemen* and *Unconditional Surrender*, the trilogy described by Cyril Connolly as 'unquestionably the finest novels to have come out of the war'.

☐ **The Honorary Consul** Graham Greene   £1.95

In a provincial Argentinian town, a group of revolutionaries kidnap the wrong man . . . 'The tension never relaxes and one reads hungrily from page to page, dreading the moment it will all end' – Auberon Waugh in the *Evening Standard*

☐ **The First Rumpole Omnibus** John Mortimer   £4.95

Containing *Rumpole of the Bailey*, *The Trials of Rumpole* and *Rumpole's Return*. 'A fruity, foxy masterpiece, defender of our wilting faith in mankind' – *Sunday Times*

☐ **Scandal** A. N. Wilson   £2.25

Sexual peccadillos, treason and blackmail are all ingredients on the boil in A. N. Wilson's new, *cordon noir* comedy. 'Drily witty, deliciously nasty' – *Sunday Telegraph*

A CHOICE OF PENGUINS

☐ **Stanley and the Women** Kingsley Amis £2.50

'Very good, very powerful . . . beautifully written . . . This is Amis *père* at his best' – Anthony Burgess in the *Observer*. 'Everybody should read it' – *Daily Mail*

☐ **The Mysterious Mr Ripley** Patricia Highsmith £4.95

Containing *The Talented Mr Ripley*, *Ripley Underground* and *Ripley's Game*. 'Patricia Highsmith is the poet of apprehension' – Graham Greene. 'The Ripley books are marvellously, insanely readable' – *The Times*

☐ **Earthly Powers** Anthony Burgess £4.95

'Crowded, crammed, bursting with manic erudition, garlicky puns, omnilingual jokes . . . (a novel) which meshes the real and personalized history of the twentieth century' – Martin Amis

☐ **Life & Times of Michael K** J. M. Coetzee £2.95

The Booker Prize-winning novel: 'It is hard to convey . . . just what Coetzee's special quality is. His writing gives off whiffs of Conrad, of Nabokov, of Golding, of the Paul Theroux of *The Mosquito Coast*. But he is none of these, he is a harsh, compelling new voice' – Victoria Glendinning

☐ **The Stories of William Trevor** £5.95

'Trevor packs into each separate five or six thousand words more richness, more laughter, more ache, more multifarious human-ness than many good writers manage to get into a whole novel' – *Punch*

☐ **The Book of Laughter and Forgetting**
Milan Kundera £3.95

'A whirling dance of a book . . . a masterpiece full of angels, terror, ostriches and love . . . No question about it. The most important novel published in Britain this year' – Salman Rushdie

A CHOICE OF PENGUINS

☐ *The Complete Penguin Stereo Record and Cassette Guide*
Greenfield, Layton and March   £7.95

A new edition, now including information on compact discs. 'One of the few indispensables on the record collector's bookshelf' – *Gramophone*

☐ *Selected Letters of Malcolm Lowry*
Edited by Harvey Breit and Margerie Bonner Lowry £5.95

'Lowry emerges from these letters not only as an extremely interesting man, but also a lovable one' – Philip Toynbee

☐ *The First Day on the Somme*
Martin Middlebrook   £3.95

1 July 1916 was the blackest day of slaughter in the history of the British Army. 'The soldiers receive the best service a historian can provide: their story told in their own words' – *Guardian*

☐ *A Better Class of Person* **John Osborne**   £1.95

The playwright's autobiography, 1929–56. 'Splendidly enjoyable' – John Mortimer. 'One of the best, richest and most bitterly truthful autobiographies that I have ever read' – Melvyn Bragg

☐ *The Winning Streak* **Goldsmith and Clutterbuck**   £2.95

Marks & Spencer, Saatchi & Saatchi, United Biscuits, GEC.... The UK's top companies reveal their formulas for success, in an important and stimulating book that no British manager can afford to ignore.

☐ *The First World War* **A. J. P. Taylor**   £3.95

'He manages in some 200 illustrated pages to say almost everything that is important ... A special text ... a remarkable collection of photographs' – *Observer*

A CHOICE OF PENGUINS

☐ *Man and the Natural World* Keith Thomas   £4.95

Changing attitudes in England, 1500–1800. 'An encyclopedic study of man's relationship to animals and plants . . . a book to read again and again' – Paul Theroux, *Sunday Times* Books of the Year

☐ *Jean Rhys: Letters 1931–66*
  Edited by Francis Wyndham and Diana Melly   £3.95

'Eloquent and invaluable . . . her life emerges, and with it a portrait of an unexpectedly indomitable figure' – Marina Warner in the *Sunday Times*

☐ *The French Revolution* Christopher Hibbert   £4.50

'One of the best accounts of the Revolution that I know . . . Mr Hibbert is outstanding' – J. H. Plumb in the *Sunday Telegraph*

☐ *Isak Dinesen* Judith Thurman   £4.95

The acclaimed life of Karen Blixen, 'beautiful bride, disappointed wife, radiant lover, bereft and widowed woman, writer, sibyl, Scheherazade, child of Lucifer, Baroness; always a unique human being . . . an assiduously researched and finely narrated biography' – *Books & Bookmen*

☐ *The Amateur Naturalist*
  Gerald Durrell with Lee Durrell   £4.95

'Delight . . . on every page . . . packed with authoritative writing, learning without pomposity . . . it represents a real bargain' – *The Times Educational Supplement*. 'What treats are in store for the average British household' – *Daily Express*

☐ *When the Wind Blows* Raymond Briggs   £2.95

'A visual parable against nuclear war: all the more chilling for being in the form of a strip cartoon' – *Sunday Times*. 'The most eloquent anti-Bomb statement you are likely to read' – *Daily Mail*

A CHOICE OF PENGUINS

☐ *The Diary of Virginia Woolf*
 Edited by Quentin Bell and Anne Olivier Bell

'As an account of the intellectual and cultural life of our century, Virginia Woolf's diaries are invaluable; as the record of one bruised and unquiet mind, they are unique' – Peter Ackroyd in the *Sunday Times*

☐ Volume One	£4.50
☐ Volume Two	£4.50
☐ Volume Three	£4.95
☐ Volume Four	£5.50
☐ Volume Five	£5.95

These books should be available at all good bookshops or news-agents, but if you live in the UK or the Republic of Ireland and have difficulty in getting to a bookshop, they can be ordered by post. Please indicate the titles required and fill in the form below.

NAME _____ BLOCK CAPITALS

ADDRESS _____

_____

_____

Enclose a cheque or postal order payable to The Penguin Bookshop to cover the total price of books ordered, plus 50p for postage. Readers in the Republic of Ireland should send £IR equivalent to the sterling prices, plus 67p for postage. Send to: The Penguin Bookshop, 54/56 Bridlesmith Gate, Nottingham, NG1 2GP.

You can also order by phoning (0602) 599295, and quoting your Barclaycard or Access number.

Every effort is made to ensure the accuracy of the price and availability of books at the time of going to press, but it is sometimes necessary to increase prices and in these circumstances retail prices may be shown on the covers of books which may differ from the prices shown in this list or elsewhere. This list is not an offer to supply any book.

This order service is only available to residents in the UK and the Republic of Ireland.

● ● ●